Art
Song

Linking
Poetry
and
Music

Art Song

Linking Poetry and Music

By
Carol Kimball

ISBN 978-1-6177-4080-0

Hal Leonard Corporation
7777 W. Bluemound Rd.
P.O. Box 13819
Milwaukee, WI 53213

Libray of Congress Cataloging-in-Publication Data has been applied for.

Printed in the U.S.A.

Visit Hal Leonard Online at **www.halleonard.com**

Contents

Foreword

Bright is the ring of words
When the right man rings them
Fair the fall of songs
When the singer sings them.

—Robert Louis Stevenson

In an art song recital the singer faces the ultimate challenge: to sustain an audience's interest by communicating drama, emotion, mood, and stories throughout a program of varied song styles and composers. During the course of the evening, the singer must play myriad roles and transmit numerous emotions and states of mind. The singer becomes a storyteller *par excellence*: the link between the composer, the poet, and the listener. When the singer is able to draw the listener into the song on an emotionally responsive level, the ultimate artistic goal is achieved and he has "ringed the ring of words."

In order to achieve this goal, singers have to do their research. They must plumb the depths of the poetry, be fastidious in their delivery of the words, and find the dramatic images and emotional moments submerged in the words they are singing. A precise approach on the singer's part yields a performance rich in commitment and communication. Musical and technical details are key in this process. Gifted interpreters are usually addicted to the work of dissecting details of music and text in order to explore the layers of meaning that make up a song's totality, then bringing everything together again in performance.

Why write this book? My first book, *Song: A Guide to Art Song Style and Literature*, was a survey of art song repertoire and an overview of the history of art song in various countries. *Art Song: Linking Poetry and Music* book goes further than a broad overview of song literature. It deals fundamentally with what the art song genre *is*.

In my teaching and in numerous conversations with professional colleagues and university/college students over the years, I have become aware that though we work with song repertoire constantly, when performance time rolls around, many times the groundwork of preparing *the entire song* has been neglected. I have had young singers in master classes self-consciously read the poem they are about to sing or stumble over the poetic phrases with all the elegance of reading a grocery list. Often they cannot define lesser-known words found in the text. I doubt that every student takes every song they sing and dismantles its musical parts, exploring how the composer has re-created the poem as an art song.

So this book became a collection of thoughts on how to prepare an art song for performance—what its basic parts are and how they merge to create the song itself, which links a poem to a musical setting by a composer. By understanding the component parts of an art song and studying how they complement and balance one another, singers can uncover details about the magical fusion created when words are linked to music.

As performing artists, we are in the business of creating and transmitting beauty. We need to be committed to working beyond memorizing notes and words. We must remain open to new and/or different ideas about performance and performance preparation. In the final analysis, our goal must be an honest re-creation of the song.

We especially need to work with poetry, which is the answer to the question "Which came first—the chicken or the egg?" Singers need to fall in love with poetry and become fluent reading it. This step is quite often omitted or glossed over in performance preparation. The first section of the book explores how we can begin to read poetry and contains lists of poems that may be used for study and reading. There are also suggestions that might be helpful in becoming comfortable working with the texts we sing.

The musical score is the framework for the poem—its partner and the other half of the art song equation. Studying the score and seeing how the composer has set the words in a musical context is vital to preparing song repertoire. Working with style is another important component of the preparation puzzle. Looking at the broad components or musical characteristics of the song and breaking them into smaller sub-headings can help us see how the composer has intuited the poem and has translated its imagery into sound.

The next section of the book centers on working with recital formats of differing designs and content, and discusses building recitals of varied, interesting, and engaging repertoire. The ideas presented here are intended to spark interest in working with repertoire in ways that will produce a committed, organic performance.

After all the preparation is completed, the songs we have worked on so diligently must be communicated to our listeners in performance. Our presentation must reflect our preparatory work, our vocal sound, and our artistic sensibilities.

Interpretation is an intangible word and shares a relationship to the singer's emotional response in the moment of performance. Distinguished interpreter of the French *mélodie* and renowned teacher Pierre Bernac wrote: "In the art of music, it is the interpreter's performance which we come to regard as the work itself." [1] In order to produce imaginative and artistic performances, singers must have done extensive preliminary work with words and music. Then, armed with the knowledge that they have uncovered, abandon themselves in the moment of performance to being the final conduit for the voices of the poet and the composer.

The last chapter of the book is an annotated list of selected repertoire for undergraduate collegiate students. Three appendices follow, dealing with the recital program in print, a poetry poll of some professional musicians, and a selection of sample recital programs. Finally, there is an annotated bibliography organized by topics having to do with art song.

In today's fast-paced world, there are master classes, young artist programs, and all manner of summer programs, as well as books, articles, and videos that present ideas on performance preparation. This book contains some of my thoughts on the subject. Most of them are not new, but they are still workable suggestions for singers who care enough to adopt them. Hopefully these will cultivate renewed commitment to studying art song on the part of every singer whose goal in singing is artistry.

—Carol Kimball
May, 2012

NOTES

1   Pierre Bernac, *The Interpretation of French Song* (New York: W.W. Norton Co., 1970), 1.

Acknowledgements

Sincere thanks are due the following people who, at various points along the way to publication, served as my "consulting team": Juline Barol-Gilmore, Wanda Brister, Thomas Grubb, Debra Greschner, Judith Cloud, Serdar Ilban, Veera Asher, Debbie Siebert, and Lori Laitman. When I needed a sounding board for my ideas, they generously weighed in on questions about content and format, and were a source of encouragement to me.

A word of gratitude goes to those singers, composers, collaborative pianists, and teachers who participated in my "Poetry Poll" (see Appendix 1), and to the colleagues and former students for permission to include material from their song recitals and program notes. Thank you to those who supplied me with programs from which I drew examples (see Appendix 3).

Thanks also go to the editorial team at Hal Leonard Corporation for their willingness to answer any random questions I had, or respond to other publication issues as they arose. I am deeply indebted to Richard Walters for his sound ideas about purpose and content, and to Joshua Parman for his thorough, helpful editing.

And always, my heartfelt thanks go to my husband, Ralph Kimball, for his steady presence in navigating through another project with me.

For permission to reprint parts of previously published material from the articles listed below, much of which has been revised, I am most grateful to Dr. Richard Sjoerdsma, Editor-in-Chief of the *Journal of Singing*, formerly *The NATS Journal.*

Carol Kimball, "The Song File: Art Songs Oubliées (Part 3)," *Journal of Singing* 68, no. 5 (May/June 2012).

————, "The Song File: Art Songs Oubliées (Part 2)," *Journal of Singing* 68, no.3 (January/February 2012).

————, "The Song File: Art Songs Oubliées (Part 1)," *Journal of Singing* 68, no.1 (September/October 2011).

————, "The Song File: Made in the U.S.A.: Some Thoughts on American Song," *Journal of Singing* 67, no. 4 (March/April 2011).

————, "The Song File: A Suggested List of French Song for Young Singers," *Journal of Singing* 67, no.2 (November/December 2010).

————, "The Song File: A Smorgasbord of Song Groups," *Journal of Singing* 66, no. 3 (January/February 2010).

————, "The Song File: Tweaking the Song Recital," *Journal of Singing* 66, no. 2 (November/December 2009).

————, "The Song File: Bright Is the Ring of Words," *Journal of Singing* 66, no.1 (September/October 2009) .

————, "Working With Song Literature: The Journey to Performance," *Journal of Singing* 53, no. 3 (January/February 1997).

————, "Jane Bathori's Interpretive Legacy," *Journal of Singing* 57, no. 3 (January/February 2001).

————, "Unity from Contrast: Poulenc's *La Fraîcheur et le feu*," *The NATS Journal* 44, no. 5 (May/June 1988).

————, "Poulenc's *Le Travail du peintre*: A Synthesis of the Arts," *The NATS Journal* 44, no. 2 (November/December 1987).

Finally, I dedicate this book to all singers and pianists who have been profoundly moved by reading a poem, or by singing or playing an art song. In your hands is the safekeeping of the future of this treasured art form. In some quarters, *art song* may be considered an endangered species, but in the performances of inspired and competent creators, it will continue to have a long life and remain a vibrant part of our artistic lives.

—Carol Kimball
May, 2012

Chapter 1

What is Art Song?

*Songs represent the composer's purest utterance,
his most private being, unadorned, uncluttered,
devoid of posturing, spontaneous, distilled.* [1]

—Dominick Argento

Art Song: A Unique Hybrid

Art song is a unique hybrid of poetry and music, fashioned of two arts that from earliest times were considered "sister arts." Poetry and music share similar sound characteristics: rhythmic patterns, accents (stresses), variations in tempo, pitch inflection (speech), and melodic phrases (song). In the best of art songs, the composer's musical "re-creation" or "transformation" of the text unites the poetry and music in such a way that it is impossible to think of them apart. We do not hear poetry set to music, we hear an art song.

An art song's poetry existed *before* the song was written. Though there are some composers who have written their own art song texts, this is the exception and not the rule. The great art songs of the nineteenth century in Germany and France proliferated due to the high quality of poetry being written during that time. Early art songs depended upon the singer to be the primary interpreter of the poem; however, by the nineteenth century, poets and their poetry had reached a higher level of artistic expression and the art song's development was on its way. This explosion in poetry's maturity and progress took place notably in Germany, then in France. The "new" poetry made possible freer forms, more lyric vocal declamation, and increased expressiveness in the accompaniment. These factors, fused with poems of high literary quality, caused the art song to flourish. As this continued, a greater unity of tone and word was reached. By the end of the nineteenth century, art song was a firmly established musical form.

When we hear an art song, we experience it as a complete entity—and we get an overall impression. This impression is stimulated by the images in the song, which composers create with settings of words, melodies, harmonies, and rhythms. All the images of the poem *merge* with the images in the music, creating the distinctive *overall* images of the song—a unique blend of word and sound, poetry and music. As we listen, we respond to those images, we form mental pictures, and we experience emotions.

The big component in both poetry and art song is imagery. When we read a poem, we react to its images; when we listen to an art song, the same thing takes place; however, in an art song, the words have been subsumed into a musical texture, and the combination of the two creates new and heightened images.

Art Song and Popular Song

Art song is another term for classical song—a musical composition, usually for voice and piano—the result of a composer choosing an existing poem or section of prose and then setting it to music. The "art song" is the composer's musical response to those words—their meaning or implied meanings—in a free and expressive manner. [2] Depending on its country of origin, it might be called art song, *Lieder*, *mélodie*, *romanza*, *romanser*. Art songs are usually composed for voice and piano and sung by professional or trained voices.

Art song is not like popular song. Words to popular songs or musical theater songs are properly called "lyrics" and are the products of a collaborative process between a lyricist and a composer working as a team. The song is usually created with a specific subject or an existing story upon which both words and music are based. Some examples of collaborative teams that created popular songs—now considered "classics" in the field—are Richard Rodgers and Lorenz Hart, Richard Rodgers and Oscar Hammerstein II, George and Ira Gershwin, Jerome Kern and Oscar Hammerstein II plus other lyricists, and numerous others. Some composers write their own lyrics; among them are Stephen Sondheim, Cole Porter, Irving Berlin, and Frank Loesser. Many of these songs belonged to musical scores of musical productions which have long since disappeared from performance, but the quality of the lyrics and melody have kept the songs alive.

Distinguished art song composer Ned Rorem differentiates poetry from lyrics this way: "Poetry is self-contained, while lyrics are made to be sung, and don't necessarily lead a life of their own. The best lyricists are collaborative craftsmen." [3]

Irving Berlin, considered one of the greatest American popular songwriters in history, had this to say when asked when asked whether he ever studied lyrical writing:

> I never have, because if I don't know them, I do not have to observe any rules and can do as I like, which is much better for me than if I allowed myself to be governed by the rules of versification. In following my own method I can make my jingles fit my music or vice versa with no qualms as to their correctness. Usually I compose my tunes and then fit words to them, though sometimes it's the other way about. [4]

Notice that Berlin uses the word "jingles" for the words he writes. In later years he still emphasized his ignorance about prosody, saying, "it's the lyric that makes a song a hit, although the tune, of course, is what makes it last." [5]

An art song then, is a composer's reaction to a poem—a response that compels him to set the words of the poem to music. Again, Ned Rorem writes: "People always ask if second-rate poems can make first-rate songs. Yes, but only if the composer thinks the poems are first-rate." [6]

Why Sing Art Songs?

Singing art songs demands that we focus on some of the most celebrated and beautiful poetry in the world. In working with the poems we sing, we learn to appreciate the pleasures of word sounds. If we have not done this sort of work before in preparing our music, it adds a new and rewarding dimension to our studies.

Singing art songs stretches and develops our imaginations as musicians. A major challenge of song study is exploring the "why" of the musical/poetic setting, formulating ideas, and fitting everything together like pieces in a puzzle. Finding as many pieces to the puzzle as we can ultimately produces a performance of expressive and potent communication, where the singer really "crawls inside the song" versus one in which the singer performs the song beautifully on a one-dimensional level.

When we sing art songs, we use our total musicianship and intelligence. Working with the words of the poet and the music of the composer calls not only for intelligence but imagination. The singer becomes a storyteller or narrator, bringing the images of the words and the music to the listener. Performance demands the totality of our artistry.

Singing art song requires us to focus on details. A precise, thorough approach on the singer's part yields a performance rich in commitment and communication. Musical and vocal details are key in this process. Composer Daron Hagen, who has composed both operas and many art songs, compares the two genres using this analogy: "An opera is a mural; an art song is an exquisite miniature, requiring the tiniest of brush strokes." [7]

Preparing an art song for performance demands that we uncover and identify as many of these "tiniest of brush strokes" as possible. When we do, we come closer to unlocking what the poet meant when he penned the words, and what the composer intended when he set the words to music. Becoming "one" with our performance repertoire is the ultimate goal. When the singer finally adds his voice and persona to the song, that is the final piece of the puzzle.

Pared down to the bare essentials, singing art songs is creating art. It is one way of creating beauty, which is a basic need for humankind. We are constantly evolving, and so we continue to find new musical and poetic facets in the repertoire we sing. This is the delight of singing art songs.

Poetry as the Basis for Art Song

Poem and music is a DNA combo. [8]

—Lori Laitman

When a composer sets a poem to music, the words acquire another format. They are encased in musical sound, which adds its own pitch, rhythm, and textures to those the poem already possesses. French composer Jacques Leguerney (1906–1997) put it this way: "The words and music are of equal importance. Their conjunction results in a poem that is not the same as it was before." [9]

Creating a Musical Framework for Poems

How do composers choose their texts? What draws them to a particular poem, poet, or poetic theme? Most composers of art songs have a strong love of literature and a keen knowledge about what sort of poems attract them as composers. Often a composer will set poetry by colleagues and contemporaries, as did Francis Poulenc and Ned Rorem, or may have a strong predilection for setting prose, as in the case of Dominick Argento. In many cases, a composer may be strongly attracted to poetry from a specific period in history; with few exceptions, Jacques Leguerney used Renaissance poetry for all his *mélodies*. Some composers prefer the works of specific poets; for instance, the poetry of William Shakespeare, Emily Dickinson, Walt Whitman, and Paul Verlaine are found in numerous art songs. Still other composers prefer highly dramatic poems; Carl Loewe is chiefly remembered for his ballads, which present gripping stories of high intensity and emotion.

Since art song composers have to find poems that stimulate their musical creativity, many are voracious readers. Looking for the right poem to react to musically takes a great amount of time, and should be considered part of the compositional process. In looking at many sources to discover composers' thoughts about the connection of words and music in their vocal compositions, all of them were in general agreement, although they expressed their feelings in slightly different ways:

Samuel Barber

"The text means a great deal to me. I read lots of poetry anyway, so I go through tons and tons of poems that could possibly be songs. It's very hard to find them— they are either too wordy, too introverted, or what have you." [10]

Ned Rorem

"The composer's initial job is to find an appropriate poem. The test of this is a poem's final enhancement by music; it is contrariwise inappropriate when both words and music add up to an issue of mutual confusion. One poem may be so intrinsically musical that a vocal setting would be superfluous.

Another may be so complex that an addition of music would mystify rather than clarify its meaning." [11]

Francis Poulenc

"When I have chosen a poem, the musical realization of which often does not follow until months later, I examine it from all angles . . . I recite the poem to myself many times. I listen to it, I look for traps, I sometimes underline the difficult parts of the text. I note the pauses, I try to discover the internal rhythm through a line *which is not necessarily the first*. Then I try setting it to music, bearing in mind the different densities of the piano accompaniment." Elsewhere, with typical Gallic *panache*, Poulenc contradicted himself by stating: "The musical transposition of a poem should be an act of love, and never a marriage of reason." [12]

Jacques Leguerney

"I wrote a *mélodie* first of all because I loved the poem. It is very difficult to find suitable poems. Sometimes one writes a song in order to set two verses, or because one loves one verse . . . The relationship of text to music is the raison d'être of my music." [13]

Lori Laitman

"…there are certain factors I consider when choosing a text. It's easier when a poem isn't too long or too short… It's good if the poem is not too complex, because the audience has to be able to grasp of the meaning of the poem through the song… Most importantly, it is good if the poem has some emotional 'breathing space'—so that the music can take over what is left unsaid." [14]

Daron Hagen

"The poem already has a music of its own. It is my duty to find that music and cooperate with that structure and express it melodically and harmonically." [15]

John Duke

"In the course of reading literally thousands of poems in English in my quest for song texts, I have developed an ability to sense quickly usually after a single reading, the possibilities of a poem as musical material, at least as far as my own musical sensibilities are concerned. What do I look for? Lines which immediately suggest a 'singable' phrase; stanzas which offer contrasts in mood and suggest varieties of musical treatment; open vowels at climactic points; variety and subtlety in the spoken rhythms. But the most important thing of all is the ability to sense the possibility of assimilating *all* of the material which the poem offers into a strong and concise musical form." [16]

Libby Larsen

"Each poem I work with must be considered on its own terms. Great poetry already has its meticulously crafted music—strong and intact. I feel that I have a serious responsibility to work as diligently as I can to discover the music of the poem (or prose) as the first part of my process. If I do that work well, I move through the discovery of poetic devices to discover the melodic contour, meter (usually polymeter), syntax, counterpoint, and musical form of the poem.

I find that if I stop my process at the point of analyzing poetic device, I am more likely to force my music on the poem. But if I complete my process of discovery to find the music of the poem itself, I open up to the meaning of the poem in an entirely different way, resulting in the poem directing the writing of its own unique and innate music." [17]

Eric Whitacre

"The really great poetry is full of music already. You just need to quiet yourself enough and listen to what the poet is telling you to do. You know, one takes the credit as the composer, but really, the poet does all of the heavy lifting." [18]

Judith Cloud

"One quality of a poem that convinces me I must set it—not *might* set it, but *must* set it—is: The opening line immediately suggests music… that delicious quality of consonant and vowel combinations tethered to the meaning of individual words draws me in to the sound world I seek." [19]

Pierre Bernac, distinguished French baritone and pedagogue, commented on the harmonious fusion of words and music in *The Interpretation of French Song*, his classic reference to French *mélodie*:

In vocal music, the sonority and the rhythm of the words are an integral part of the music itself. The word itself is a musical sound. The sonority and stress and rhythm of words inspire music no less, and at times even more, than the emotion they express . . . the music of the poem is as important as the music set to the poem. The music of the words and the music itself are one and the same; they should not be disassociated. [20]

Are all poems equal? No. But a first-rate composer who is compelled to set a less-than-stellar poem can still produce a wonderful art song. Another composer can take a wonderful poem and the setting might not be as powerful a blend of poetic and musical elements as that of a more skillful composer. The chief reason for *any* composer's choice of poem is that the words—their emotions, moods, and images—spoke to his artistic sensibilities.

Take some time and compare settings of the same poem by several composers and you probably will be drawn to one above the rest. We gravitate to that which touches us and communicates emotion clearly.

Working With Art Song: The Singer's Task

Stephen Sondheim's *Sunday in the Park with George* is a musical theater work that dramatizes, among other things, the emotions associated with creating art. In Act 2, French painter Georges Seurat's fictional grandson makes a shrewd observation about the "how" of producing an art work:

Bit by bit,
Putting it together...
Piece by piece—
Only way to make a work of art.
Every moment makes a contribution,
Every little detail plays a part.
Having just the vision's no solution,
Everything depends on execution:
Putting it together—
That's what counts. [21]

These lyrics also pinpoint the journey of exploration and discovery that takes place in working toward a performance of song. It is painstaking work, often frustrating, frequently elusive, and habitually exciting.

Distinguished recitalist and passionate advocate of American song, tenor Paul Sperry describes a song recital as "an evening of stories set to music" and continues, "the bridge between speaking to people and singing to people should be as close as possible." [22]

Artistic singing does not just "happen." It results from merging preparation with talent. Skilled interpreters are willing to lose themselves in dissecting the details of music and text that combine to create a song—which will live again through their performance. After thoughtful study of text and music, the singer interprets his findings in the light of prior knowledge and experience.

It is interesting to note that a synonym for **interpretation** is **understanding**. That is exactly what happens before we step on the stage to sing. We have gathered everything we have learned about the song into our consciousness and have reached a point of understanding it to the fullest level possible at that specific moment.

As we mature and perform that particular song again, our understanding will reach another level and we will find new meanings and nuances in songs we consider "old friends."

Several years ago, I observed that "instant gratification is too slow for most people. Our hyper-paced society often promotes and reinforces the idea that everything needs to happen 'right now.' We need to slacken our pace and proceed toward every performance, slowly but surely, letting our talents and abilities develop evenly and thoughtfully…" In the last decade our society has literally exploded into one that is even more technologically oriented. More than ever, we need to proceed in studying art song repertoire with a plan and an eagerness to find out as much as possible about the song or song cycles we will be presenting to an audience.

In a recital performance, the singer and pianist create a moment in time in which a poem and its musical setting come to life again, channeled through their artistic sensibilities. A program of twenty-odd songs is essentially a form of time travel involving the creation of characters, situations, and emotions that may or may not be linked by some thematic thread. We need to have a systematic plan for working with the repertoire we perform.

A Roadmap for Working With an Art Song

Discovering the *inner life* of an art song must be our goal before we attempt to perform/interpret it. If song is (as Stanislavski said) "a microcosm of drama," then the dramatic interaction of text and music is the perfect starting place. The combination of the two is most easily perceived in imagery—pictures or sensations imparted by the words or by the way the musical texture functions. In a performance, these images are most powerfully transmitted by the singer who has excellent vocal technique, diction, musicality, and dramatic sensibilities.

Optimum communication of musical and poetic imagery requires solid vocal technique, good diction and language skills, musicianship, a sense of drama, and an inquiring mind. These are the big signs on our "roadmap":

- WORK WITH THE POETRY
- WORK WITH THE MUSIC
- PARTNER WITH THE PIANIST
- ABSORB and UNDERSTAND YOUR DISCOVERIES
- BLEND THESE INTO YOUR PERFORMANCE

Our journey to discover the inner life of a song, or a "GPS for the recitalist" begins in the chapters that follow, which discuss making friends with poetry as an art form, working with poetry and the poetry you sing, working with the musical framework or the other half of the art song equation, and thinking about interpretation. In his diminutive but treasurable book entitled *Interpretation in Song*, published in 1912, Harry Plunket Greene cautions: "There are no shortcuts in art." [23]

Involving ourselves totally in studying a song and its textual and musical components means we are making an aesthetic investment. We are dealing with a set of principles concerned with the nature and appreciation of beauty—indeed, we are committing ourselves to creating beauty. This is a distinct privilege presented to the musical performer, and we need to give it our best efforts.

NOTES

1   Dominick Argento, "The Composer and the Singer," Keynote address, National Association of Teachers of Singing (NATS) National Conference, San Antonio, Texas, 1986.

2   The author is indebted to Richard Walters for his "What Is An Art Song?" preface to *Classical Contest Solos* (Hal Leonard Corp., 2011) for high school singers. The definition for art song is based on that material. Used by permission.

3   Ned Rorem, "Poetry and Music" in *Settling the Score: Essays on Music* (New York: Doubleday, 1988), 294.

4   "The Story of Irving Berlin," *New York Times*, January 2, 1916.

5   Philip Furia, *Irving Berlin: A Life in Song* (New York: Schirmer Books, 1998).

6   Ned Rorem, "Fauré's Songs" in *Setting the Tone: Essays and a Diary* (New York: Limelight Editions, 1984), 248.

7   Daron Hagen, "Writing Opera with Paul," Liner notes to *Bandanna*: World Premiere Recording, ARSIS Audio 128, 2002.

8   Lori Laitman, Master class and open forum on her songs, University of Nevada, Las Vegas, March 31, 2008.

9   Mary Dibbern, Carol Kimball, and Patrick Choukroun, *Interpreting the Songs of Jacques Leguerney : A Guide for Study and Performance* (Hillsdale, NY: Pendragon Press, 2001), 34.

10 Samuel Barber, from a 1978 interview with Robert Sherman for WQXR, published in *Samuel Barber Remembered: A Centenary Tribute*, ed. Peter Dickinson (University of Rochester Press, 2010).

11 Ned Rorem,"Writing Songs" in *Setting the Tone: Essays and a Diary* (New York: Limelight Editions, 1983), 300.

12 Francis Poulenc, *Entretiens avec Claude Rostand* (Paris: René Julliard, 1954), 69–70. Quoted in Keith Daniel, *Francis Poulenc: His Artistic Development and Musical Style* (Ann Arbor, MI: UMI Research Press, 1980), 249.

13 Jacques Leguerney, quoted in Mary Dibbern, Carol Kimball, and Patrick Choukroun, Interpreting the Songs of Jacques Leguerney: A Guide to Study and Performance (Hillsdale, NY: Pendragon Press, 2001), 36.

14 Lori Laitman, "How Do You Select Your Poetry?" Frequently asked questions, Lori Laitman website, www.artsongs.com (accessed January 7, 2013).

15 Daron Hagen, quoted in Carol Kimball, *Song: A Guide to Art Song Style and Literature* (Milwaukee, WI: Hal Leonard Corp., 2005), 346.

16 John Duke, "Some Reflections on the Art Song in English," in Ruth C. Friedberg and Robin Fisher, eds., *The Selected Writings of John Duke 1917–1984* (Lanham, MD: The Scarecrow Press, 2007), 177.

17 Libby Larsen, "How do you go about setting text to music?" Frequently Asked Questions, Libby Larsen website, www.libbylarsen.com (accessed July 16, 2011).

18 Eric Whitacre, quoted in James McCarthy, "Choir Master, Sounds of America," *Gramophone* (August 2010), iii.

19 Judith Cloud, "In Search of the Perfect Words," *The Journal of Singing 67*, no. 5 (May/June 2011), 612, 613.

20 Pierre Bernac, *The Interpretation of French Song* (New York: W. W. Norton, Inc., 1978), 3–4.

21 *Sunday in the Park with George*. Music and lyrics by Stephen Sondheim. Book by James Lapine (New York: Dodd Mead & Company, 1986), 163–164.

22 Paul Sperry, Quote from a master class, International Festival of the Art Song, University of Wisconsin, Milwaukee, July 7–11, 1983.

23 Harry Plunket Greene, *Interpretation in Song* (London: Macmillan and Co., 1912), xii.

Chapter 2

Poetry Basics for Singers

*Poetry is not a special language. It is, rather,
a special way in which language is used.* [1]

—Charles B. Wheeler

What Is Poetry?

Of all people, singers need to know about poetry. Without poetry, there would be no art songs. Poet Maya Angelou said it well: "Poetry is music written for the human voice." [2]

As singers, we know many poems. The art songs we have studied and/or performed are memorized poems set in a musical structure. We may not have thought of the poetry apart from the music, but the words were a poem before a composer set them as an art song. This chapter is about paying attention to poetry *as poetry*.

What sort of opinions do you have about the poetry you sing? Is it simply a number of lines of words strung together that somehow relates to the title of the poem? Did you choose the song because you were especially drawn to the title? Perhaps to the poem? Or did you choose the song because you thought the music would make you sound "fabulous?" After you have internalized poetry and music, you most probably *will* sound impressive, but *only* as a result of having read and studied the poem, then the musical setting, and finally using this information subconsciously with your imagination as you perform the art song.

Poetry began as a vocal art, and has roots as ancient as those of music—in fact, the two arts were linked together as "sister arts." From the earliest times, poems were chanted or sung and were meant to stimulate the senses and the memory. They became a means of preserving cultural values and beliefs. Much later, most poems were sung, many by troubadours or lyric poets who fashioned verses to the musical accompaniment of a lute or lyre. When writing replaced memory as a way of preserving thoughts, poetry and music diverged and essentially became separate arts.

Here is a definition of poetry by poet/author Babette Deutch:

> *Poetry*: The art which uses words as both speech and song, and more rarely, as typographical patterns, to reveal the realities that the senses record, the feelings salute, the mind perceives, and the shaping imagination orders. [3]

Poet Dana Gioia identifies poetry as a basic human art: "As long as we use speech to communicate, poetry will be important to us. It is the art of refining our language. It teaches us the skills of imagination and empathy." [4] It is helpful to take some time and look up other definitions of poetry by other poets. Reading a few of these will probably kindle your interest in reading poetry. Here are a few examples:

> *"…poems are not, as people think, simply emotions—they are experiences."* [5]
> —Rainer Maria Rilke

> *"Art happens every time we read a poem."* [6]   —Jorge Luis Borges

> *"Poetry is a way of taking life by the throat."* [7]   —Robert Frost

> *"Art is the means we have of undoing the damage of haste. It's what everything else isn't…"* [8]
> —Theodore Roethke

> *"If I read a book and it makes my whole body so cold no fire can warm me, I know that is poetry. If I feel physically as if the top of my head were taken off, I know that is poetry. These are the only ways I know it. Is there any other way?"* [9]   —Emily Dickinson

Who's Afraid of Poetry?

We should not be afraid to read poetry. We tend to be suspicious of things that make us uncomfortable. What we really distrust is ourselves. We have misgivings about our ability to make sense of a poem the first time we read it; we are anxious about being labeled as pretentious, as though poetry belonged to only those of superior intellect and talent. Nothing could be further from the truth.

Poetry is not some ivory tower art form intended only for the few; poetry is a form of communication. Discard any ideas that poetry is an "elitist" art having nothing to do with everyday life and emotions. It has *everything* to do with everyday life and especially with emotions. We need to approach poetry, not with a sense of dread, but with a sense of expectancy. Again, Dana Gioia states: "Poetry is only fractionally intellectual. A poem speaks to you holistically—simultaneously to your mind, your heart, your physical senses, and your memory." [10]

Every reader brings his unique background and emotional makeup to the words of the poem being read, so there are countless responses to a poem's content, all of them inextricably tied to the individual reader. The power of poetry to speak to our imagination is what differentiates it as an art, and not just written language.

As you read poetry, you will find that your imagination stretches and becomes an active part of the work. Imagination is one of the most essential abilities in interpreting art songs; the information you collect from working with poetry integrates seamlessly into your study of the art song as a fusion of poetry and the composer's musical setting.

The Power of Language

*Poetry is the art of using words charged
with their utmost meaning.* [11]

—Dana Gioia

Poetry is simply language. Properly spoken, language can be extremely musical; all words have a rhythm and sound inflection of their own. Poems are full of verbal music and good poets create this verbal music in countless ways. When we read a poem, we immediately begin to see how this works; words sound differently from the way we use them in everyday conversation; the colors and shapes that are part of a word's core makeup start to appear.

We can take part in this celebration of language by reading a poem aloud. When we give ourselves over to the *sounds* of the words, we start to feel the energy that exists in the arrangement of words in poems. We also begin to feel comfortable with the poetic structure in which those words operate.

Poet Muriel Rukeyser:

> The movement of meaning is surely the music of poetry. There isn't any music as we mean music, but there is that movement in the body and the soul, if you like. And one longs for it; it is a deep pleasure and a deep life to us, and there is this union of a physical life and a mental life that comes to us in poetry, and the physical life is bound up with sound in that way. [12]

In his *Poetic Manifesto*, distinguished poet Dylan Thomas described his first encounters with poetry:

> The first poems I knew were nursery rhymes, and before I could read them for myself I had come to love just the words of them, the words alone. What the words stood for, symbolized, or meant, was of very secondary importance. What mattered was the sound of them as I heard them on the lips of the remote and incomprehensible grownups who seemed, for some reason, to be living in my world. And these words were, to me, as the notes of bells, the sounds of musical instruments, the noise of wind, sea and rain, the rattle of milk carts, the clopping of hooves on cobbles, the fingering of branches on a window pane, might be to someone, dead from birth, who has miraculously found his hearing. I did not care what the words said, overmuch. . . I cared for the shapes of sound that their names, and the words describing their actions, made in my ears; I cared for the colors the words cast on my eyes. [13]

Perks from Poetry

Reading poetry offers many "perks" to singers. Some are listed below. All of them assimilate with singing art song.

- Poetry challenges our imagination and kindles our memory.

- Poetry enlarges our understanding of life and humanity.

- Poetry is a means of time travel to places we have not been before.

- Poetry can be exhilarating, disturbing, joyful, poignant, thought-provoking, gloomy, humorous, unusual, reflective—the list could keep going indefinitely through countless adjectives.

- Poetry is a way of developing and training our emotional intelligence. [14]

- Reading poems stocks the mind with powerful images and ideas expressed in unforgettable language. [15]

- Poetry gives us a deeper appreciation of language, the power of words, and how they can function. We learn to think about *how* poetry says something, as well as *what* it says.

- Reading poetry aloud improves our speaking voice and our sense of identity.

- When we work with the sounds of words, we develop a keener sense of clarity and color, which transfers into our interpretation in performance. In a sung phrase we make choices as to color, weight, and vocal inflection. These become more expanded and more effective as a result of working with poems.

It is not the purpose of this chapter or this book to teach you how to analyze poetry, but only how to embrace it for its beauty and for the intrinsic role it plays in creating an art song. In the section at the end of the next chapter entitle "Working with Poetry," there is a selected glossary of terms and definitions having to do with poetry which may prove helpful as you read the poems in this book. At some point, you may want to acquire a dictionary of poetic terms that will help organize your thinking about poems and poetic form.

Beginning to Look at Poems

Poems hang out where life is. [16]

—Susan Goldsmith Wooldridge

How do we become proficient at experiencing poems? Where do we start? Obviously, the first task is to choose a poem to read and work with it. You may want to take the poem from an art song (in English) that you especially like to sing. Copy the poem out away from the musical setting, and begin to look at the poem for word sounds and imagery. Concentrate on the words, or the musical setting of the poem will keep you from experiencing the poem as a *poem*.

There may be a specific poet whose work you have heard and liked; if not, take a poem anthology and browse through it until you see a poem you think you might like to read. If you are really at a loss, begin with a poem in this book, choosing from the list of poems in English in Chapter 3.

Anyone who can read can read a poem. Part of poetry's power is in the sound of the spoken word, so after you have read it silently, you *have* to read it again aloud. One time won't do it. More than one time reading aloud will put you on the right path. You will find upon re-reading a poem that you begin to convey meaning through vocal stress, that you begin to parse the poem's literal and figurative meanings, and that your imagination actively engages in associative feelings. It is actually like having a conversation with the poet, since what his artistic mind and ear created is interacting with your imaginative mind and ear. The more you read, the more you will realize that poems do not have *just one* meaning. Readers make subjective and imaginative choices when they read, and these can change upon re-reading a poem. Unlike prose, a poem read just one time is not fully read.

Guidelines for Beginning Readers of Poetry

Here are a few guidelines for reading poetry:

1. Poems are written in lines. There are punctuation marks to help you read. If the line ends with a comma, the reader should make a pause; if there is a period, there is a full stop. Emily Dickinson's poems contain many dashes, both within and at the ends of lines. Dashes somehow have more vitality than a comma; they seem to drive the poem forward. If there is no punctuation at the end of a poetic line, make a very small pause—to stress or accentuate the last word in the line, but *do not stop*. Keep reading! Sometimes the line doesn't come to an end, but its sense or meaning flows over into the following line.

2. First read the poem silently, then aloud. Read slowly and in a normal tone of voice. Pay attention to the word sounds. Especially notice the verbs, which move the poem's ideas forward. Notice the rhyme scheme. If you read in a relaxed manner, the word sounds of the poem will fall into place, and each word will become easier to hear and understand.

3. "The sound must be an echo to the sense," wrote Alexander Pope. [17] Sound is there to implement meaning and to link it with our senses. The round sounds of open vowels, the clicking of consonants and plosives; the gliding, sliding sounds of fricatives and sibilants—sounds create feeling, atmosphere, and intensity in a poem.

4. Use a dictionary and look up any unfamiliar word or words that are difficult to pronounce. A confident reader must know the literal meaning of every word in the poem.

When you read a poem, don't be afraid to participate with your imagination, your experience, and your intelligence. Poetry is like concentrated energy, waiting for a reader to bring it to life with the sound of their voice and the force of their imagination.

Each reader brings his own set of experiences and imagery to the reading. Just as no two singers sing an art song in exactly the same way, so no two readers react similarly to every detail in a poem.

Things to Notice:

How does it look?

Even before you begin to read it, the poem has a certain appearance or shape on the page. Some poems appeal to the eye and some do not. How does the poem *look*? Is it written in four-line stanzas? In couplets? Is it one long narrative? Does the title make you want to know more about the poem? The first line might immediately catch your attention and draw you into the poem. The poet's name might be familiar or somewhat familiar to you, or not.

An Unusual Poetic Form

One of the most unusual and interesting poetic forms is the pattern poem or the shaped poem. French poet Guillaume Apollinaire often wrote in this style, calling his poems *calligrammes*. In this form, the layout and typography of words, letters, and phrases forms a typographic visual, or picture of the poem's theme. Apollinaire had a keen eye for the visual; he used the blank page to experiment with spatial relationships, which in turn became actual images. Composer Francis Poulenc chose seven of Apollinaire's *calligrammes* to set in a song cycle of the same name. Here is Apollinaire's poem titled "Il pleut" ("It is raining").

Il Pleut

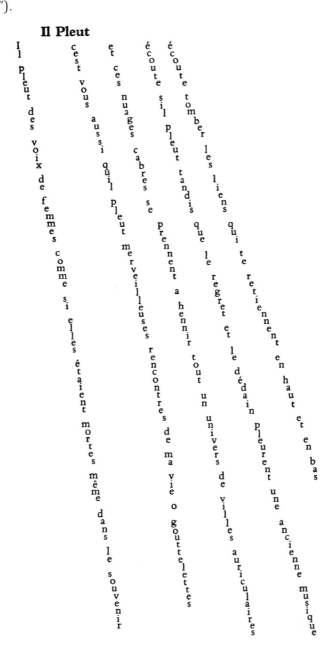

Il pleut

Il pleut des voix de femmes comme si elles étaient mortes même
  dans le souvenir

C'est vous aussi qu'il pleut merveilleuses rencontres de ma vie
  ô gouttelettes

Et ces nuages cabrés se prennent à hennir tout un univers de villes
  auriculaires

Écoute s'il pleut tandis que le regret et le dédain pleurent une
  ancienne musique

Écoute tomber les liens qui te retiennent
  en haut et en bas

—Guillaume Apollinaire (1880–1918)
*Calligrammes—Poèmes de la paix et de
la guerre in Ondes*, published 1918.

It is raining

It is raining women's voices as if they had died even
  in one's memory.

It is raining you too, marvelous encounters of my life,
  oh droplets.

And these reared clouds begin to neigh a whole universe
  of auricular cities.

Listen if it rains while regret and disdain weep an
  ancient music.

Listen to the bonds fall that restrain you
  up and down.

—Translation by Thomas Grubb and Pierre Bernac
Tanglewood Festival, 1979. Used by permission.

Important Basics

There are several component parts of poetry that the novice reader should be aware of:

- WORD SOUNDS
- TEXTURE
- IMAGERY
- RHYTHM

Once you pick up a poem to read it, you can immediately identify these four components, since the same features—in different guises— are found in art songs. They are differentiated only by their respective art forms; poetry is fashioned only of words, and art songs are a blend of both words and music.

Word Sounds

The sound of a poem is the sound of words coming together in an interesting way. [18]

—Carole Kiler Doreski and William Doreski

Poems are alive, as language is alive. Words have shapes, colors, and inflections. Words reverberate with energy. The intensity of that energy is due to the sound of each word, and is bound up with its literal meaning. The totality of the mood of a poem is created in great part by word sounds.

Words in combination with other words can not only move us intellectually, but can also trigger remembered emotions and experiences. So, while reading a poem, the reader adds imagination and experience in response to the words. In a split second, we thread these sensations into the poem without really ever leaving the reading of it. Poet Dylan Thomas wrote that "the best craftsmanship always leaves holes and gaps in the work of the poem so that something that is *not* the poem can creep, crawl, flash, or thunder in." [19]

Of course, Thomas is speaking of a reader's connection with the words. When we are drawn into a poem, we "flesh it out" with experiences from our own life. In reading or listening to poetry, the mind can move backward and forward through the work; it can subconsciously accept or discard several possibilities of meaning and interpretation; it is constantly busy making comparisons and refining relationships.

Some poetry is easy to read, and some is more difficult. It is not necessary to like every poem you read, but if you do read frequently, you will accumulate a list of poems with which you connect emotionally and to which you will return regularly to read again. Poems to which we relate have an immediate appeal to us—words tied together that speak to our emotions and our senses.

Texture

One definition of texture is the quality created by the combination of the different elements in a work of music or literature. In an art song, texture generally refers to the density or sparseness of the piano accompaniment combined with the vocal line. Texture is the accompaniment fabric, woven with harmony, lines of melody, or other distinctive figures.

A poem's texture is a mixture of the sounds of words, the weight of their metrical stress, and the way the poet has combined them to create images. The more detailed the figurative language (imagery), the more interesting and rich the poetic texture. Texture can be vibrant, creating a fabric of words that immediately draws the reader into the poem, or it can be a matter-of-fact informative presentation.

Texture is an essential part of every poem. It makes the poem an experience. All of the poems in the next section ("Imagery") show clearly how detailed imagery produces extraordinary poetic texture.

Imagery

Imagery is a basic component of all poetry, and is often thought of as its most important characteristic. Much of poetry's potent appeal to the reader is through images fashioned from the poet's choice of words. Strung together into lines of poetry, they can become images that appeal to the senses, the imagination, or the memory of the reader. Images in poetry tend to be fluid, and can change with re-readings.

In an interview, poet Louise Glück spoke of imagery this way:

> ...if you can properly frame an image or a verbal gesture in white space, in silence, you can make of that whole movement something equivalent to a single word; that is, the way a word, a contained word, explodes into meaning. It's like those little Japanese stones that you drop into water. They become flowers. That's a metaphor very attractive to me—the idea that something small should ramify.* [20]

As we read poems, the sound of the words and the images they shape belong to us at *that* point in time. We enter the world of the poem and based on the sounds of the words, their meanings, and the way in which the poet has used them, our imaginations become engaged in crafting images.

*ramify: spread out/branch out

Here is a poem by Sara Teasdale. Its images are particularly vivid in their appeal, not only to the mind, but also to the senses. Read the poem, first silently to yourself, then aloud. Notice that when you read aloud, the word sounds cause the images become more vibrant and dramatic.

Barter
Life has loveliness to sell,
  All beautiful and splendid things,
Blue waves whitened on a cliff,
  Soaring fire that sways and sings,
And children's faces looking up
Holding wonder like a cup.

Life has loveliness to sell,
  Music like a curve of gold,
Scent of pine trees in the rain,
  Eyes that love you, arms that hold,
And for your spirit's still delight,
Holy thoughts that star the night.

Spend all you have for loveliness,
  Buy it and never count the cost;
For one white singing hour of peace
  Count many a year of strife well lost,
And for a breath of ecstasy
Give all you have been, or could be.

—Sara Teasdale (1884–1933)

A much older example of a poem filled with sensory images is one from sixteenth-century poet Ben Jonson (1572–1637). It is from *A Celebration of Charis*, and was set as a lute song by an anonymous composer, who titled it "Have you seen but a whyte lilie grow?" Its manuscript is in the British Museum. There are other art song settings of Jonson's poem, including one by Frederick Delius. Jonson uses sensory images one after another: lilies, newly fallen snow, beaver fur, swan's-down, flower's scent, incense, and honey. For the poet, all these images converge to suggest a woman who is the embodiment of everything the words describe: white, soft, and sweet.

Have you seen but a bright lilie grow

Have you seen but a bright lilie grow,
  Before rude hands had touch'd it?
Have you mark'd but the fall of the snow
  Before the Earth hath smutched it?
Have you felt the wool of Beaver,
  Or Swans-down ever?
Or have smelt of the Bud o' the Brier?
  Or the Nard in the fire?
Or have tasted the Bag of the Bee?
O so whyte, O so soft, O so sweet is she!

—Ben Jonson (1572–1637)

The poetry of seventeenth-century poet Robert Herrick is elegantly sensual in its images. In "Upon Julia's Clothes" (see Chapter 3), the poet is so smitten with the lady that her clothes become equally bewitching. As she moves, her dress (perhaps of satin or taffeta) "flows" and "glitters" as if liquid and alive ("That liquefaction of her clothes"). Herrick's poetry was set in two cycles by composer Roger Quilter: *To Julia*, Op. 5 (six settings); and *Five Lyrics of Robert Herrick*, Op. 7; by Ned Rorem in his first song cycle *Flight for Heaven*; and by many other composers as well.

Below is another poem about the captivating Julia, titled "Upon Julia's hair fill'd with dew," wherein Herrick's descriptions are again rich in imagery that appeals to the senses.

Upon Julia's hair fill'd with dew

Dew sat on Julia's hair
And spangled too,
Like leaves that laden are
With trembling dew:
Or glittered to my sight,
As when the beams
Have their reflected light
Danc'd by the streams.

—Robert Herrick (1591–1674)

Once we have spent some time with them, poems belong to us; we can return to them again and again, and find continuous interpretations. When we read a poem, we are in a unique and personal moment, away from our daily routine. Susan Wooldridge writes that poems take her to a place out of normal time and thought: "The poem speaks in confidence, the reader feels included, honored, and keeps the secret." [21]

Rhythm and Rhyme

The rhythm of the poem moves the mind, and rhythm generates meaning. That's one of the splendors of poetry, that it moves the reader's mind in a way it wouldn't move by itself. And maybe it's why we need poetry. [22]

—C. K. Williams

Can you think of nursery rhymes or poems you learned as a child? They remain in our memory almost solely because of their rhythm:

> Baa baa, black sheep,
> Have you any wool?
> Yes sir, yes sir,
> Three bags full.
> One for the master,
> One for the dame,
> And one for the little boy
> Who lives down the lane.

> **OR:**

> Hickory, dickory, dock,
> The mouse ran up the clock.
> The clock struck one,
> The mouse ran down,
> Hickory, dickory, dock.

Most poems are not as elementary in their rhyme schemes as the old nursery rhymes; however, it is generally not difficult to find rhyming schemes in many poems.

Below is a humorous poem by American poet Richard Wilbur. [23] Read it aloud at a fairly relaxed pace. Look for the rhyme scheme; in each stanza each of the four quatrains has the same pattern (ABCB). Wilbur's clever poetic observance of the guards in the art museum provides a wry commentary on fine art and its impact on artists and those whose work puts them in close proximity to art.

Museum Piece   —Richard Wilbur
(set by Stephen Paulus)

The good gray guardians of art
Patrol the halls on spongy <u>shoes</u>,
Impartially protective, though
Perhaps suspicious of <u>Toulouse</u>.

Rhyme Scheme for each
quatrain (Stanza) ABCB

Here dozes one against the wall,
Disposed upon a funeral <u>chair</u>.
A Degas dancer pirouettes
Upon the parting of his <u>hair</u>.

See how she spins! The grace is there,
But strain as well is plain to <u>see</u>.
Degas loved the two together:
Beauty joined to <u>energy</u>.

Edgar Degas purchased once
A fine El Greco, which he <u>kept</u>
Against the wall beside his bed
To hang his pants on while he <u>slept</u>.

Discovering the rhyme scheme of poems involves scansion of poetic lines for patterns of stress. If you are interested in going deeper into studying poetic forms, there are many texts to help you do this. The purpose of this book is to identify some of the elements in poetry that easily connect with elements in music. When an art song evolves from the union of a poem and a composer's musical setting of that poem, the singer's preparation of the poem *as a poem* will yield excellent results when the singer moves on to study the words in the musical framework the composer has created for them.

Noticing Dramatic Qualities

Do not try to be too analytical reading a poem for the first time. Enjoy the word sounds, notice the imagery that pleases you, and appreciate the rhythm of the phrases. In order to begin to think dramatically about the poem—which will help you begin to think about interpreting it as a reader and later as a singer—there are three questions to try and answer. Try and define simply: who is speaking, to whom they are speaking, and the setting in which they speak. These are the three main questions to answer first; there is a longer list with which to work in the following chapter.

With these questions in mind, take an art song in English that you are particularly fond of singing and read its poem *away* from its musical setting—that is, read the poetry *as poetry*. Try and answer the questions above. Read the poem again. You might have a different slant on the poem's meaning as a result of looking for the information above.

Reading Poetry—Pleasure Through Sound

...the subject in most poems doesn't matter; a poem is a singing; it's an enactment of the human voice singing... What's important is how the poet sings. [24]

—C. K. Williams

Sound in poetry *does* give us pleasure; it creates the atmosphere in which the words can work and in which the poet can create his magic. If you read the example poems in the "Imagery" section of this chapter, you can begin to understand how figurative language holds sway in a poem and its effect upon the reader or listener.

Every poem has its own verbal soundscape tied in part to the historical time in which it was written. Some poems use words which we consider archaic today; Shakespeare's sonnets are love poems of the sixteenth century; Elizabeth Bishop's "Sonnet (1928)" is a contemporary poem but uses the sonnet form; cowboy poetry and rap poetry are light years away from the work of Pablo Neruda. Poetry for the last 100 years or so has largely been unmetered and quite free; only the texture and vitality of the word sounds, the intent of the poet, and the power of the way he uses those sounds makes the poetry speak.

Poetry is an art, but like music, it is inanimate on the page until the reader or singer gives it life. Therefore, the reading of poetry is an art, just as is the performance of art song, which gives poetry a new structure of sound to live in—that of music.

Your goal is to enter the life of the poem. There really is no set of rules to follow or formula that will guarantee success every time you read, but like practicing vocal technique, consistent practice will bring results.

Reading Poetry—Pleasure Through Association

When we read poetry, the words form images. We also call up images from our past experiences or our imagination creates newly minted pictures that spin off the poem's literal images. It is akin to a miniature chain reaction—one so blazingly fast that we might not realize it is happening. Our minds, writes Frances Mayes, are naturally associative, and one thing brings to mind another, without logical connection. [25] This is one way—perhaps the most important way—our imagination creates pleasure as we read poetry.

Hearing Poems—Pleasure Through Listening

If the idea of beginning to read poetry on a regular basis is a bit overwhelming, then a comfortable way to begin might be to access websites on the Internet that have audio and video files of poets reading their own works, or actors reading poems. There are also CDs of poetic readings available.

It has become increasingly easy to research poetry on the Internet. You can search on YouTube for "poets reading their poetry," "poets reading their poems," by the name of the poet, or even the name of the poem. Inevitably, as usually happens on these searches, you will find peripheral pictures/names to click on and you're off and running on a wonderful listening experience. Hearing poems read aloud by their creators is always special, and often helps the listener understand the poem better. Word sounds also tend to fall on the listening ear with more power than when a newcomer to reading poetry is reading.

In addition to YouTube for videos and audio files of poetry readings, there are two really excellent websites that are tended by The Academy of American Poets (poets.org) and The Poetry Foundation (poetryfoundation.org), that offer the explorer an abundance of riches for listening *and* reading (see "Some Helpful Resources" below).

This section has touched on pleasure and what poetic qualities produce it; however, pleasure itself needs no justification. Pleasure— especially aesthetic pleasure—is synonymous with beauty, and beauty is a basic need of humankind. Poet Wallace Stevens observed: "The purpose of poetry is to contribute to man's happiness. Children know this essential truth when they ask to hear their favorite nursery rhymes again and again. Aesthetic pleasure needs no justification, because a life without such pleasure is one not worth living." [26]

Reading and Memorizing Poems

After you have read a poem that you really like, you may find that after many readings you have memorized—or almost memorized—all of it. After we have memorized a poem, we can say with confidence that we "know" the poem—or, child-like, we say: "I know it by heart." That is an interesting little phrase; it not only implies that we can recite the poem without looking at the printed words, but that we have also internalized the poem's emotional content. The poem has become ours. When we begin to study the musical setting of an art song that we sing, the words are already a part of our spirit. When we memorize poetry, the words undergo a personal transformation; they become part of our stored feelings and experiences.

Some Helpful Resources

Websites to Visit

The Academy of American Poets (www.poets.org)

The website, at this writing, features the biographies of more than 500 poets, news about poets, poems, essays and interviews on poetry, audio and video, and *Life Lines—Vital Words*—about the lines of poetry people from all walks of life carry with them for comfort or laughter, and why. You can also keep your own "Notebook" on the site—for storing items you want to keep track of—biographies, poems, audio clips, and events.

The Poetry Foundation (www.poetryfoundation.org)

This website is sponsored and maintained by the Poetry Foundation, and has a wealth of information about poets and poetry. The website also supports monthly poetry lectures, talks given by notable scholars and critics on poets, poetry, and their intersections with other art forms. In addition to live events, these talks feature recordings from historic archives.

A project sponsored by the Poetry Foundation and the National Endowment for the Arts is titled "Poetry Out Loud" (poetryoutloud. org) and is a national recitation competition. The 2006 finals were televised and are available on the website in an eleven minute video. The final contestants were all young people. The memorized recitations, the emotional commitment, and passion that the young finalists brought to their readings are inspiring. This would be an excellent video for young singers to watch.

PBS Newshour Poetry Series, featured on PBS, was founded by the Poetry Foundation, and engages a broader audience with poetry through a series of thoughtful, in-depth reports and interviews on contemporary poets and poetry.

The Poetry Archive (www.poetryarchive.org)

The Poetry Archive is the world's premier online collection of recordings of poets reading their work. You can listen to the voices of contemporary English-language poets and of poets from the past. The Poetry Archive, based in the United Kingdom, is dedicated to preserving, as far as is possible, sound archives of poets and their work. The website will guide the researcher (you) to explore the Archive through individual poems, selected by title, poetic forms, or poetic themes. There are also a number of video interviews with poets. Hearing the poet reading or talking about his own work is unique; it helps the listener to better understand the poem as well as to enjoy it.

All three of these websites are fascinating, extensive, informative, and entertaining sites to browse for poetry and for inspiration.

Poetry Books with Recordings or Videos

Robert Pinsky and Maggie Dietz, eds. *An Invitation to Poetry: A New Favorite Poem Project Anthology* (New York: W. W. Norton & Co., 2004). Includes a DVD featuring project participants reading their favorite poems from Shakespeare to Szymborska. The readers are people from a cross-section of professions across the United States—a construction worker, a Supreme Court justice, a glass blower, a Marine—each speaking about his or her connection to the poem.

There are 200 poems in the book. An excellent anthology—something for everyone.

John Lithgow, ed. and compiler, ***Poet's Corner: The One-and-Only Poetry Book for the Whole Family*** (New York: Grand Central Publishing, 2007). Lithgow has chosen fifty poets, and included short biographies and poems by each. A bonus MP3 CD of poetry readings by Lithgow and twelve distinguished actors is included—among them: Morgan Freeman, Lynn Redgrave, Susan Sarandon, Helen Mirren, Glenn Close, Sam Waterston, and Kathy Bates.

Some Foreign Language Resources for Listening to Poetry

If you spend a small amount of time on the Internet and in the library, you can locate very helpful information about reading in a foreign language. Using these aids does not exclude nor excuse *your* participation as a reader of poems! But hearing a native speaking reader recite poems in the original language will put the prosody and inflection in your ear and facilitate your own efforts.

Here are some other resources to consult:

- **Song anthologies with accompanying CDs**, with the song texts read by native speakers. These are very helpful as a starting point for reading the poems yourself.

- **Spend some research time on the Internet** to locate audio materials on the topic of foreign language poetry set as art songs. There might be some helpful materials that could be downloaded.

- ***106 French Recitations by Martial Singher***, a set of two CDs or tapes with a book of texts and translations is an excellent resource for French poetry. Singher, a distinguished French baritone, reads the French poems that encompass a list of important French *mélodie* repertoire. Singher's mellifluous voice will draw you into the French language in no time. (Published by Pocket Coach, Inc., this can be found on the publisher's website: www.pocketcoach.com) The website also offers a set of two German CDs in the same format as above, read by Dietrich Erbelding.

Applications (Apps) for Electronic Devices

Because smartphones, tablets, and computers arrive, disappear, and change with such dizzying speed, the applications (apps) listed here should be looked up on the Internet for applicability and availability for your personal devices.

- *Poem Flow* (Initial download free)

  Each day a new poem flows to thousands of screens around the world. Each device receives the same poem on the same day creating an instant, invisible community of simultaneous readers. When you click on the poem of the day, the screen displays the place where the last reader lives and how long ago they read the poem. If you're not certain that people *really* read poetry on a daily basis, this should convince you.

  The poems are chosen from the greatest poems in English, many contemporary. Turn the screen in your hand, and each poem dissolves into a gentle reading animation. Turned back, the original poem format returns. You begin with twenty poems to keep and share and may purchase additional poems for a very nominal free. The Academy of American Poets created this app.

- *Poetry Everywhere* (free app.) WGBH Interactive and Dave Grubin Productions in association with the Poetry Foundation. A collection of short poetry videos, featuring contemporary poets reading their own works, introduced by Garrison Keillor.

- *Discover Poetry* (free app.) The Poetry Foundation also made this application available, and it is another interactive app. that allows you to choose poems by "themes" (nature, love, spirituality, celebrations, joy, humor, gratitude, and so on).

Selected Bibliography for this Chapter

The books listed below are a good beginning list of references from which to continue exploring the ideas in this chapter and the next. The books on this list contain example poems, but with one exception, they are *not* anthologies of poetry. Please note that most of these books also appear in the **Selected Bibliography** at the end of this book.

Edward Hirsch, *How to Read a Poem and Fall In Love with Poetry* (New York: A Harvest Book, Harcourt, Inc., 1999).

John Lithgow, compiler. *The Poet's Corner: The One-and-Only Poetry Book for the Whole Family* (New York: Grand Central Publications, Hachette Book Group USA, 2007). Comes with an accompanying CD with various actors reading selected poetry from the book.

Frances Mayes, *The Discovery of Poetry: A Field Guide to Reading and Writing Poems* (New York: A Harvest Original, Harcourt, Inc., 2001).

Mary Oliver, *Rules for the Dance: A Handbook for Writing and Reading Metric Verse* (Boston, MA: A Mariner Original, Houghton Mifflin Co., 1998).

Laurence Perrine, *Sound and Sense: An Introduction to Poetry* (New York: Harcourt, Brace & World, Inc., 1963).

Susan Goldsmith Wooldridge, *poemcrazy: freeing your life with words* (New York: Three Rivers Press, 1995).

Article:

This reference belongs in this section, although it is not a book of poetry. Its content speaks to working with poetry in the voice studio.

Gerald Seminatore, "Teaching Poetry Through Song: A Modest Proposal," *Journal of Singing* 66, no. 5 (May/June 2010): 515–525. A helpful article on working with poetry in the voice studio.

NOTES

1   Charles B. Wheeler, *The Design of Poetry* (New York: W. W. Norton & Co., 1966), 6.

2   Maya Angelou, quoted in Carolyn Lindley Cooley, *The Music of Emily Dickinson's Poems and Letters* (Jefferson, NC: McFarland and Company, 2003), introductory page to the Preface.

3   Babette Deutsch, *Poetry Handbook: A Dictionary of Terms*, 4th edition (New York: HarperResource, 1974), 126.

4   Dana Gioia, "An Afternoon with the Poet," a videotaped address at UCSD TV, found on www.songofamerica.net/cgi-gin/iowa/writer/134.html (accessed December 4, 2011). Dana Gioia is former chairman of the National Endowment for the Arts (2003–2008), and an articulate advocate for poetry. He is himself a much-admired poet.

5   Rainer Maria Rilke, quoted on the website of the Academy of American Poets www.poets. org; www.poets.org/page.php/prmlD/59 (accessed November 19, 2011).

6   Jorge Luis Borges. *This Craft of Verse*, The Charles Eliot Norton Lectures, ed. Cǎlin-Andrei Mihǎilescu (Cambridge, MA: Harvard University Press, 2000), 6.

7   Robert Frost, quoted in Good Poems, selected and edited by Garrison Keillor (New York: Penguin Books, 2002), 442.

8   Theodore Roethke, quoted in Keillor, 454.

9   Robert N. Linscott, ed., *Selected Poems and Letters of Emily Dickinson* (New York: Anchor Books, a division of Random House, 1959), 19. In a letter to Thomas Higginson.

10 Gioia, ibid.

11 Dana Gioia, "Can Poetry Matter?" in *Essays on Poetry and American Culture*. (Saint Paul, MN: Graywolf Press, 1992), 20.

12 Muriel Rukeyser, quoted in Alexander Neubauer, ed., *Poetry in Person: Twenty-five Years of Conversation with America's Poets* (New York: Alfred A. Knopf, 2011), 29. These are transcriptions of audiotapes of Pearl London's poetry class at the New School in NYC, in which she interviewed contemporary poets and discussed their newest poems.

13 Dylan Thomas, from *Poetic Manifesto*, quoted in Frances Mayes, *The Discovery of Poetry: A Field Guide to Reading and Writing Poetry* (New York: Harcourt, Inc., 2001), 28.

14 Dana Gioia, "The Power of Poetry"; www.poetryoutloud.org/poems-and-performance/ listen-to-poetry (accessed November 11, 2011).

15 Goia, ibid.

16 Susan Goldsmith Wooldridge, *poemcrazy: freeing your life with words* (New York: Three Rivers Press, 1996), 4.

17 Alexander Pope, from *An Essay in Criticism*, quoted in Laurence Perrine, *Sound and Sense: An Introduction to Poetry* (New York: Harcourt, Brace & World, Inc., 1963), viii.
    True ease in writing comes from art, not chance,
    As those move easiest who have learned to dance.
    'Tis not enough no harshness gives offense,
    The sound must seem an echo to the sense.

18 Carole Kiler Doreski and William Doreski, *How to Read and Interpret Poetry* (New York: Arco, a division of Simon & Schuster, Inc.,1988), 1.

19 Dylan Thomas, quoted in Mayes, *The Discovery of Poetry*, 428.

20 Louise Glück, quoted in Neubauer, *Poetry in Person*, 52–53. Glück has twice served as Poet Laureate of the United States.

21 Susan Goldsmith Wooldridge, ibid., 75.

22 C. K. Williams, quoted in Neubauer, *Poetry in Person*, 190.

23 Richard Wilbur (b. 1921) was the second Poet Laureate of the United States (1987), and twice a winner of the Pulitzer Prize for Poetry. He was Leonard Bernstein's librettist for the1956 version of Leonard Bernstein's musical *Candide*. He is also a translator, specializing in seventeenth-century French comedies.

24 C. K. Williams, quoted in Neubauer, *Poetry in Person,* 189.

25 Frances Mayes, ibid., 437.

26 Wallace Stevens, quoted in Dana Gioia, "Can Poetry Matter?," the title essay from *Can Poetry Matter? Essays on Poetry and American Culture* (St. Paul, MN: Graywolf Press MN: 1992), 34 (accessed on danagioia.net/essays/ecgm.htm).

Chapter 3

Working With Poetry

*Savoring the original texts as poetry is
the way to the heart of songs.* [1]

—Philip L. Miller

Making Poetry a Part of
Your Performance Preparation

Poetry is the touchstone component in art song, and as such,
deserves more than a cursory glance from singers who sing those words
in performance. In a sense, the singer *becomes* the poet, re-creating his
poem in a texture of musical sound. We are not just singing words, *we
are singing poems*.

Working with and understanding poetry is the cornerstone
of building a strong musical interpretation, based on the following
guidelines:

- Thorough understanding and familiarity with the text

- Complete mastery of pronunciation and articulation

- Flexibility of vocal inflection, coupled with word meaning

- Ability to read the text aloud, superimposing the dynamics
  and tempos that the composer has used in creating his musical setting

The Sounds of Words

No other choices the poet makes—
subject, structure, speaker—are more important
than the quality of individual words. [2]

—Frances Mayes

The presence of words defines art song as a musical genre. Composers begin with the words and so must singers. When we sing, that fusion of text and tone is filtered through our emotions and intellect. We need to work with the poetry as poetry before fast forwarding to musical interpretation. A singer who works carefully with the poem, sees how the composer's musical conception transmits the words, and is able to communicate that to the listener, is usually an excellent recitalist. This does not happen without a systematic investigative process.

Singers are wordsmiths. Words are our stock in trade. Words are thoughts made audible, images minted from vowels and consonants. When we sing songs, we are singing poems. Both poetry and music appeal to the ear through their rhythms, and to the senses through the images they transmit. Reading poetry sharpens our awareness of how these elements work together. The more we stimulate our imagination, the more nuances we add to our performance.

Poet Dana Gioia suggests: "Poems should be memorized, recited, and performed. The sheer joy of the art must be emphasized. The pleasure of performance is what first attracts children to poetry, the sensual excitement of speaking and hearing the words of the poem." [3] As singers, we need to tap into this forgotten childhood talent. If poems and nursery rhymes were not a part of your childhood experience, it is never too late to discover the joy of reading poems.

In a lecture at the 1996 National Association of Teachers of Singing National Conference in Seattle, prominent singer/teacher Glenda Maurice observed that "poetry teaches us the enormous force of a few words, speaking through the music. The composer is inspired by the poem. The genesis of song is the poem. The singer must serve the poetry also." She went on to say: "Beautiful sound is useless until it defines a thought" and that "words have a shape, a texture, and a color . . . In every musical phrase we sing, we can choose the vowel sound we want to emphasize, the word(s) we want to stress, and the vocal weight needed to achieve these choices." [4]

Speak the Speech, I Pray You…

Speak the speech, I pray you…trippingly on the tongue.
But if you mouth it, as many players do, I had as
lief the town crier spoke my lines.

—William Shakespeare (*Hamlet*)

Reading Poems Aloud

How can we hope to *sing* a poem well unless we can first *read* it well? Reading *aloud* is the answer. Taking the poem in hand and flinging the words into the air *aloud* as a good actor might do, helps us discover the fluidity in a string of words. We physically experience the sounds in the poem's phrases in a way that is different from reading them silently on the printed page. We notice even more the sound and rhythm, and the word order in the poetic phrase. Reading aloud produces the same rhythmic give and take of verbal sound that the composer has set to music, adding yet another layer of sound to the words on the page.

How do we begin to learn to read aloud? One way is to listen to others read poems—perhaps even the poems that we are singing as art songs. Listening to poets read their poems aloud, listening to actors read poetry, or seeking out commercial records of poetry being read help the novice reader to get started reading poetry.

The Internet offers an often bewildering array of information. Perhaps the best place to start is to access the websites of poetry organizations, specifically the Poetry Foundation (www.poetryfoundation.org) and the Academy of American Poets (www.poets.org). These two sites offer a fabulous range of subjects having to do with poetry.

Go to the Poetry Foundation website and watch the videos offered there in connection with their program *Poetry Out Loud*. Watching these young people recite poems or listening to the recorded examples is energizing. The more you listen to poets, actors, and peers read poems aloud, the less intimidating it will seem.

Also, there are many recorded and video examples on the Internet of poets reading their own works and talking about their craft. Many of these can be found on YouTube. Your search should uncover other information that will help in your exploration. There is an extensive list of poems (which have also been set as art songs) at the end of this chapter. These will help in making choices of poems to practice reading aloud.

Reading song texts aloud as an exercise builds awareness of *what the words mean* without the barrier of singing at the same time. Singers need to read the poem as the composer has set it, with all the expressive musical markings indicated in the music—tempos, dynamics, mood, and any guidelines for performance. Reading in this manner heightens our response to word meaning, vowel color, and phrase nuance. We become *aesthetically* aware of the text we will be singing—its emotional and dramatic content are instantly intensified. If we read the text in full-voiced phrases that allow the vowels to resonate freely, we free the speaking voice in the same way we will do when we sing.

It may seem daunting at first, to read words aloud with dramatic inflection. In today's culture, we are accustomed to communicating with each other mumbling into electronic phones held so close to the ear that we need not articulate very well or, we dispense completely with vocal sound as we tap on electronic keyboards that hurl our messages to their destinations via cyberspace.

Commenting on how most students read metrical poetry today, distinguished poet Mary Oliver has this to say:

> They read for comprehension and hear little if anything of the interwoven pleasures of the sound and the pattern of the poem, which are also deeply instructive concerning the statement of the poem, along with the meanings of the words themselves. Not knowing how to listen, they read the poem but they do not hear it sing, or slide, or slow down, or crush with the heel of sound, or leap off the line, or hurry, or sob, or refuse to move from the self-pride of the calm pentameter no matter what fire is rustling through it. [5]

We have lost the art of shaping words aloud and we have lost the experience of tasting consonants and feeling the space of vowels as we say them aloud. Of all people, singers need to regain this skill. Reading aloud helps us discover the fluidity in a string of words. We experience the shape and movement of the poetic lines through inflected pitch, correct pronunciation, and clear articulation. Our diction improves and our imaginations are stretched when we read aloud. Out of this will emerge a sort of verbal melody, one that will serve the interpreter well when he examines how the composer has translated the poem's rhythms into *musical rhythms.*

In master classes, I am accustomed to asking singers to read the poem aloud for the listening audience, and I am always delighted when the poetry is declaimed as though the speaker were improvising it on the spot, with all the engaged vocal energy and honest dramatic inflection that good poetry reading should have. I always know that the song to follow will be sung with the same dramatic commitment and imagination.

The more you work with the poetry you sing, the more liberating you will find it to be. Claire Croiza, distinguished French soprano renowned in later life for the many master classes she gave, affirmed that the poem and the poet were of utmost importance in performance preparation:

> Once everything is in order from the vocal and musical point of view, the tempo, nuances and rhythm, we must think only of the poet. If we think more about the music than of the poetry, we worry about the voice, and about all the obsessive physical difficulties. *We must always think of the poet—it is he who delivers us.* [6]

Working With Foreign Language Texts

Singers need not only to work with poetry in their native language, but with poetry in foreign languages as well. We are expected to have gone beyond correct pronunciation and have worked with the foreign texts we are singing so that we are able to interpret the poetic/ vocal lines with understanding and expressive communication.

If you do not speak the language, get a good dictionary and look up each word that you do not know for correct pronunciation and literal meaning. Do a word-by-word translation of the entire text.

You will also benefit by *listening* to foreign language texts, just as we did for texts in English. There are good reasons for listening to foreign language texts read aloud. Hearing a French or German text being read by a native speaker helps get the sound of the language in our ears, and also serves as a model for our own reading.

After you are able to read the text in the original language, you should then read it in an English translation. There are many translations to choose from—in song anthologies, poetry books, or music publications (see the Bibliography at the end of the book for some ideas). Find and read *several* translations and see which one captures what you think is the truest mood, emotional state, and dramatic impulse of the words' literal meaning.

The most helpful translation is the one you make yourself. When translating foreign texts, first do a word-by-word translation. Do not settle for a paraphrase of the poem or an English version printed in the musical score designed for singing. These are "fitted to the musical line" and are often unrelated to the actual meaning of the poetry.

Also, be careful when accessing translations on the Internet. Some of the poetry sites found there accept submissions from anyone who wishes to post them, and more often than not, they are not "refereed" (judged) before they are posted. They may contain inaccuracies—among them: misspellings, upper/lower case mistakes, or stanza indents which are not in the original poem. If you have done a word-by-word translation on your own, you will be able to put it into a workable translation. Just keep your foreign language dictionary handy. Each time you do this, it becomes easier.

Admittedly, working with poetry in a foreign language is much different and more difficult for English-speaking singers unless they are fluent in the foreign language. In order to feel comfortable working with poetry as outlined above, work with English texts first, then move on to foreign language texts.

American composer Ned Rorem wrote in 1974 that "Americans [voice students/singers] illogically, learn songs in foreign languages first (languages which they neither speak nor think in), often to the exclusion of American—or even English—works . . . 'English is bad to sing in,' say American singers. Because they comprehend the words they can no longer hear them . . . our singers have been geared to language as medium, not message." [7]

Exercises for Working With Texts

The complete vocal artist must cultivate and refine this sensitivity to the word, to poetry, and to literature in general...The singer is always working through a text that in some way or another inspired the vocal line and its texture. [8]

—Thomas Grubb

Exercise 1: Descriptors

In working with a poetic text, this exercise is perhaps the easiest and most elementary. Based on your initial reading and understanding of the poem, list or verbalize in free association:

- Adjectives or adverbs that describe the poetic/dramatic content

- Emotions evoked by the text

This list will vary in length according to the poem, but every poem should yield several descriptors as to content and mood. Some poems are more complex in content and may contain shifts in emotional content. Doing this exercise is excellent preparation for creating subtexts*, since you are working with the images created by the literal meaning of the words in the poem.

Remember when doing this exercise, work with the words *apart* from any musical setting you might know.

Here is a short example list of "descriptors" that might immediately call to mind a song text.

lyrical	vague	playful	bland
charming	bitter	frightening	angry
dramatic	serious	reflective	graceful
powerful	repentant	humorous	passionate
potent	mysterious	seductive	tender

---

*An underlying imagined paraphrase that serves as an exercise in working with texts

Here are five song texts by American, British, German, French, Italian and Spanish poets. The first poem of each national section has been done for you, listing some descriptors that might be used for each poem. Not every person's descriptors will match since our individual imaginations will function differently as we read the poems. When you have made your list, read the poem aloud.

If you are working with a poem in a foreign language, put the English translation to the right of the poem on the page, with the phrases in each language lining up.

Example 1: Five American Poems for Defining Descriptors

Heart, we will forget him   —Emily Dickinson

(set by Aaron Copland, John Duke, Arthur Farwell)

	Descriptors
Heart, we will forget him	Mood: dramatic, determined
You and I, tonight!	
You may forget the warmth he gave,	evocative recollection
I will forget the light.	
When you have done, pray tell me,	anxious
That I my thoughts may dim;	
Haste! lest while you're lagging,	emotional
I may remember him!	poignant

Sonnet (1928)   —Elizabeth Bishop

(set by Lori Laitman, Ben Moore, Judith Cloud, Perry Brass, Tobias Picker)

Descriptors (add your own)

I am in need of music that would flow
Over my fretful, feeling finger-tips,
Over my bitter-tainted, trembling lips,
With melody, deep, clear, and liquid slow.
Oh, for the healing swaying, old and low,
Of some song sung to rest the tired dead,
A song to fall like water on my head,
And over quivering limbs, dream flushed to glow!

There is a magic made by melody:
A spell of rest, and quiet breath, and cool
Heart, that sinks through fading colors deep
To the subaqueous stillness of the sea.
And floats forever in a moon-green pool,
Held in the arms of rhythm and of sleep.

Stopping by Woods on a Snowy Evening —Robert Frost

(set by Ned Rorem, John Duke, Margaret Bonds)

Descriptors (add your own)

Whose woods these are I think I know.
His house is in the village, though;
He will not see me stopping here
To watch his woods fill up with snow.

My little horse must think it queer
To stop without a farmhouse near
Between the woods and frozen lake
The darkest evening of the year.

He gives his harness bells a shake
To ask if there is some mistake.
The only other sound's the sweep
Of easy wind and downy flake.

The woods are lovely, dark, and deep,
But I have promises to keep,
And miles to go before I sleep,
And miles to go before I sleep.

Richard Cory —Edwin Arlington Robinson

(set by John Duke, Charles Naginski)

Descriptors (add your own)

Whenever Richard Cory went down town,
We people on the pavement looked at him:
He was a gentleman from sole to crown,
Clean favored, and imperially slim.

And he was always quietly arrayed,
And he was always human when he talked;
But still he fluttered pulses when he said,
"Good morning," and he glittered when he walked.

And he was rich—yes, richer than a king—
And admirably schooled in every grace:
In fine, we thought that he was everything
To make us wish that we were in his place.

So on we worked, and waited for the light,
And went without the meat, and cursed the bread;
And Richard Cory, one calm summer night,
Went home and put a bullet through his head.

Sure on this shining night   —James Agee

(set by Samuel Barber)

Descriptors (add your own)

Sure on this shining night
Of star-made shadows round,
Kindness must watch for me
This side the ground.

The late year lies down the north,
All is healed, all is health.
High summer holds the earth.
Hearts all whole.

Sure on this shining night
I weep for wonder
wand'ring far alone
Of shadows on the stars.

Example 2: Five British Poems for Defining Descriptors

Upon Julia's Clothes   —Robert Herrick

(set by Ned Rorem [*Flight for Heaven*], John Corigliano, Edwin Penhorwood)

Descriptors (add your own)
Mood: sophisticated, lyrical

Whenas in silks my Julia goes,
Then, then, methinks, how sweetly flows
That liquefaction of her clothes!

fluid, graceful

Next, when I cast mine eyes and see
That brave vibration each way free,
O how that glittering taketh me!

provocative

passionate

He wishes for the cloths of heaven   —W. B. Yeats

(set by Rebecca Clarke, Ivor Gurney, Peter Warlock)

Descriptors (add your own)

Had I the heavens' embroidered cloths,
Enwrought with golden and silver light,
The blue and the dim and the dark cloths
Of night and light and the half-light,
I would spread the cloths under your feet:
But I, being poor, have only my dreams;
I have spread my dreams under your feet;
Tread softly because you tread on my dreams.

Winter   —William Shakespeare

(set by Dominick Argento)

Descriptors **(add your own)**

When icicles hang by the wall,
  And Dick the shepherd blows his nail
And Tom bears logs into the hall,
  And milk comes frozen home in pail,
When blood is nipp'd and ways be foul,
Then nightly sings the staring owl,
Tu-whit!
Tu-who! — a merry note,
While greasy Joan doth keel* the pot.

When all aloud the wind doth blow,
  And coughing drowns the parson's saw,
And birds sit brooding in the snow,
  And Marian's nose looks red and raw,
When roasted crabs** hiss in the bowl,
Then nightly sings the staring owl,
Tu-whit!
Tu-who!—a merry note,
While greasy Joan doth keel the pot.

*skim
** crab apples

Bright Is the Ring of Words
—Robert Louis Stevenson

(set by Ralph Vaughan Williams [*Songs of Travel*];
Ivor Gurney ["Song and Singer"];
Peter Warlock ["To the Memory of a Great Singer"])

Descriptors **(add your own)**

Bright is the ring of words
  When the right man rings them,
Fair the fall of songs
  When the singer sings them.
Still they are carolled and said—
  On wings they are carried—
After the singer is dead
  And the maker buried.

61

Low as the singer lies
  In the field of heather,
Songs of his fashion bring
  The swains together.
And when the west is red
  With the sunset embers,
The lover lingers and sings
  And the maid remembers.

The House of Life: 19. Silent Noon
—Dante Gabriel Rossetti

(set by Ralph Vaughan Williams, Charles Orr, Elinor Remick Warren)

<u>*Descriptors*</u> (add your own)

Your hands lie open in the long fresh grass,—
  The finger-points look through like rosy blooms:
  Your eyes smile peace. The pasture gleams and glooms
'Neath billowing clouds that scatter and amass.
All round our nest, far as the eye can pass,
  Are golden kingcup fields with silver edge
  Where the cow-parsley skirts the hawthorn-hedge.
'Tis visible silence, still as the hour-glass.

Deep in the sun-search'd growths the dragon-fly
Hangs like a blue thread loosened from the sky:—
  So this wing'd hour is dropt to us from above.
Oh! clasp we to our hearts, for deathless dower,
This close-companioned inarticulate hour
  When twofold silence was the song of love.

Foreign Language Texts

Below are some poems in German, French, Italian, and Spanish. Read the poems in the original foreign language, then read the English translation. Do not be in a hurry to get through each line of poetry. If there are any words about which you're in doubt, look up the correct pronunciation or definition.

Example 3: Five German Poems for Defining Descriptors

Das verlassene Mägdlein   —Eduard Möricke
(The forsaken serving maid)

(set by many composers, including Hugo Wolf, Robert Schumann, Robert Franz, Hans Pfitzner)

		Descriptors
Früh, wann die Hähne kräh'n,	Early, at cock-crow,	**Mood: ineffable sadness, resignation**
Eh' die Sternlein verschwinden,*	before the little stars disappear,	
Muß ich am Herde stehn,	I must be at the hearth;	**dreary**
Muß Feuer zünden.	must light the fire.	
Schön ist der Flammen Schein,	The flames blaze beautifully,	**hopeless**
Es springen die Funken,	the sparks fly upward,	
Ich schaue so drein**	I stare at them	
In Leid versunken.	lost in sorrow.	
Plötzlich, da kommt es mir,	Suddenly, it comes to me,	**longing**
Treuloser Knabe,	unfaithful boy,	
Daß ich die Nacht von dir	that all last night	
Geträumet habe.	I dreamt of you.	
Träne auf Träne dann	Tear upon tear then	**desolate**
Stürzet hernieder;	falls down;	
So kommt der Tag heran –	so the day begins –	
O ging er wieder!	would it were gone again!	

* "schwinden" in Wolf, Pfitzner and Schumann
** "darein" in Wolf, Pfitzner and Schumann

Widmung (Dedication)   —Friedrich Rückert

(set by Robert Schumann)

Du meine Seele, du mein Herz,	You my soul, you my heart,
Du meine Wonn', o du mein Schmerz,	You my bliss, oh you my pain
Du meine Welt, in der ich lebe,	You my world in which I live,
Mein Himmel du, darein ich schwebe,	You my heaven, into which I float,
O du mein Grab, in das hinab	Oh you my grave, into which
Ich ewig meinen Kummer gab.	I cast my grief forever.
Du bist die Ruh, du bist der Frieden,	You are repose, you are peace,
Du bist vom Himmel mir beschieden.	You are bestowed upon me from Heaven.
Daß du mich liebst, macht mich mir wert,	Your love for me gives me my worth,
Dein Blick hat mich vor mir verklärt,	Your eyes transfigure me in mine,
Du hebst mich liebend über mich,	You raise me lovingly above myself,
Mein guter Geist, mein beßres Ich!	My guardian spirit, my better self!

Descriptors (add your own)

Der Tod, das ist die kühle Nacht (Death is the cool night)   —Heinrich Heine

(set by Johannes Brahms, Peter Cornelius, Max Reger)

Der Tod, das ist die kühle Nacht	Death is the cool night,
Das Leben ist der schwüle Tag,	Life is the sultry day,
Es dunkelt schon, mich schläfert,	It is growing dark, I am sleepy;
Der Tag hat mich müd gemacht.	The day has made me tired.
Über mein Bett erhebt sich ein Baum,	Above my bed a tree rises,
Drin singt die junge Nachtigall;	where the young nightingale sings;
Sie singt von lauter Liebe,	it sings only of love—
Ich hör es sogar im Traum.	I hear it even in my dream.

Descriptors (add your own)

Liebst du um Schönheit   —Friedrich Rückert
(If you love for beauty)

(set by Gustav Mahler, Clara Schumann, César Cui)

Liebst du um Schönheit,	If you love for beauty,
O nicht mich liebe!	Oh, do not love me!
Liebe die Sonne,	Love the sun,
Sie trägt ein gold'nes Haar!	She has golden hair!
Liebst du um Jugend,	If you love for youth,
O nicht mich liebe!	Oh, do not love me!
Liebe den Frühling,	Love the spring,
Der jung ist jedes Jahr!	It is young every year!
Liebst du um Schätze,	If you love for riches,
O nicht mich liebe!	Oh, do not love me!
Liebe die Meerfrau,	Love the mermaid,
Sie hat viel Perlen klar !	She has many shining pearls!
Liebst du um Liebe,	If you love for love,
O ja—mich liebe!	Oh yes—love me!
Liebe mich immer,	Love me always,
Dich lieb' ich immerdar!	As I will always love you!

Descriptors (add your own)

Das Veilchen —Johann Wolfgang von Goethe
(The Violet)

(set by Wolfgang Amadeus Mozart)

Ein Veilchen auf der Wiese stand,	A violet stood in the meadow,
Gebückt in sich und unbekannt;	modest, and known to none;
Es war ein herzigs Veilchen!	It was a charming violet!
Da kam ein' junge Schäferin	There came a young shepherdess
Mit leichtem Schritt und munterm Sinn	light of step and merry of heart
Daher, daher,	this way, this way
Die Wiese her, und sang.	Along the meadow, and sang.
Ach! denkt das Veilchen, wär ich nur	Oh! thought the violet, if only I were
Die schönste Blume der Natur,	the most beautiful flower in nature,
Ach, nur ein kleines Weilchen,	Oh, just for a little while
Bis mich das Liebchen abgep- flückt	so that this sweet girl might pick me
Und an dem Busen matt gedrückt!	And press me until limp to her bosom!
Ach nur, ach nur	Ah only, only
Ein Viertelstündchen lang!	for a quarter of an hour!
Ach! aber ach! das Mädchen kam	Oh! but alas! the maiden came
Und nicht in acht das Veilchen nahm,	and did not notice the violet—
Ertrat das arme Veilchen.	and crushed the poor violet underfoot.
Es sank und starb und freut' sich noch:	It sank, and died, but still was happy:
Und sterb' ich denn, so sterb' ich doch	For though I die, yet still I die
Durch sie, durch sie,	through her, through her,
Zu ihren Füßen doch.	right at her feet.

Descriptors (add your own)

Example 4: Five French Poems for Defining Descriptors

Clair de lune (Moonlight)　　　—Paul Verlaine

(set by Gabriel Fauré, Claude Debussy, Jósef Szulc,
J.Canteloube, Gustave Charpentier)

		Descriptors
Votre âme est un paysage choisi	Your soul is a chosen landscape	Mood: lyrical, intimate
Que vont charmant masques et bergamasques,	Charmed by masks and bergamasks	
Jouant du luth et dansant, et quasi	Playing the lute and dancing, and almost	
Tristes sous leurs déguisements fantasques.	Sad beneath their fantastic disguises.	
Tout en chantant sur le mode mineur	While singing in the minor key	expressive
L'amour vainqueur et la vie opportune.	Of victorious love and the good life,	subtle, graceful
Ils n'ont pas l'air de croire à leur bonheur,	They do not seem to believe in their happiness,	
Et leur chanson se mêle au clair de lune,	And their song blends with the moonlight.	
Au calme clair de lune triste et beau,	With the calm moonlight, sad and beautiful,	sensual
Qui fait rêver, les oiseaux dans les arbres,	That makes the birds dream in the trees,	
Et sangloter d'extase les jets d'eau,	And the fountains sob with rapture,	evocative
Les grands jets d'eau sveltes parmi les marbres.	The tall slender fountains among the marble statues.	

Mandoline (Mandolin) —Paul Verlaine

(set by Gabriel Fauré, Claude Debussy, Jósef Szulc,
Reynaldo Hahn, Poldowski [Lady Dean Paul])

Les donneurs de sérénades	The serenaders
Et les belles écouteuses	And their lovely listeners
Échangent des propos fades	Exchange trivial banter
Sous les ramures chanteuses.	Under the singing boughs.
C'est Tircis et c'est Aminte,	It is Tircis and Aminte,
Et c'est l'éternel Clitandre,	And the tiresome Clitandre,
Et c'est Damis qui pour mainte	And Damis, who for many a
Cruelle fait maint vers tendre.	Cruel woman writes many a tender verse.
Leus courtes vestes de soie,	Their short silken jackets,
Leurs longues robes à queues,	Their long dresses with trains,
Leur élégance, leur joie	Their elegance, their joy
Et leurs molles ombres bleues,	And their soft blue shadows,
Tourbillonnent dans l'extase	Whirl wildly in the rapture
D'une lune rose et grise,	Of a pink and gray moon,
Et la mandoline jase	And the mandolin chatters on
Parmi les frissons de brise.	Amid the shivering breeze.

Descriptors (add your own)

Si mes vers avaient des ailes (If my verses had wings)   —Victor Hugo

(set by Reynaldo Hahn)

Mes vers fuiraient, doux et frêles,	My verses would fly, fragile and gentle,
Vers votre jardin si beau,	To your beautiful garden,
Si mes vers avaient des ailes,	If my verses had wings,
Comme l'oiseau.	Like a bird.
Ils voleraient, étincelles,	They would fly, like sparks,
Vers votre foyer qui rit,	To your cheery hearth,
Si mes vers avaient des ailes,	If my verses had wings,
Comme l'esprit.	Like my spirit.
Près de vous, purs et fidèles	Pure and faithful, to your side
Ils accourraient nuit et jour,	They would hasten night and day
Si mes vers avaient des ailes,	If my verses had wings,
Comme l'amour.	Like love.

Descriptors (add your own)

Lamento (Lament)   —Théophile Gautier

(set by Henri Duparc, Hector Berlioz ["Au cimitière"])

Connaissez-vous la blanche tombe	Do you know the white tomb
Où flotte avec un son plaintif	Where with a plaintive sound, floats
L'ombre d'un if?	The shadow of a yew tree?
Sur l'if une pâle colombe,	On the yew a pale dove
Triste et seule au soleil couchant,	Sad and alone in the setting sun,
Chante son chant.	Sings its song.
On dirait que l'âme éveillée	As though the awakened soul
Pleure sous terre à l'unisson	Weeps, under the earth, in unison
De la chanson,	With the song,
Et du malheur d'être oubliée	And from the unhappiness of being forgotten
Se plaint dans un roucoulement,	Moans in cooing sounds
Bien doucement.	Very softly.

Ah! jamais plus près de la tombe	Ah! nevermore near the tomb
Je n'irai, quand descend le soir	Shall I go, when night descends
Au manteau noir,	In its black cloak,
Écouter la pâle colombe	To hear the pale dove
Chanter, sur la branche de l'if	Sing on the branch of the yew
Son chant plaintif?	Its plaintive song.

Descriptors (add your own)

Lydia —Charles-Marie-René Leconte de Lisle

(set by Gabriel Fauré)

Lydia sur tes roses joues	Lydia, onto your rosy cheeks
Et sur ton col frais et si blanc,	And onto your neck, so fresh and white
Roule étincelant	There rolls down, gleaming
L'or fluide que tu dénoues;	The flowing gold that you loosen.
Le jour qui luit est le meilleur;	The day that is dawning is the best;
Oublions l'éternelle tombe.	Let us forget the eternal tomb.
Laisse tes baisers de colombe	Let your kisses, your dove-like kisses
Chanter sur ta lèvre en fleur.	Sing on your blossoming lips.
Un lys caché répand sans cesse	A hidden lily ceaselessly spreads
Une odeur divine en ton sein:	A divine scent in your bosom.
Les délices comme un essaim	Delights, like swarming bees
Sortent de toi, jeune déesse.	Emanate from you, young goddess!
Je t'aime et meurs, ô mes amours.	I love you and die, oh my love,
Mon âme en baisers m'est ravie!	My soul is ravished in kisses
O Lydia, rends-moi la vie,	O Lydia, give me back my life,
Que je puisse mourir toujours!	That I may die, die forever!

Descriptors (add your own)

Example 5: Five Italian Poems for Defining Descriptors

Amarilli   —Anonymous

(set by Giulio Caccini)

		Descriptors
Amarilli, mia bella,	Amarilli, my beautiful one	**Mood: romantic, persuasive**
Non credi, o del mio cor dolce desio,	Do you not believe, my heart's sweet desire,	
D'esser tu l'amor mio?	That it is you I love?	**intimate**
Credilo pur: e se timor t'assale,	Do believe it: and if fear assails you,	**assertive**
Dubitar non ti vale,	You should have no doubts	
Aprimi il petto e vedrai scritto in core:	Open my breast and see what is written on my heart	
Amarilli è il mio amore.	Amarilli is my love.	**ecstatic**

Delizie contente   —Giacento Andrea Cicognini

(set by Francesco Cavalli)

Delizie contente, che l'alma beate, fermate.
Su questo mio core deh più non stillate le gioie d'amore.
Delizie mie care, fermatevi qui:
non so più bramare, mi basta così.

In grembo agli amori fra dolci catene, morir, mi conviene.
Dolcezza omicida a morte, mi guida, mi guida in braccio
   al mio bene.
Dolcezze mie care, fermatevi qui: non so più bramare,
   mi basta così.

Joyful delights, making my soul happy, cease.
Upon this heart of mine
do not tickle the joys of love any more.
Dear pleasures, come to an end now:
I cannot desire anymore, it is enough.
In the lap of love, in sweet chains, it is better for me to die.
Murderous sweetness, lead me to death
in the arms of my beloved.

—English translation by Martha Gerhart

Descriptors (add your own)

71

Intorno all'idol mio   —Anonymous
(Around my idol)

(set by Marc'Antonio Cesti)

Intorno all'idol mio spirate pur, spirate,	Blow, sweet and pleasant breezes
Aure, Aure soavi e grate,	Around my idol,
E nelle guancie elette	And on his dear cheeks
Baciatelo per me,	Kiss him for me,
Cortesi, cortesi aurette!	Kind little breezes!
Al mio ben, che riposa	And my love who sleeps
Su l'ali della quiete,	On the wings of peace
Grati, grati sogni assistete	with pleasant dreams
E il mio racchiuso ardore	Reveal to him for me,
Svelate gli per me,	My secret ardor,
O larve, o larve d'amore!	O spirits of love!

Descriptors (add your own)

Se tu m'ami, se sospiri   —Paolo Antonio Rolli
(If you love me, if you sigh)

(set by Alessandro Parisotti [misattributed to Giovanni Battista Pergolesi], Corona Schröter, Antonio Vivaldi)

Se tu m'ami, se sospiri	If you love me, if you sigh
Sol per me, gentil pastor,	Only for me, gentle shepherd
Ho dolor de' tuoi martiri,	I am pained by your sufferings,
Ho diletto del tuo amor,	Yet I delight in your love.
Ma se pensi che soletto	But if you think that
Io ti debba riamar,	I must in return love only you
Pastorello, sei soggetto	Dear little shepherd, you simply
Facilmente a t'ingannar.	Deceive yourself.
Bella rosa porporina	A beautiful red rose
Oggi Silvia sceglierà,	Sylvia will choose today,
Con la scusa della spina	Then, with the excuse of its thorns,
Doman poi la sprezzerà.	Tomorrow she will discard it.
Ma degli uomini il consiglio	The advice of men
Io per me non seguirò.	I will not follow—

| Non perché mi piace il giglio | Just because the lily pleases me |
| Gli altri fiori sprezzerò. | I do not have to dislike all other flowers. |

<u>*Descriptors*</u> (add your own)

Malinconia, ninfa gentile   —Ippolito Pindemonte (Melancholy, gracious nymph)

(set by Vincenzo Bellini)

Malinconia, ninfa gentile,	Melancholy, gracious nymph,
la vita mia consacro a te;	I devote my life to you.
i tuoi piaceri chi tiene a vile,	Whoever scorns your pleasures
ai piacer veri nato non è.	is not born for true pleasures.

Fonti e colline chiesi agli dei;	I asked the gods for fountains and hills,
m'udiron alfine, pago io vivrò,	At last they heard me, and I shall live satisfied,
né mai quel fonte co' desir miei	I shall never desire to pass beyond
né mai quel monte trapasserò.	that spring or that mountain!

<u>*Descriptors*</u> (add your own)

Example 6: Five Spanish Poems for Defining Descriptors

El tra la la y el punteado   —Fernando Periquet (Tra la la and the plucked guitar)

(set by Enrique Granados)

		<u>*Descriptors*</u>
Es en balde, majo* mío,	It is useless, my majo	**Mood: teasing, playful**
que sigas hablando,	To continue talking,	
porque hay cosas que contesto	because there are some things I answer	
yo siempre cantando.	Only by singing.	**flirtatious**
Tra la la . . .	Tra la la . . .	
Por más que preguntes tanto,	No matter how much you ask	**mocking**
tra la la . . .	tra la la . . .	
en mí no causas quebranto	You'll not interrupt me	

73

ni yo he de salir de mi canto,	nor cause me to stop my song.	**triumphant**
tra la la . . .	tra la la . . .	

*A man of eighteenth-century Madrid

Pámpano verde
(Green vine)

—Francisco de la Torre

(set by Arne Dørumsgaard)

Pámpano verde	Green vine
razimo alvar;	white cluster;
¿Quién vido dueñas *	Whoever saw duennas
a tal ora andar?	out at this hour?
Enzinueco entr'ellas	In their midst
entre las donzellas.	the young girls are seen.
Pámpano verde	Green vine
razimo alvar;	white cluster;
¿Quién vido dueñas	Whoever saw duennas
a tal ora andar?	out at this hour?

*An older woman who serves as a governess/companion to young girls

Descriptors (add your own)

Paño murciano (Cloth from Murcia)

—Anonymous

(set by Joaquín Nin)

Diga usted, señor platero,	Tell me, Mister Silversmith,
Cuanta plata es menester	How much silver is needed
Para engarzar un besito	to set a little kiss
De boca de una mujer.	From my lover's lips?
Señor platero, he pensado	Mister Silversmith, I've heard
Que usted sabe engarzar;	that you are a master of your art;
Por eso le venga a dar	I've come to give you
Una obrita de cuidado.	a little job worthy of your craftsmanship.
A mí un besito me ha dado	A most tempting little kiss
Mi novia con gran salero.	my sweetheart gave me,
Engarzarlo en plata quiero,	I want to set it in silver
Porque soy su fiel amante.	since I'm her faithful lover.
¿Qué plata sera bastante?	How much silver would it take?
Diga usted señor platero.	Please tell me, Mister Silversmith.

Descriptors (add your own)

Del cabello más sutil (From the finest hair)

—Anonymous

(set by Fernando Obradors)

Del cabello más sutil	From the finest hair
Que tienes en tu trenzado	In your braided tresses
he de hacer una cadena	I want to make a chain
Para traerte a mi lado.	So I may draw you to my side.
Una alcarraza en tu casa,	A water jug in your house
Chiquilla, quisiera ser,	Little one, I'd like to be,
Para besarte en la boca,	so that I might kiss your lips,
Cuando fueras a beber.¡Ay !	whenever you take a drink. Ah!

Descriptors (add your own)

El vito *   —Anonymous

(set by Joaquín Nin, Fernando Obradors)

Una vieja vale un real **	An old woman is worth a real
y una muchacha dos cuartos, ***	and a young girl two cuartos,
y yo, como soy tan pobre	and I, because I'm so poor
me voy a lo más barato.	I'll go for the cheapest.
Con el vito, vito, vito,	On with the dancing,
con el vito, vito, va.	with the dancing, dancing, ole!
No me jaga 'usté' cosquillas,	Stop your teasing, now
que me pongo 'colorá'.	your tickling makes me blush!

* *Vito.* A fiery dance performed in the taverns by a woman standing on a table before an audience of bullfighters.

** *Real.* A silver coin.

*** *Cuarto.* A copper coin

(Unless indicated, translations of foreign texts by Carol Kimball)

Exercise 2: Getting in Touch With Your Speaking Voice

All the fun's in how you say a thing. [9]

—Robert Frost

Texture = Sound Quality

Poetry, like music, is an aural medium. As listeners, we react to the resonance of words as we hear them. Author Francis Mayes writes: "sound alone tells a lot about the poem . . . It is as if you could run your hand over the poem's surface." [10] Word sounds may be flowing or choppy, smooth or harsh, heavy or light. Their sound characteristics help define the poem's texture.

Below are five poems with distinctively different sound qualities, rhythms, and images. Practice reading them aloud. Use crisp articulation, but try and capture the overall sound quality and overall mood of the poem. This exercise is not meant to be analytical, but simply to give the reader pleasure from experiencing the texture of the words. As you read aloud, you will find that you are translating the words into images and that you are applying your imagination simultaneously with the sound of your voice.

Just as a song is recreated in performance, so a poem is revitalized each time it is read. Each time we read a poem, it becomes new again; each time we sing a song, it is re-created

As in Exercise 1, the names of some composers who have set these texts are given in parentheses after the poet's name.

Example 1: Reading Aloud to Experience Texture

Dover Beach

The sea is calm to-night.
The tide is full, the moon lies fair
Upon the straits; — on the French coast the light
Gleams and is gone; the cliffs of England stand,
Glimmering and vast, out in the tranquil bay.
Come to the window, sweet is the night-air!
Only, from the long line of spray
Where the sea meets the moon-blanched land,
Listen! you hear the grating roar
Of pebbles which the waves draw back, and fling,
At their return, up the high strand,
Begin, and cease, and then again begin,
With tremulous cadence slow, and bring
The eternal note of sadness in.

Sophocles long ago
Heard it on the Aegean, and it brought
Into his mind the turbid ebb and flow
Of human misery; we
Find also in the sound a thought,
Hearing it by this distant northern sea.

The Sea of Faith
Was once, too, at the full, and round earth's shore
Lay like the folds of a bright girdle furled.
But now I only hear
Its melancholy, long, withdrawing roar,
Retreating, to the breath
Of the night-wind, down the vast edges drear
And naked shingles of the world.

Ah, love, let us be true
To one another! for the world, which seems
To lie before us like a land of dreams,
So various, so beautiful, so new,
Hath really neither, joy, nor love, nor light,
Nor certitude, nor peace, nor help for pain;
And we are here as on a darkling plain
Swept with confused alarms of struggle and flight,
Where ignorant armies clash by night.

—Matthew Arnold (1822–1888)
from *New Poems*, published 1867
(set by Samuel Barber, Op.3, published 1936,
for medium voice and string quartet)

Example 2: Reading Aloud to Experience Texture

Jabberwocky

'Twas brillig, and the slithy toves
    Did gyre and gimble in the wabe;
All mimsy were the borogoves,
    And the mome raths outgrabe.

"Beware the Jabberwock, my son!
    The jaws that bite, the claws that catch!
Beware the Jubjub bird, and shun
    The frumious Bandersnatch!"

He took his vorpal sword in hand:
    Long time the manxome foe he sought—
So rested he by the Tumtum tree,
    And stood awhile in thought.

And, as in uffish thought he stood,
    The Jabberwock, with eyes of flame,
Came whiffling through the tulgey wood,
    And burbled as it came!

One, two! One, two! And through and through
    The vorpal blade went snicker-snack!
He left it dead, and with its head
    He went galumphing back.

"And, hast thou slain the Jabberwock?
  Come to my arms, my beamish boy!
O frabjous day! Callooh! Callay!"
  He chortled in his joy.

'Twas brillig, and the slithy toves
  Did gyre and gimble in the wabe;
All mimsy were the borogoves,
  And the mome raths outgrabe.

—Lewis Carroll (1832–1898)
from *Through the Looking-Glass and
What Alice Found There*, published 1871
(set by Lee Hoiby, John Duke)

Example 3: Reading Aloud to Experience Texture

O mistress mine, where are you roaming?

O mistress mine, where are you roaming?
O, stay and hear, your true love's coming,
  That can sing both high and low.
Trip no further, pretty sweeting;
Journeys end in lovers' meeting,
  Ev'ry wise man's son doth know.

What is love? 'Tis not hereafter.
Present mirth hath present laughter;
  What's to come is still unsure.
In delay there lies no plenty;
Then come kiss me, sweet-and-twenty,
  Youth's a stuff will not endure.

—William Shakespeare (1564–1616)
from *Twelfth Night*, Act II, Scene 3
(set by many composers including
Roger Quilter, Gerald Finzi, Erich Korngold,
Amy Beach, Peter Warlock, Mario Castelnuovo-Tedesco,
Lee Hoiby, Mervyn Horder, Ralph Vaughan-Williams)

Example 4: Reading Aloud to Experience Texture

Loveliest of trees, the cherry now

Loveliest of trees, the cherry now
Is hung with bloom along the bough,
And stands about the woodland ride
Wearing white for Eastertide.

Now, of my threescore years and ten,
Twenty will not come again,
And take from seventy springs a score,
It only leaves me fifty more.

And since to look at things in bloom
Fifty springs are little room,
About the woodlands I will go
To see the cherry hung with snow.

—A. E. Housman (1859–1936)
from *A Shropshire Lad*, No. 2, published 1896
(set by many composers including
John Duke, Ivor Gurney, Mervyn Horder,
Charles Orr, Celius Dougherty)

Example 5: Reading Aloud to Experience Texture

Recuerdo

We were very tired, we were very merry—
We had gone back and forth all night on the ferry.
It was bare and bright, and smelled like a stable—
But we looked into a fire, we leaned across a table,
We lay on a hill-top underneath the moon;
And the whistles kept blowing, and the dawn came soon.

We were very tired, we were very merry,
We had gone back and forth all night on the ferry;
And you ate an apple, and I ate a pear,
From a dozen of each we had bought somewhere;
And the sky went wan, and the wind came cold,
And the sun rose dripping, a bucketful of gold.

We were very tired, we were very merry,
We had gone back and forth all night on the ferry.
We hailed "Good morrow, mother!" to a shawl-covered head,
And bought a morning paper, which neither of us read;
And she wept, "God bless you!" for the apples and pears,
And we gave her all our money but our subway fares.

—Edna St. Vincent Millay (1892–1950)
from *A Few Figs from Thistles*, published 1920
(set by John Musto, Mario Castelnuovo-Tedesco, Ricky Ian Gordon)

Exercise 3: Be a Poetry Detective

Make a list of three to five songs you have sung or are presently studying. Work with one poem at a time. Extract the poetry and write it in poetic form (the capital letters will tell you where the next poetic line begins). Read the poem aloud.

In order to communicate a poem artistically, it is necessary to cultivate the ability to work with it dramatically. Isolating information that the poem provides broadens the dramatic scope of your thinking and stretches the limits of your imagination.

So then, as the poem allows, answer the following questions: [11]

- What does the title suggest?

- Where does the poem take place? Give an adjective that might describe the location.

- Who is speaking? Is it a named character? An implied character? The voice of the poet?

- Is he/she alone? If not, to whom is he/she speaking?

- Can you determine the emotional state of the character?

- What might have happened before the poem begins?

- Or—what is happening at present?

- Can you tell what kind of inner "rhythm" the character has? Does he/she move or think fast or slowly? Is this the result of the dramatic situation or his/her personality?

- Is sound an active element of the poem? If so, what atmosphere does it create?

- Are there unusual words in the poem?

- Does the imagery in the poem produce a particular effect? Does the poem have its own vernacular? Does it speak from a specific culture?

- Is the poem the result of an identifiable historical moment?

Asking questions about any poem based on what you can observe from the words and how the poem is structured will give you a starting place to understanding the poem. Not every poem will have the answers to the questions above. Some modern poetry is much more abstract and does not lend itself to this sort of exercise; however, learning to look at a poem in this manner gives you "clues" about the poem's content. Think about the information you were able to glean by asking these questions about the poem and read the poem again. You have identified a certain amount of information about the words you will eventually sing, and what they mean *as a poem*.

Exercise 4: Reciting to Music

This exercise will require the help of your pianist. Choose an art song you are familiar with, and try reciting the poem as the pianist plays the accompaniment of the song. Repeat this at least two times, perhaps more. You have to become an actor, reacting to the words in their musical setting, with the tempo, mood, and dynamics the composer has written. You are adding the composer "into the picture."

To be able to do this exercise well takes the unselfconsciousness of an actor. You will probably be more successful if you begin with a song you know or have sung. You could use a recording of the piano part (available on many CDs that accompany musical anthologies) and read to that until you become comfortable with the exercise. As you progress, you will begin to "hear the poem" as part of the musical texture of the art song. You are absorbing some of the composer's point of view before you get to the notes the composer has written for you to sing.

Take the Poetry Pledge: Read a Poem a Day

Poetry is a river; many voices travel in it; poem after poem moves along in the exciting crests and falls of the river waves.[12]

—Mary Oliver

Below is a list of poems that can serve as practice material for reading poetry aloud. These were chosen because all of them have been set as art songs. Many of these can be found in poem anthologies, others may be accessed by individual poet in library catalogs or on the Internet. As a beginning goal, pick a poem every day or so for your "reading practice." It will be easiest to begin with poetry by American or British poets and then move on to foreign language texts. Take the poetry pledge: try to work your way up to reading a poem every day. As daily reading becomes a habit, you will soon identify poets whose work you enjoy reading, who are "on the same wave length." Perhaps you will be drawn to a specific historical period and a group of poets, or one specific poet who wrote at that time. These discoveries are useful in building recital groups and/or programs.

Reading a poem daily becomes a habit that yields excellent results in our study of songs. If singers took the time to read poems aloud each day, just as they schedule time in the practice room to warm up their voices, and to learn and practice their music, imagine what cumulative dividends it would pay in terms of their performances.

Choose any poem to begin your work. Do not feel you have to complete the entire list. Do not be in a hurry to move on to another poem until you are satisfied that you have done a thorough job with the poem you are working with and have mastered reading it aloud. As you work, it might be useful to record yourself; it might also be valuable to read aloud for another person (perhaps another singer also engaged in reading poetry aloud) so that you can gather constructive comments on your reading.

Although many of these poems have been set by several composers (some are listed in parentheses after the poem's title), this list is for practice reading the poems *aloud*, and *this goal should be accomplished apart from any musical setting*. Copy the poem apart from the musical score or read it from a poetry anthology. Do not use the musical score for your reading practice! Remember, you are reading aloud for fluency and for pleasure. Derek Attridge advises in his book *Poetic Rhythm*: "When possible, read aloud. Even when you read a poem silently, it should take up the same amount of time reading aloud would give it." [13]

A list of books to help further your goals of reading poetry may be found in the Bibliography at the back of the book (see "Poetry: References for Study"). An abridged glossary of helpful poetic terms can be found at the conclusion of this chapter.

Recommended American Poetry for Reading Aloud
HENRY WADSWORTH LONGFELLOW (1807–1882)
The Children's Hour   (Charles Ives)

WALT WHITMAN (1819–1892)
Beginning my studies   (Lee Hoiby)
To what you said   (Leonard Bernstein [*Songfest*])

EMILY DICKINSON (1830–1886)
Dear March, come in!   (Aaron Copland, Lori Laitman)

Wild nights! Wild nights!   (Ernst Bacon, Lee Hoiby, Lori Laitman, Richard Pearson Thomas)

It's all I have to bring today   (Ernst Bacon, Lori Laitman)

Will there really be a morning?   (Ernst Bacon, Ricky Ian Gordon, Richard Hundley, Vincent Persichetti, André Previn, Lori Laitman)

There came a wind like a bugle   (Aaron Copland, Ernst Bacon [titled "A wind like a bugle"], Lee Hoiby, Thomas Pasatieri)

I'm Nobody! Who are you?   (Lori Laitman, Arthur Farwell, Vincent Persichetti, Ernst Bacon)

Heart! we will forget him   (John Duke, Arthur Farwell, Aaron Copland, Richard Hundley)

Ample make this Bed—   (Daron Hagen, Jake Heggie, Arthur Farwell, Gerald Ginsburg)

ROBERT FROST (1874–1963)
The Rose Family   (John Musto, Elliott Carter)
Stopping by the Woods on a   (Ned Rorem)
   Snowy Evening
The Pasture   (Charles Naginski, Henry Cowell)

CARL SANDBURG (1878–1967)

Omaha	(Ernst Bacon)
Fog	(Roy Harris, Alan Hovhaness)

JAMES JOYCE (1882–1941)

In the dark pine-wood	(Samuel Barber, Ben Moore)
I hear an army charging upon the land	(Samuel Barber, David Del Tredici [titled "I hear an army"])
Strings in the earth and air	(Richard Hundley, Luciano Berio, Jean Coulthard)

SARA TEASDALE (1884–1933)

The Metropolitan Tower	(Lori Laitman)
The Mystery	(Lori Laitman)

ELINOR WYLIE (1885–1928)

Let us walk in the white snow	(Randall Thompson [titled "Velvet Shoes"], Mary Howe, John Duke, Richard Hageman)
Little Elegy	(Lori Laitman, John Duke, Mary Howe, Ned Rorem)

EDNA ST. VINCENT MILLAY (1892–1950)

Recuerdo	(John Musto, Mario Castelnuovo-Tedesco)
Afternoon on a Hill	(Arthur Farwell)
Pity me not because the light of day	(William Bolcom)
Sonnet XLIII: What lips my lips have kissed, and where, and why	(Jake Heggie, Leonard Bernstein, Jack Beeson)

E. E. (EDWARD ESTLIN) CUMMINGS (1894–1962)

meggie and milly and molly and may	(Richard Hundley, John Musto, Vincent Persichetti)
i carry your heart with me…	(John Duke [titled "i carry your heart"])
who knows if the moon's a balloon	(Dominick Argento, Vincent Persichetti, Lee Hoiby [titled "always, it's spring"])
when faces called flowers float out of the ground	(Dominick Argento, John Duke)

ROBERT HILLYER (1895–1961)

Early in the Morning	(Ned Rorem, John Duke [titled "Morning in Paris"])

(JAMES MERCER) LANGSTON HUGHES (1902–1967)

Song for a Dark Girl	(Ricky Ian Gordon)
Genius Child	(Ricky Ian Gordon)
Dream Variations	(Margaret Bonds)
The Dream Keeper	

THEODORE ROETHKE (1908–1963)

The Waking	(Ned Rorem, William Bolcom, Judith Cloud)
My Papa's Waltz	(Ned Rorem, David Diamond)

ELIZABETH BISHOP (1911–1979)

Sonnet (I am in need of music)	(Ben Moore, Chris DiBlasio, Judith Cloud, Tobias Picker, Lori Laitman [set as a duet])
We lived in a pocket of time	(Lee Hoiby [titled "A pocket of time"])

PAUL GOODMAN (1911–1972)

The Lordly Hudson	(Ned Rorem)
Such beauty as hurts to behold	(Ned Rorem)

TENNESSEE WILLIAMS (1911–1983)

The Cabin	(Paul Bowles)
Heavenly Grass	(Paul Bowles)
Three	(Paul Bowles)

RICHARD WILBUR (b.1921)

Museum Piece	(Stephen Paulus)
For C	(Lori Laitman [titled "A Wild Sostenuto"])
It must be me	(Leonard Bernstein [Candide])

MARY OLIVER (b.1935)

Last Night the Rain Spoke to Me	(Lori Laitman)
Blue Iris	(Lori Laitman)

DANA GIOIA (b. 1950)

The Apple Orchard	(Lori Laitman)
Pentecost	(Lori Laitman)
House (Insomnia No. 2)	(Tom Cipullo)

Recommended British Poetry for Reading Aloud
WILLIAM SHAKESPEARE (1564–1616)

When icicles hang by the wall	(Dominick Argento)
O mistress mine	(Gerald Finzi, Roger Quilter)
It was a lover and his lass	(Peter Warlock [titled "Pretty ring time"], Erich Korngold [titled "When birds do sing"], Madeleine Dring, Gerald Finzi)
Fear no more the heat o' the sun	(Gerald Finzi, Roger Quilter)
Come away, come away death	(Ralph Vaughan Williams, Erich Korngold, Gerald Finzi [titled "Come away, death"], Dominick Argento [titled "Dirge"], Jacques Leguerney [titled "Come away, come away"], Lee Hoiby, Madeleine Dring, Roger Quilter)

BEN JONSON (1572–1637)

To Celia (Drink to me only with thine eyes)	(Richard Faith, Roger Quilter)

ORLANDO GIBBONS (1583–1625)

The Silver Swan	(Lori Laitman, Ned Rorem, Eric Thiman)

ROBERT HERRICK (1591–1674)

Whenas in silks my Julia goes	(Ned Rorem, John Corigliano [titled "Upon Julia's Clothes"])
To the virgins, to make much of time	(Madeleine Dring, Ben Moore, Mervyn Horder, Thomas Pasatieri: [titled "Gather ye rosebuds"], Roger Quilter [titled "To the virgins"])
To Music, to becalm his Fever	(Ned Rorem, Paul Hindemith)

EDMUND WALLER (1606–1687)

Song	(Roger Quilter, Ned Rorem, [both titled "Go lovely rose"])

PERCY BYSSHE SHELLEY (1792–1822)

Music, when soft voices die	(Richard Faith, Ernest Gold, David Diamond, Peter Warlock, Roger Quilter, Libby Larsen, Frank Bridge)

JOHN KEATS (1795–1821)

A Thing of Beauty
(William Schuman [titled "Beauty"], Mario Castelnuovo-Tedesco)

ROBERT BROWNING (1812–1889)

Grow old along with me!
(Lori Laitman [titled "Along with me"], Jake Heggie)

The year's at the spring
(Amy Beach, Ned Rorem [titled "Pippa's Song"])

CHRISTINA ROSSETTI (1830–1894)

Echo
(Lori Laitman, John Musto, Richard Faith, Thomas Pasatieri)

When I am dead, my dearest
(Ralph Vaughan Williams, Richard Hageman, Lori Laitman [titled "Song"], Roger Quilter [titled "A song at parting"])

My heart is like a singing bird
(Ned Rorem, Mario Castelnuovo-Tedesco, Richard Faith)

LEWIS CARROLL (1832–1898)

Jabberwocky
(Lee Hoiby, John Duke)

ROBERT LOUIS STEVENSON (1850–1894)

I will make you brooches…
(Ralph Vaughan Williams [titled "The Roadside Fire"])

Bright is the Ring of Words
(Ralph Vaughan Williams)

The Vagabond
(Ralph Vaughan Williams)

A.E. HOUSMAN (1859–1936)

Loveliest of trees
(John Duke, George Butterworth, Ivor Gurney, Celius Dougherty, Mervyn Horder)

When I was one-and-twenty
(George Butterworth, John Duke, Ivor Gurney, Mervyn Horder)

The Half-Moon Westers Low
(Jake Heggie)

WILLIAM BUTLER YEATS (1865–1939)

The Cloths of Heaven
(Rebecca Clarke, Ivor Gurney)

Down by the Salley Gardens
(Rebecca Clarke, Benjamin Britten, Ivor Gurney)

KATHLEEN RAINE (1908–2003)

Lament
(Judith Cloud, Geoffrey Bush)

Nocturn
(Judith Cloud)

PHILIP LARKIN (1922–1985)

Within the dream you said	(Daron Hagen)
Friday Night in the Royal Station Hotel	(André Previn)
Talking in Bed	(André Previn, Daron Hagen)

Reading Poetry in Foreign Languages

For English speakers, working with poetry apart from its musical setting may be more difficult in foreign languages such as German, French, or Italian. You may have studied and/or performed repertoire in these languages, but it is quite different to extract the poetry and work with it as previously outlined. As singing artists we need to go beyond just being able to sing with correct pronunciation. We need to be able to determine the meaning of the poetic line and read it with resonance and inflection just as we would sing a vocal phrase applying the same criteria.

Before beginning work with the foreign text, have an English translation handy. This *should not* be a translation intended to be sung, but a translation *in poetic form*. Most of these selections will have a number of English translations from which to choose. The reader is directed to Philip Miller's classic book *The Ring of Words: An Anthology of Song Texts* (New York: W. W. Norton Co. 1973), a collection of German, French, Italian, Russian, and Scandinavian poems that have been set as songs. Every text has an English translation on the facing page. Other books of foreign language texts with translations may be found in the Bibliography (see "Texts and Translations").

Below are lists of some well known examples of *Lieder, mélodie,* and Italian and Spanish art song texts. Most of these contain specific imagery, some present a definite story with delineated characters, and others are more sophisticated in content. Work with these texts in the same way as outlined for texts in English.

Begin with a selection you are familiar with or have sung before. If you have not heard the musical setting for the poem you choose, listening to a recording might provide a good starting place. In parentheses, following the poems, are the names of some composers who have set the text as an art song.

Recommended German Poetry for Reading Aloud

CHRISTIAN FRIEDRICH DANIEL SCHUBART (1739–1791)

Die Forelle	(Franz Schubert [stanzas 1–3])

JOHANN WOLFGANG VON GOETHE (1749–1832)

Kennst du das Land	(Hugo Wolf, Robert Schumann)
Das Veilchen	(W.A. Mozart, Clara Schumann)
Erlkönig	(Franz Schubert, Carl Loewe)
Gretchen am Spinnrade	(Franz Schubert, Richard Wagner)

JOSEPH EICHENDORFF (1788–1857)

Waldesgespräch	(Robert Schumann)
Mondnacht	(Robert Schumann)
Nachtwanderer	(Erich Korngold)

FRIEDRICH RÜCKERT (1788–1866)

Liebst du um Schönheit	(Gustav Mahler, Clara Schumann)
Ich atmet' einen linden Duft'	(Gustav Mahler)
Du bist die Ruh	(Franz Schubert)

FRANZ SCHOBER (1796–1882)

An die Musik	(Franz Schubert)

HEINRICH HEINE (1797–1856)

Die beiden Grenadiere	(Robert Schumann)
Die Lotosblume	(Robert Schumann, Robert Franz, Charles Ives)
Schlechtes Wetter	(Richard Strauss)

EDUARD MÖRICKE (1804–1875)

Das verlassene Mägdlein	(Hugo Wolf, Robert Schumann, Robert Franz)
Er ist's	(Robert Schumann, Hugo Wolf)

RICHARD DEHMEL (1863–1920)

Die stille Stadt	(Alma Mahler)
Befreit	(Richard Strauss)

RAINER MARIA RILKE (1875–1926)*

Bei dir ist es traut	(Alma Mahler)
Un cygne avance sur	(Samuel Barber [titled "Un cygne"],
l'eau toute entouré	Louis Durey, Paul Hindemith)

* the second poem is in French, but listed here under poet's name

Recommended French Poetry for Reading Aloud
PIERRE DE RONSARD (1524–1585)

A sa guitare	(Francis Poulenc, Judith Cloud)
Ne nous tenons	(Jacques Leguerney)
Mignonne, allons voir si rose	(Cécile Chaminade)
Bonjour, mon cœur	(Pauline Viardot, Judith Cloud)

VICTOR HUGO (1802–1885)

Guitare	(Georges Bizet, Camille Saint-Saëns, Franz Liszt [titled "Comment, disaient-ils"], Édouard Lalo)
O quand je dors	(Franz Liszt)
Si mes vers avaient des ailes	(Reynaldo Hahn)

THÉOPHILE GAUTIER (1811–1872)

Villanelle	(Hector Berlioz)
Lamento	(Henri Duparc, Hector Berlioz [titled "Au cimetière"])

LECONTE DE LISLE (1818–1894)

Le Colibri	(Ernest Chausson)
Lydia	(Gabriel Fauré)

CHARLES BAUDELAIRE (1821–1867)

La Vie antérieure	(Henri Duparc)
Les Hiboux	(Deodat de Sévérac)
L'Invitation au voyage	(Henri Duparc, Emmanuel Chabrier)

STÉPHANE MALLARMÉ (1842–1898)

Sainte	(Maurice Ravel)
Soupir	(Claude Debussy, Maurice Ravel)

PAUL VERLAINE (1844–1896)

Green	(Gabriel Fauré, Claude Debussy, Reynaldo Hahn [titled "Offrande"])
Mandoline	(Gabriel Fauré, Claude Debussy, Reynaldo Hahn, Poldowski [Lady Dean Paul], Józef Szulc)
Clair de lune	(Gabriel Fauré, Claude Debussy, Józef Szulc, J. Canteloube, Gustave Charpentier)
Sur l'herbe	(Maurice Ravel)

La Lune blanche	(Gabriel Fauré, Reynaldo Hahn [titled "L'heure exquise"])
En Sourdine	(Claude Debussy, Gabriel Fauré, Reynaldo Hahn, Józef Szulc)
Fantoches	(Claude Debussy)

ALBERT SAMAIN (1858–1900)
Arpège	(Gabriel Fauré)

LÉON-PAUL FARGUE (1876–1947)
La Statue de bronze	(Erik Satie)
Air du rat	(Erik Satie)

GUILLAUME APOLLINAIRE (1880–1918)
Hôtel	(Francis Poulenc)
La Grenouillère	(Francis Poulenc)
Bleuet	(Francis Poulenc)
Montparnasse	(Francis Poulenc)

RENÉ CHALUPT (1885–1957)
Le Chapelier	(Erik Satie)
Sarabande	(Albert Roussel)

PAUL ELUARD (1895–1952)
Ce doux petit visage	(Francis Poulenc)
Georges Bracque	(Francis Poulenc)

LOUIS ARAGON (1897–1982)
C	(Francis Poulenc)
Fêtes galantes	(Francis Poulenc)

LOUISE DE VILMORIN (1902–1969)
Fleurs	(Francis Poulenc)
Le Garçon de Liège	(Francis Poulenc)

Recommended Italian Poetry for Reading Aloud
ANONYMOUS
Sento nel core	(Alessandro Scarlatti, Stefano Donaudy)
Tu lo sai	(Giuseppe Torelli)
Intorno all'idol mio	(Marc Antonio Cesti)

La regata veneziana   (Gioachino Rossini)
  Anzoleta avanti la regata
  Anzoleta co passa la regata
  Anzoleta dopo la regata
O leggiadri occhi belli   (Marc Antonio Cesti)
Placido zeffiretto   (Vincenzo Righini)
Caro mio ben   (Giuseppe Giordani)
Vaga luna, che inargenti   (Vincenzo Bellini)

GIOVANNI BATTISTA GUARINI (1538–1612)

Amarilli, mia bella   (Giulio Caccini)
Con que soavità, labbra odorate   (Claudio Monteverdi)

NICCOLÒ MINATO (c.1627–1698)

O cessate di piagarmi   (Alessandro Scarlatti)
Và godendo   (George Frideric Handel)

PAOLO ANTONIO ROLLI (1687–1765)

Se tu m'ami, se sospiri   (Giovanni Battista Pergolesi)

PIETRO METASTASIO (1698–1782)

La promessa   (Gioachino Rossini)
Ma rendi pur contento   (Vincenzo Bellini)

RANIERI DE' CALZABIGI (1714–1795)

O del mio dolce ardor   (Christoph Willibald Gluck)
Spiagge amati   (Christoph Willibald Gluck)

IPPPOLITO PINDEMONTE (1753–1828)

Malinconia, ninfa gentile   (Vincenzo Bellini)

LUIGI BALESTRI (1808–1863), trans. from the German of Johann Wolfgang von Goethe

Perduta ho la pace   (Giuseppe Verdi)

ALBERTO DONAUDY (1880–1941)

Vaghissima sembianza   (Stefano Donaudy)
O del mio amato ben   (Stefano Donaudy)

S. MANFREDO MAGGIONI (n.d.)

Lo spazzacamino   (Giuseppe Verdi)

LORENZO PAGANS (n.d.)

Danza danza fanciulla gentile   (Francesco Durante)

Recommended Spanish Poetry for Reading Aloud
ANONYMOUS/FOLK POETRY

¿Con que la lavare?	(Joaquín Rodrigo)
Viniendo de Chilecito	(Carlos Guastavino)
El paño moruno (1)	(Manuel de Falla [numbered poems
Asturiana (3)	are from *Siete canciones populares*
Jota (4)	*españolas*])

FERNANDO PERIQUET (1873–1940)

Amor y odio	(Enrique Granados)
La maja dolorosa (2)	(Enrique Granados)
El majo discreto	(Enrique Granados)

PABLO NERUDA (1904–1973)

Si no fuera porque tus ojos tienen color de luna	(Peter Lieberson, Judith Cloud [in English translation by Stephen Tapscott])
Ya eres mía. Reposa con tu sueño en mí sueño	(Lieberson, Judith Cloud [see above])

FRANCESCO SILVA (n.d.)

La rosa y el sauce	(Carlos Guastavino)

A Selected List of Helpful Poetic Terms

Below is a brief glossary that may be helpful as you begin to read poetry. As you become a more experienced reader, I recommend acquiring a dictionary of poetic terms that will be more extensive and detailed, or almost all textbooks on poetry contain an informative introduction that will provide good information. One very handy book is Mary Oliver's *Rules for the Dance: A Handbook for Writing and Reading Metrical Verse*. Oliver, an acclaimed poet and Pulitzer Prize winner, has written a succinct and beautiful presentation of poetry's elements. While readers of this book probably do not seek to become poets, this book is user-friendly and full of effectively presented information for *readers* of poems.

Poetry textbooks are also good resources. Most are easy to read and understand, and also contain informative introductory chapters. A little time in the library examining college and high school poetry texts will pay handsome dividends in terms of your comfort level as a reader. There are also dictionaries available on the websites of the Academy of American Poets (poets.org) and the Poetry Foundation (poetryfoundation.org).

BASIC TERMS

Literal meaning The simplest, clearest, most obvious meaning of a word.

Rhyme (or Rime) Repetition of the end syllable sounds in successive words, either as full rhymes or as part rhymes in which the end consonants match but not the vowels; at the end of lines or internal to them.

Masculine rhyme (between single stressed syllables): *sheep, release, fleece, neat.*

Feminine rhyme (matches 2 syllables, one stressed and one usually unstressed): *stinging, singing, clinging, ringing.*

Rhyme Scheme	Patterns of recurring rhymes in a poem at the ends of lines. Letters are assigned to these and are called rhyme schemes. If four poetic lines end in *leather, well, bell, weather* it would be said to have a rhyme scheme of ***abba***.
Meter	A poem's basic rhythm. Meter depends on the number and placement of stressed syllables in each line. The stresses usually fall into a pattern, and the patterns are given specific names (example: *iambic pentameter*). When we scan a poem we are looking for the stress patterns in order to determine in what meter the poem was written.
Texture	The quality created by the combination of all the elements of a work of literature or music. In a poem: the words, word sounds (consonants and vowels), rhythm, stress, etc.
Diction	Specifically refers to word choice and encompasses all the words in a poem. Mayes describes diction as "somewhat analogous to a recipe a chef devises from his entire familiarity with cuisines. A fiery pepper on a clam has consequences, as does a hot word in a cold poem. The chef wants his dish to balance and contrast tastes for the entire experience. The quality of every ingredient contributes to this." [14]
Prose	Non-metrical written language generally lying midway between verse and spoken language. Samuel Taylor Coleridge articulated the difference between prose and poetry in his advice to young poets, saying: "prose—words in their best order; poetry—the best words in their best order." [15]
Prosody	The patterns and sound used in poetry, including meter, stanza, rhyme; the patterns of stress and intonation in a language.

Syntax	Sentence structure; the way in which words are arranged to form phrases, clauses, or sentences.
Scansion	The detailed analysis of the metrical pattern of lines and stanzas to determine poetic meter. This is done by marking stressed and unstressed syllables.
Tone	In a poem, the speaker's attitude toward his subject. Tone involves all the elements in the poem which create the emotional meaning of the work.
Rhythm	In verse, the organized rhythm of accented and unaccented syllables; the more or less regular recurrence of units of sound.

FIGURATIVE LANGUAGE

Hyperbole	Exaggeration or overstatement—added emphasis.
Imagery (image)	Visually descriptive or figurative language, which uses figures (images) to simplify a thought. Imagery is a basic component of all poetry, and is often thought of as its defining characteristic. Imagery may appeal to the senses, the imagination, the memory.

Examples:
Sara Teasdale:
"Blue waves whitened on a cliff
Soaring fire that sways and sings"
Richard Wilbur:
"The good gray guardians of art
Patrol the halls on spongy shoes."

Metaphor	A direct comparison between two unlike things.

Examples:
Matthew Arnold:
"Retreating, like the breath of the night wind"
Carl Sandburg:
"The fog comes on little cat feet"

Symbol	Something meaning more than what it is; standing for something else.

Perrine disposes of the three terms very neatly in his textbook *Sound and Sense*: "Image, metaphor, and symbol shade into each other and are sometimes difficult to distinguish. In general, however, an **image** means only what it is; a **metaphor** means something other than what it is; and a **symbol** means what it is and something more too." [16]

Allegory	A poem that can be interpreted to reveal a hidden meaning beneath the surface one.
Personification	Attributing human characteristics to something non-human—an animal, object, or idea.

Example:
Emily Dickinson:
"It was not Night, for all the Bells
Put out their Tongues, for Noon"

Simile	A figure of speech (explicit comparison) in which two dissimilar things are compared by the use of *like, as, as if, than, similar to,* or *resembles.*

Examples:
William Wordsworth:
"I wandered, lonely as a cloud"
Robert Burns:
"My luv is like a red, red rose"

POETIC DEVICES

Alliteration

The repetition of initial consonant sounds.

Example:
Robert Herrick:
   "So smooth, so sweet, so silv'ry is thy voice,"

Caesura (cesura)

A natural pause in a line of poetry. Emily Dickinson was one poet who made extensive use of dashes in her poetry—these act as pauses.

Example:
   Safe in their Alabaster Chambers—
   Untouched by Morning
   And untouched by Noon—
   Lie the meek members of the
      Resurrection—
   Rafter of Satin—and Roof of Stone!

   Grand go the Years—in the Crescent—above them—
   Worlds scoop their Arcs—
   And Firmaments—row—
   Diadems—drop—and Doges—
      surrender—
   Soundless as dots—on a Disc of Snow—
      —Emily Dickinson (Version of 1861)

Assonance

The repetition of stressed vowel sounds in words.

Example:
   "High r<u>ow</u>, the b<u>oa</u>tmen r<u>ow</u>
   Fl<u>oa</u>tin' down the river, the <u>O</u>hi<u>o</u>"

Consonance

A form of alliteration in which *both initial and interior sounds* of words are repeated.

Example:
   <u>bl</u>ue<u>b</u>erry, <u>w</u>hippoor<u>w</u>ill

Cacophony	A harsh or unpleasant sound. In poetry, a line or phrase that is deliberately rough in meter or full of clashing vowels or consonants.
	Example: Alexander Pope: "The hoarse, rough verse should like the torrent roar"
Euphony	Pleasant-sounding language, easy on the ear. more or less the opposite of *cacophony*.
	Example: Alexander Pope: "Soft is the strain when Zephyr gently blows"
Enjambment	The continuation of a poetic phrase without a pause beyond the end of a line, couplet, or stanza, so that the grammatical structure of the phrase is completed in the next line.
	Examples: Robert Frost: "My little horse must think it queer To stop without a farmhouse near"
	Wallace Stevens: "One must have a mind of winter To regard the frost and the boughs Of the pine-trees crusted with snow"
Onomatopoeia	Words that communicate sound and sense (the sound of the word imitates its meaning). They are used for verbal effect. Mayes describes them as "noise words." [17]
	Examples: hiss, slap, rip, thud, buzz, sizzle, gargle, hum, thunderstorm

POETIC FORMS

Ballad

A brief narrative poem with a song-like quality, written in four line-stanzas that rhyme and often include repeated refrains (***abcb***).

Closed verse

Poems with a formal structure, meter, rhyme scheme, and repetition.

Open verse

Poems with no consistent or strict pattern of meter or rhyme scheme.

Couplet

A pair of adjacent lines of poetry that form a complete unit either because of some relationship such as end-rhyme or because of their sense or meaning. They are usually of the same length.

Tercet

A unit of three lines that may be rhymed or unrhymed.

Quatrain

A unit of four lines of verse—one of the most common units in English poetry, usually ***abcb***.

Free verse

Verse without regular metrical form or set sound pattern. Also called **nonmetrical** verse, it was a favorite form of many twentieth-century poets.

Dramatic poem

A drama entirely in verse, intended to be read rather than performed on stage.

Dramatic monologue

A speech for a single character, delivered to a silent listener or audience. It resembles a speech or soliloquy in a play.

Narrative poem

A poem that tells a story.

Lyric poetry

Includes all poetry that is about a subject and contains little narrative. The speaker in a lyric poem is usually the poet himself and the words are his subjective expression of emotions, ideas, or descriptions of a person or place.

Epitaph

A short poem to be inscribed on a tombstone.

Epic	A long narrative poem, usually on a dignified or noble historical, mythological, or religious subject.
Refrain	A regularly recurring phrase or verse in a poem or song, found within or at the end of each stanza.
Shaped poem	(also **pattern poem**) A poem composed so that its typographical appearance on the page copies the shape of its subject. French poet Guillaume Apollinaire referred to his shaped verses as "calligrammes." Composer Francis Poulenc set a group of these as a cycle of *mélodies* (*Calligrammes*).
	Example: See "Il pleut" in Chapter 2.
Sonnet	The most popular pattern for a complete poem in English verse originated in the sixteenth century. As originally borrowed from Italian poetry of the day, the sonnet is fourteen lines long. The first unit consists of two linked quatrains, ***abbaabba***, plus a sestet, a six-line grouping of either two or three rhymes: ***cdcd*** or ***cdecde*** are most common patterns. This form is known as the **Petrarchan sonnet**, named after the Italian poet Petrarch, who originated it. In the sixteenth century, the English devised a new form, the **Shakespearean sonnet**. This was three quatrains and a final couplet. The usual rhyme scheme was ***abab–cdcd–efef–gg***.
Stanza	A unit of poetry, usually four lines, set off typographically by spaces above and below it, and repeated throughout the poem.
Strophic	A poem organized by stanza groupings.
Verse	A line in a poem, especially one that has formal structure; also, a stanza in a hymn.

NOTES

1   Philip L. Miller, compiler and translator, *The Ring of Words: An Anthology of Song Texts* (New York: W.W. Norton & Co., 1973), Introduction, xxviii.

2   Frances Mayes, *The Discovery of Poetry: A Field Guide to Reading and Writing Poems* (Orlando, FL: Harcourt, Inc., 2001), 26.

3   Dana Gioia, "Can Poetry Matter?" in *Essays on Poetry and American Culture* (Minneapolis, MN: Graywolf, 1992), 41–42.

4   Glenda Maurice, "When Poetry Becomes Music," lecture given at the National Association of Teachers of Singing National Conference, Seattle, WA, 1996. From notes taken by the author.

5   Mary Oliver, *Rules for the Dance* (Boston: Houghton Mifflin Co.,1998), viii.

6   Betty Bannerman, editor, *The Singer as Interpreter: Claire Croiza's Master Classes* (London: Victor Gollancz, 1989), 52.

7   Ned Rorem, "Song," in *An Absolute Gift: A New Diary* (New York: Simon and Schuster, 1978), 161, 162.

8   Thomas Grubb, *Singing in French: A Manual of French Diction and French Vocal Repertoire* (New York: Schirmer Books, 1979), 99–100.

9   Robert Frost, quoted in Frances Mayes, ibid., 363.

10 Mayes, 26.

11 These questions are based on a list found in "How to Read a Poem," reproduced in partnership with the Great Books Foundation; on the website of the American Academy of American Poets, www.poets.org (accessed October 10, 2011), and from a discussion about creating subtexts in Carol Kimball, "Working With Song Literature: The Journey to Performance," *Journal of Singing* 53, no. 3 (January/February 1997), 5–6.

12 Mary Oliver, *A Poetry Handbook* (New York: Harcourt Brace & Co. 1994), 9.

13 Derek Attridge, *Poetic Rhythm: An Introduction* (Cambridge, UK: The Cambridge University Press, 1995), 19.

14 Mayes, 42.

15 Jack Myers and Don C. Wukasch, eds., *Dictionary of Poetic Terms* (Denton, TX: University of North Texas Press, 2003), 201.

16 Laurence Perrine, *Sound and Sense* (New York: Harcourt, Brace & World, Inc., 1963), 69.

17 Mayes, 31.

Chapter 4

Working With Music

Musick and Poetry have ever been acknowledg'd Sisters,
which walking hand in hand, support each other:
As Poetry is the harmony of Words, so Musick is that of Notes;
and as Poetry is a Rise above Prose and Oratory, so is Musick
the exaltation of Poetry. Both of them may excel apart, but sure
they are most excellent when they are joyn'd because nothing
is then wanting to either of their Perfections: for thus they
appear like Wit and Beauty in the same Person. [1]

—Henry Purcell (John Dryden)

Music is a step farther than poetry. If the singer can
find the place where poetry and music converge then
he will have found the entity of the song. [2]

—Glenda Maurice

The Musical Framework for the Poem

Words by themselves do not an art song make. No matter how much work you do with the poetry, it is the addition of music to those words that make an art song, and working with the music is the next step in performance preparation. Looking at the musical framework the composer has created is of major importance in our exploration of the art song.

Most composers strive to create a synthesis of music and words by using melody, rhythm, harmony, and accompaniment to transform poetic images into musical images—that is, blending musical elements into a texture that gives the words a musical framework and mirrors the poetic images in sound. By combining words and music into an art song, the unique components in both arts function concurrently and "the place where poetry and music converge" will have been reached.

The "Why" of the Musical Setting

Ultimately there can be only one justification for the serious composition of a song: it must be an attempt to increase our understanding of the poem. [3]

—Edward T. Cone

Figuring out the "why" of a musical setting is paramount to understanding the art song as a complete entity—by discovering the way the composer has achieved the fusion of words with music.

Just as an artist paints with a palette of many colors that may be subtly changed by mixing them together, or by varying the type of brush strokes he uses, a composer may create musical textures with melodic lines, rhythms, harmonic structures, or accompaniment figures, combining them in ways that reflect the words of the poem and its meaning as he perceives it. Since no two readers read a poem in the same way, no two composers share the same response to a text. Listen to some of the many settings of Shakespeare's "It was a lover and his lass" to hear the different musical responses composers have had to this text.

How has the composer "felt" or "experienced" the poem? You will be able to answer this with some amount of certainty when you explore the composer's musical setting for the text in question. The composer's instinctual reaction to the words of the poet engenders a musical response that ultimately results in the art song. The manner in which a composer reacts to the poem ultimately shapes their setting of the words. Some settings are centered on the sense and meaning of the words; some settings are derived from the rhythms of the poetry rather than the literal meaning of the words. Each of these reactions will produce a very different musical setting. Composer Lori Laitman spoke about this, adding the performer(s) into the mix: "Composing an art song is an interesting sequential collaboration. First between the composer and the poet; and then between the performers and the music—and each person adds more to the interpretation of the poem." [4]

Setting Words to Music

Chapter 1 offered a number of composers' thoughts about choosing poems to set to music as art songs. Once a poem has been chosen, the act of setting it to music begins. Composers have their own thoughts and timetables regarding this process. Here are thoughts of a few composers, speaking about putting words to music.

Composer Ned Rorem, whose catalogue of art songs numbers in the hundreds, writes about the process of fusing poetry and music:

> Song is the reincarnation of a poem that was destroyed in order to live again in music. The composer, no matter how respectful, must treat poetry as a skeleton on which to borrow flesh, breaking a few bones in the process. He does not render a poem more musical (poetry isn't music, it's poetry); he weds it to sound, creating a third entity of different and sometimes greater magnitude than either parent. [5]

> If you sing words as you would speak them, if you develop a viewpoint about the verse, if you care about sense, then the music—or at least my music—will automatically fall into place around the poem like a velvet cloak around a naked form. [6]

French composer Francis Poulenc, who composed over 150 *mélodies*, the largest body of song to be added to French vocal literature in the twentieth century, was quite knowledgeable about poetry and chose his texts with care. The charm and sophistication of his songs derive from their poetic inspirations. His gift of divining the inner life of the texts he set produced songs that do more than just illustrate the poems. As he commented. "It is not only the lines of the poem that must be set to music, but all that lies between the lines and in the margins." [7]

American composer Scott Wheeler offered interesting insight on composer Virgil Thomson's teaching of text setting:

> Virgil's teaching of text setting focused on syllable lengths and the stresses of both words and word groupings... He taught that

to set a text is to give a line reading, as an actor does. As with an actor's line reading, the object isn't to show how deeply you feel the emotion of the words but rather to project the text in a way that is clear, so the audience may feel that emotion. These principles seem simple enough, but I've spent much of the rest of my composing life exploring their implications in setting poetry and prose in song and in opera. [8]

In an interview, composer Lori Laitman described her approach to text setting this way:

I am guided by both the sound and the meaning [of words in a poem]. I try to figure out what will work best vocally and set each word so that its sounds are set well. The sound of the poem can, and often does, influence the rhythm of the music; yet it is the meaning of the words that drives my musical interpretation... It's great when the poem leaves some emotional space for the music to fill in. [9]

Jeffrey Ryan, associate composer of the Canadian Music Centre, shared his thoughts on working with poetry in a podcast posted on the website of the Vancouver International Song Institute:

In terms of looking for poetry, I'm always on the lookout for a good poem. And what makes a good poem for a song text? A big question. There are a lot of really a lot of fantastic poems that don't speak to me musically... sometimes it's a few words, or [it's the] form—the way it's set up on the page. It might be too structured, or too long. I won't change a published poem. I feel pretty strongly about that. I think it's an issue of respect. The poet has spent a lot of time thinking about each word—has chosen that word for a reason—just as I choose each note for a reason . . . I think it's important to respect the poet's vision.

To me, the music has to serve the text and the style of the music springs from the text. I set the words so they can be understood... I take a lot of time to find a poem where the words really speak to me, and I want to make sure that the listener can understand those words. Also, I think it's really important that I really look at what's going on in the poem and what's going on underneath the poem, because I think the music can provide that subtext that can take it to a different level . . . I usually look for a single underlying image or an emotion that provides a starting point for me and then it all flows from that . . . [10]

When Composer and Poet Collaborate

Artistic collaborations between the composer and the poet are not always the norm; however, when such a situation occurs, it is fascinating to gather what information there is available as to this shared process that results in an art song.

Lori Laitman enjoys finding poems by contemporary poets to set as songs. She explains:

> Although I try to ensure that all of my settings capture the essence of the poem, it's nice to have actual feedback from a living poet. If I have questions about a poem, it's a treat to be able to email or contact the poet directly. Sometimes the poet will have a certain suggestion that can change the course of my composition. I love meeting new poets and exploring new poetry, and it's wonderful to have the opportunity to introduce their poems to a musical audience. [11]

Laitman composed "The Apple Orchard" in 2004 to a poem by her friend, poet Dana Gioia, then chairman of the National Endowment for the Arts. She was drawn to the poem's dramatic arc as well as the beautiful image of "spring's ephemeral cathedral."

Gioia's text is a modern-day *carpe diem*, describing a path not taken, a love not claimed. Laitman sets the final poignant line of the poem with an ascending figure that remains suspended in space, unfinished—mirroring the poem's last words.

The Apple Orchard

You won't remember it— the apple orchard
We wandered through one April afternoon,
Climbing the hill behind the empty farm.

A city boy, I'd never seen a grove
Burst in full flower or breathed the bittersweet
Perfume of blossoms mingled with the dust.

A quarter mile of trees in fragrant rows
Arching above us. We walked the aisle,
Alone in spring's ephemeral cathedral.

We had the luck, if you can call it that,
Of having been in love but never lovers—
The bright flame burning, fed by pure desire.

Nothing consumed, such secrets brought to light!
There was a moment when I stood behind you,
Reached out to spin you toward me…but I stopped.

What more could I have wanted from that day?
Everything, of course. Perhaps that was the point—
To learn that what we will not grasp is lost. [12]

—Dana Gioia

Some poets are opposed to having their poetry set to music, perhaps fearing that their words might be destroyed in some way by the musical setting. This is not the case with Gioia, who comments:

I have had a great many songs composed based on my poems. Usually the song—good, bad, or wonderful—becomes something quite different from my poem. That is only natural. The composer's vision transforms the text in some decisive way. With "The Apple Orchard" something extraordinary happened. Lori Laitman's setting is so perfect that it seems to have emerged naturally from the words as if the music had always been hidden in the lines. Every nuance of her setting seems absolutely inevitable. I can't imagine another possible setting of the poem. And the song is so suave, so beautiful—somehow both understated and dramatic. I loved it from the first moment I heard it. And oddly I have never heard a performance which didn't work. A collaboration this perfect is a very rare thing. [13]

Canadian poet Marilyn Lerch, speaking about having her poems set to music, observed:

It's always quite an honor to think that a composer hears something musical in the words. It's always quite a wonderful feeling to be asked to turn over your poetry to a composer. To me, music is a necessity. It's like air and breath. What does music add to my poetry? . . . It gives it a dimension that's impossible— even when poetry is read beautifully, even when it's on the page and moves people, to have a composer hear music in my words and then find an interpretation to fit those words. Actually it's like giving a different meaning to the words, through the music.

Speaking of hearing five musical settings of her poetry by composer Lloyd Burrit, she commented:

When I heard what he did with the poems, I was just blown away. In particular, one poem which has a lot of good imagery and is very dramatic—he absolutely caught . . . the full sense of what the narrator was saying . . . for me, that poem is alive in the music. I can barely read it without wanting to hear the music. [14]

The Music of Art Song: A Vocabulary List

Below is a checklist of categories and terms that may be useful in examining the musical framework of art songs. The list may come in handy for making study sheets for single songs, or for creating study sheets for the art song repertoire of a specific composer.

Not all the terms will be applicable to every song. It is not necessary to do an in-depth theoretical analysis of the songs; these terms are meant to provide points of reference for examining how musical materials are used to define or intensify the blend of poetic and musical images.

Vocabulary for Discussing the
Musical Components of Art Song:

Style(s) of text setting:
- treatment of prosody
- declamatory (speech-based)
- syllabic
- melismatic
- recitative
- arioso
- sprechgesang
- use of embellishments

Melody:
- melodic contours: scalar passages extended intervals
- phrase length
- tessitura
- range
- use of chromaticism, dissonances

Harmonic vocabulary:
- diatonic
- chromatic
- tonal
- atonal
- modal
- chord preferences
- key scheme—modulations

Rhythm:
- metric organization
- polyrhythms
- cross-rhythms with the voice
- patterns—simple, difficult, ostinato

Accompaniment:
- predominant figures:
- block chords
- arpeggiated figures
- shared materials with the voice
- use of motives (rhythmic, melodic)
- preludes, interludes, postludes

Form:	• strophic
	• modified strophic
	• through-composed
	• binary
	• ternary (usually ABA)
	• combinations of these
ALSO:	• Mood/atmosphere
	• Emotional content
	• Musical texture—sparse, thick

Style in Art Song

Style is a manner, a mode of expression, a type of presentation. In discussing art song, it is oriented toward the *relationships within the whole*. Style in an art song is a set of characteristics that blend to create a distinctive design, linking poetry and music so that each art is dependent upon the other for its overall function in the song.

Song must not be thought of as either music or poetry but rather as an amalgam that shares significantly in both arts and is equally dependent upon both. It is possible to discuss the poetry, in form and content, and it is possible to discuss the music, in form and content. But in a truly successful song they function concurrently. [15]

—Donald Ivey

Style is also conditioned by historical, social and geographical factors, performing resources and conventions.

The broad components of art song style are:

• MELODY

• HARMONY

• RHYTHM

• THE PIANO COMPONENT

• FORM

These constituent headings may be broken into smaller subsections (see "Some Criteria for Song Study," above) to help define the way a composer creates a song's imagery within each component; however, since a song blends all these components into one complete entity, they overlap, so when you are studying the musical setting of a poem, it is important to look at each component by itself and then in combination with the others.

Components of Style

Under each of the headings below there are a number of questions or statements. These are meant to guide your examination of each musical component of art song. [16] At the end of each component section, there is a short list of art songs for listening and study. They have been chosen for their distinctive treatment of that particular component. Use them in tandem with the annotations under each title to work out your ideas about each song. Before you listen to these art songs, you should have read the poem *apart* from the musical setting, and as you listen, you should *have the musical score to follow*. It is helpful to jot down notes as you listen. If you are listening to an art song in a foreign language, most CD liner notes will provide the text *and the translation*, which is helpful to follow.

Melody

Melody is a dominant focus for the listener. When we hear an art song, we generally hear the vocal line and the text most easily, but melody is not confined to the vocal line. Melodies can be found in the piano textures or in the harmonic structure, in the form of small melodic motives, pitch "cells," or melodic fragments.

Notice the contours and shapes of the melodic line: whether it is a *syllabic* setting (one syllable per note) or *melismatic* (more than several notes sung to a single syllable), and whether the rhythms assigned to the pitches add to the atmosphere or mood of the poem.

A composer may use these to emphasize a dramatic moment, accentuate an emotion, or sustain tension. The manner in which the composer sets the poem melodically will intensify different images in the poetry. Poulenc begins "Nous avons fait la nuit" (*Tel jour, telle nuit*) with a stepwise melody that rises calmly to set the initial mood—"we have made the night (turned out the light)." Musorgsky uses angular, jerky melodic shapes to bring to life the exasperated Nurse in the second song of his song cycle *The Nursery*. Schubert's stately melodic line in "An die Musik" intensifies the solemnity of the hymn to Music; Dowland portrays a lover's desire in "Come again, sweet love doth now invite" with five sequential repetitions of a rising interval, each one creating a mood of breathless expectation that finally releases on a long, extended note.

A few examples for listening and study:

DOMINICK ARGENTO: Winter (*Six Elizabethan Songs*)
Note the spiky, angular vocal lines. With few exceptions, this song is set syllabically. Melodic lines paint the poem's images of freezing cold.

FRANZ LISZT: O! quand je dors
Note the broad, flowing vocal phrases, Italianate in style, intense and sensual. Listen carefully to the last phrase, arching over a lean texture of three chords and two extended arpeggios.

FERNANDO OBRADORS: Del cabello más sutil
This is a beautiful lyric melody, with broad-lined phrases, made to seem even more sweeping by the arpeggiated piano figures.

FRANCIS POULENC: C
The opening piano line curves upward and falls, like the arch of a bridge. The bridges of Cé saw a great part of the French population flee before the invading armies (World War II). Languid, lyric melodic lines that curve like the arch of a bridge. The vocal lines are also beautifully shaped, long-lined and legato, almost as though improvised.

HENRY PURCELL: I'll sail upon the Dog-Star
The character that sings this melody is energetic and self-satisfied. The melodic part is full of melismas. Note the words on which they appear.

Harmony
Harmony in art song is generally tied to the expressive qualities of the poetry, and is a key component in creating imagery. A composer can organize harmonic materials to create mood, reinforce drama, or

illustrate poetic elements. Harmonic color or harmonic movement can illustrate text, harmonic sequences can heighten drama in the words, and dissonances can highlight one word or a group of words. When combined with melody and rhythm, harmony can produce momentum, create tension, sustain intensity, or provide release.

A beautiful example of how harmony can illustrate poetic atmosphere is found in Richard Strauss's "Die Nacht." The song begins with a single repeated note in the piano; as the singer enters, the piano part gradually becomes two notes, then three, heralding the soft approach of the night. Without losing momentum or changing rhythmic pattern, these harmonies shift imperceptibly throughout the song, building in intensity, until the final measures of the piano part bring release and closure.

Another example of harmonic text painting is the third song of *Chansons de Bilitis*, in which Claude Debussy illustrates the text "Le long du bois couvert de givre, je marchais" with a repeated harmonic pattern over a pedal point, evoking Bilitis's plodding steps along an icy path.

Other things to notice: Is the harmony tonal or atonal? Is there much use of chromaticism? Notice the key centers used. If many modulations are employed, do they link with a change in the poetic content? Melodic content and rhythmic stresses are usually related to important harmonic changes within a song.

A few examples for listening and study:

GABRIEL FAURÉ: Arpège

Listen for the fluctuations in the harmonies under the vocal line, creating shifting tonal centers that do not pause until the final measures.

CHARLES IVES: Tom Sails Away

Ives uses polyharmonies and polyrhythms in the musical texture of this wistful memory of the past. Blurred rhythms and a languid vocal line combine to create a meter-less kind of impressionism reminding us of the flow of time and a nostalgia for time past.

XAVIER MONTSALVATGE: Cuba dentro de un piano
(*Cinco canciones negras*)

Listen for the colorful harmonic twists in this song. The piano part is highly chromatic, held together by a swaying *habanera* rhythm. Chromatic harmonies and dissonances between voice and piano create a mood of sensual calm, violently interrupted by the last phrase.

FRANCIS POULENC: Dans l'herbe (*Fiançailles pour rire*)

Poulenc shifts tonality throughout this song, never fully establishing a decisive tonal center—perhaps to mirror the poetic content of the relationship.

RICHARD STRAUSS: Die Nacht

Note how Strauss begins with a single repeated note in the piano and builds a harmonic texture that approximates the soft but insistent coming of the night.

PETER WARLOCK: Sleep

Piano textures are full of subtle harmonic and rhythmic variations that perpetuate the mood of the text. The unusual changes of meter make the vocal part seem unbarred.

HUGO WOLF: Herr, was trägt der Boden hier?
(*Spanisches Liederbuch*)

In this 27-measure conversation between Christ and the sinning believer, listen for piercing dissonances in repeated rhythmic patterns, which are then resolved. The chords that accompany Christ's answers are both solemn and comforting.

Rhythm

Rhythm, which has been called "the backbone of music," is the underlying pulse of a musical work. The rhythmic duration of tones within a musical work also functions to organize tension and relaxation within the work. In an art song, rhythm is closely tied to melody, since rhythm organizes word stress or versification of the words within the melodic line.

Like a chameleon, rhythm combines with harmony; rhythmic patterns found in the harmonic texture are important in creating mood or highlighting a particular image in the poem. A simple, unchanging rhythm of repeated chords can create a calm dreamlike atmosphere, as in Fauré's "Après un rêve." Or rhythm can plunge us immediately into a dramatic scene, as in the opening of Richard Strauss's "Schlechtes Wetter," with rain and snow slapping in steady patterns against a windowpane.

Check the song to see if the composer uses simple or complex rhythm patterns. Are they rigid or flexible? Composers often build an entire song on a rhythmic motive (example: Hugo Wolf's "Das verlassene Mägdlein," built on an unwavering rhythmic figure in the piano part). Wolf uses this rhythm in the vocal line as well to reinforce the text.

A few examples for listening and study:

SAMUEL BARBER: The Monk and His Cat (*Hermit Songs*)
The playful padding movements of the cat are heard in rhythmic patterns in the piano. Both monk and cat are content to be "alone together."

CLAUDE DEBUSSY: La Flûte de Pan (*Chansons de Bilitis*)
Notice the changing rhythms Debussy uses—from the fluid, ascending scale of the beginning to syncopated chordal figures, shifting harmonies, imitative phrases of Bilitis and her "teacher."

ALBERTO GINASTERA: Gato
(*Cinco canciones populares argentinas*)
The energetic rhythms that drive this song are derived from the Argentina country dance called the *gato*. The pulsing rhythmic figures continue throughout the song, driving it to the very final measures.

CHARLES IVES: The Circus Band
Within the overall marching meter of the piece, there are rapidly changing rhythmic patterns in both voice and piano. The vocal line contains syncopation in a number of places, always tied to the text.

HENRY PURCELL: Sweeter than roses
The three sections of this song highlight different rhythmic design. First section: Melismatic text painting (primarily on the words "cool" and "warm"), rising sequential motives on "dear kiss," more text illustration on "trembling" and "freeze." A short transition section brings us to the second section, a faster tempo section with

a rising vocal phrase, repeated, that literally "shoots" the words upward. The third section praises victorious love, dancing triumphantly to the final measures.

HUGO WOLF: Der Rattenfänger

The rhythms that drive this piece are both sparkling and demonic, and help paint the images in the medieval tale of the Pied Piper. Almost the entire song is set syllabically, giving the vocal line a rhythmic energy that matches the piano and the brisk tempo.

The Piano in Art Song

A composer chooses melodic, rhythmic, or harmonic figures in the piano texture that help to set the song's emotional or dramatic mood. These figures can become participants in the poetic content and also help to create imagery as well. Staccato figures paint one image, arpeggios another. When you listen to an art song, notice the piano figures and how they are crafted to produce imagery.

Franz Schubert was a master at establishing musical atmosphere and mood in his piano writing—listen to "Die Forelle," "Gretchen am Spinnrade," and "Erlkönig"—or see how the conversation between a young girl and Death is portrayed in the piano figures in "Der Tod und das Mädchen."

A century later down the line, Gabriel Fauré also composed piano textures that etched an elegant ambience rooted in the style of the nineteenth-century French *mélodie*, while still supporting the beauty of the poem.

Another important quality to notice is the texture of the piano part. Is it dense and thick, or sparse and clear? Does the overall texture evolve from a sparse texture into one with a richer sound, as in Gabriel Fauré's "Clair de lune?" Is the texture linear, as in the first part of Strauss's "Die Nacht?" Contrapuntal (having several melodies happening at the same time)? Each of these textures, when linked to the words of the poem, can transmit different images to the listener.

Composers sometimes include *preludes*, *interludes*, or *postludes* in a song. Interludes are not as prevalent in art songs, but preludes and postludes are found frequently, usually in songs by composers who were also excellent pianists. Two example of extended preludes: Franz Joseph Haydn's "She never told her love" and Richard Strauss's "Morgen!" Postludes usually provide a "commentary" on the poem just sung. Two examples are the final song in Robert Schumann's cycle *Frauenliebe und –leben,* in which the first song is recalled in its entirety at the end of the cycle; and Richard Hundley's "The Astronomers," featuring an ethereal postlude that evokes a starry night viewed from the quiet of a graveyard.

A few examples for listening and study:

CLAUDE DEBUSSY: Green
Octaves and cascading arpeggiated figures suggest whole-tone harmonies and point up the breathlessness of the poetic content.

CHARLES IVES: Charlie Rutlage
Here the piano plays a rugged Western tune that is interrupted by the voice telling the story. As the tale progresses, the pianist punctuates the moment Charlie's horse falls on him with fists on chord clusters. The piano becomes an active participant in the dramatic action of this song.

JOHN MUSTO: Recuerdo
The piano part begins in a bluesy, ragtime style as the story of an all-night trip on the ferry is told. The piano part becomes very involved, at times densely textured, but holds the narrative together as the story progresses.

MAURICE RAVEL: D'Anne jouant de l'espinette
Piano figures create a sparkling texture as the poet's love, Anne, plays the harpsichord. The piano figures also create an archaic mood, mirroring Marot's sixteenth-century poem.

FRANZ SCHUBERT: Die Forelle
The piano figures of the leaping movements of the trout and the motion of the water are captured in Schubert's graceful, curving piano pattern. The piano part also images the action of the story throughout the song.

RICHARD STRAUSS: Morgen!
Note the sixteen-measure prelude to this lied. It perfectly sets the mood for the exquisite vocalism that follows. The last measures are a tiny coda.

Form

Form is the organization or shape of a piece of music as defined by all its pitches, rhythms, dynamics, and timbres. [17] Since structure of the poem usually determines the form of the song, many forms may be found in song literature. Here are a few:

STROPHIC applies to songs in which every stanza is sung to the same melody. Church hymns are strophic in form.

THROUGH-COMPOSED (also called **DURCHKOMPONI-ERT**) has no repeated sections throughout the song from beginning to end. It is used for dramatic or narrative texts in which the dramatic action changes with every stanza. Schubert's "Erlkönig" is through-composed.

BINARY denotes songs having two musical sections, usually AB, but more complex variations are possible, such as AA'BB'.

TERNARY divides a song into three musical sections, usually ABA or ABA'.

Things to notice: Does the musical setting follow the poetic form? If not, how does it deviate from the poem? Did the composer set the entire poem? If not, can you discover if there was a specific reason that the composer only used part of the poem? Did the composer change any of the words of the poem? Can you determine why?

Form itself is comprised of melody, harmony, rhythm, and the piano part. To these features, Erwin Stein adds *dynamics* and *color*, and stresses both the *independence* and *inter-dependence* of all these elements:

> Melody, harmony, texture, rhythm, dynamics and color are the elements of musical form and, though they are inseparable and interdependent in performance, each of the elements as well as their mutual relations must be taken into account. For performance is a function of musical form. [18]

Exercise: An Examination of Three Musical Settings

Now that you have examined the musical components of Melody, Harmony, Rhythm, The Piano Part, and Form, here is an exercise to try: listen to different musical settings of the same poem. William Shakespeare is a poet whose texts have multiple settings by art song composers. Shakespeare's "Come away, Death" (from *Twelfth Night*) is good for starters. Gerald Finzi, Roger Quilter, Ralph Vaughan Williams, Erich Korngold, and Jacques Leguerney have all set this text. Choose three settings from that list, locate recordings for each, and listen to how each composer re-creates the imagery in the text using musical means. If you can locate the musical scores for the songs you have chosen, listen again, this time with the music. Being able to hear images created with word plus tone develops a heightened sense of listening and assimilation, which will carry over into your interpretive work.

Cultural / Artistic Contexts for Studying Art Songs

Learning about the poem or text that we are singing not only provides factual information, but also helps to pull together both the background and spirit of the musical work. For instance, what can you learn about the poet that might give you further insights into the poem? What other art works (paintings, literature, music, sculpture) were being created during the composer's lifetime? Can you find out a specific reason the composer chose the poem to set as music?

Learning about the artistic climate in which the composer lived and worked can be enlightening. What events were happening artistically and culturally during the time the song or song cycle was composed; what current events surrounded the musical work's inception?

Below is an example of a song cycle by Francis Poulenc—one that is quite unusual in artistic concept, since it unites three arts in one musical work: poetry, painting, and music. The poet, composer, and artists (in the poems) all knew one another. The intermingling of artistic personalities during one of the most explosive periods of French artistic creation certainly had impact on the creation of this work.

EXAMPLE: Francis Poulenc: *Le Travail du peintre*, poetry by Paul Eluard

Francis Poulenc's imaginative song cycle titled *Le Travail du peintre* (*The Work of the Artist*), contains seven *mélodies* on poems by Paul Eluard. Each poem captures Eluard's poetic descriptions of the paintings of seven Cubist artists (Pablo Picasso, Marc Chagall, Georges Braque, Juan Gris, Paul Klee, Joan Miró, and Jacques Villon). Picasso's bold lettering serves as the cover of the published score.

Poulenc's cycle mixes style in music, poetry and painting; and while not specifically comparable, the three arts share common terminology: form, rhythm, texture, and color. Poulenc's *mélodies* and Eluard's poems are packed with imagery, and imagery is the most powerful operative element in examining any artwork—be it music, poetry, or painting.

In working with this particular cycle, the singer *must* read the poetry and *try to link the images within each poem with the work of the artist* being described poetically. Eluard's poems are full of short, fluid images; certain of these are easily seen in paintings by the artists in the poems, further strengthening the connection. In synthesizing the visual and literary with his music, Poulenc combined the diversities of all three media in a unique and most successful way, almost "painting" the work of each artist in sound.

The images and emotions in the poetry seem to exist in a state of constant transformation, which produces tension that is also translated into Poulenc's musical settings. Poulenc's accompaniment figurations and vocal line shapes also complement the poetic content. Poetry, painting, and music also share the element of color—the sonorous color of words, the shades and tints of a painting, and the harmonic "color" of the musical setting.

Going a step further is knowing that this cycle was composed in 1956, between two of Poulenc's operas: *Dialogues des Carmélites* (1956) and *La Voix Humaine* (1958). The art songs in the cycle (1956) show definite influences from *Dialogues*, which Poulenc completed orchestrating prior to beginning work on the song cycle. Poulenc's opening measures of "Pablo Picasso" feature a transposition of Mother Marie's theme from *Dialogues des Carmélites*.

In order to better understand the interrelationship of images in both poems and musical settings, the most helpful research a singer can do when working with this cycle is to become familiar with the work of each artist represented in the poetry. For example: Marc Chagall's paintings feature figures that seem to float in space, and he had favorite motifs that appear in more than one painting. Poulenc's art song features an angular vocal line coupled with an exuberant tempo marking specifying one beat per measure. Poulenc's musical setting suggests the violin and the mixture of dream and reality found in Chagall's work. Eluard's poem closes with dream images and Poulenc achieves a brief trancelike moment by pitting duplets in the vocal line against groupings of three in the accompaniment.

Le Travail du peintre is an inventive experiment of artistic synthesis that will communicate more strongly to an audience if the singer has done a little research on the artists in the poems, their paintings, and the cultural milieu in which they worked. Many singers have programmed this work as a multi-media presentation, which involved paintings by the artists in the cycle. These were either shown as slides during the performance of the songs, or used in some other type of visual presentation. Since not all audience members might be familiar with every artist in the cycle, and probably will be engrossed in looking at the translations of the poems, this is an excellent choice for a slide presentation of paintings, shown as the singer performs each song (see Appendix 3 for a list of slides that were used in one presentation).

Making a Study Sheet for a Song

In my song literature classes, I often had students make study sheets for *single* art songs. To do this, one has to look at the combination of all the song's musical parts—its melodies, harmonies, rhythms, and piano part. The form of the art song should be noted, and information about the poetry and poet should also be added to the study sheet. This is also the place to list other musical settings, if any, of this same poem/text. Each of these components may be broken down into smaller details that define the song's character. [19]

Choose an art song from your repertoire and make a study sheet for it. After you have looked carefully at all the parts of the art song and broken down the main headings into subsections, you can pull all these details together and create your study sheet for the song. It is important to note that *each study sheet will be different for every song*, and some songs will not use every subsection heading. List the information you have gathered about the song in the proper category on the study sheet. Use the subsections that apply for that particular song.

Create a study sheet for each song you are currently singing. Keep your data specific and succinct (see the "Sample Study Sheets" at the end of this section). As you work with more songs and develop study sheets for them, you will begin to identify patterns. If you find information that does not seem to fit neatly under one particular heading, but is a feature typically found in that composer's art songs, this information can be placed in a "General" heading in the study sheet. Consider these study sheets "works in progress."

What is the purpose of this exercise? Why go to the trouble of making study sheets? First, it will force you to examine details of the music and poetry that you may have glossed over before; second, it will sharpen your attention to fine points in the blend of words and music, and you will become increasingly proficient noticing their interaction in the songs you sing and ultimately, perform; last, but not least, you will have gone beyond merely learning the words and the notes. Making study sheets will make you a more intelligent interpretive artist.

Art Song Study Sheets

Here are four sample study sheets for the following art songs:
1. Charles Ives – "The Circus Band" (*Five Street Songs*)
2. Dominick Argento – "Winter" (*Six Elizabethan Songs*)
3. Aaron Copland –"Heart, we will forget him" (*Twelve Poems of Emily Dickinson*)
4. Samuel Barber – "A Nun Takes the Veil" (*Four Poems*, Op. 13)

STUDY SHEET 1:

Title: "The Circus Band"
Composed: 1894
Composer: Charles Ives (1874–1954)
Poet: Charles Ives

GENERAL

- Song belongs to a set titled *Five Street Songs* (Old Home Day, In the Alley, Son of a Gambolier, Down East, The Circus Band).

- Nostalgic memory of when the circus came to town in small town America. There was always a parade down the main street to drum up business for the evening's performance. It was an annual ritual, captured here in Ives's own words.

- One of Ives's most popular songs, inspired by his native New England.

- Villamil: for "Any voice that can cut through the piano writing." [20]

- Approximate performance time: 2:00.

MELODY

Melodic Contour/ Phrase Shape	Exuberant, rhythmically driven. Begins with a little quickstep march tune. Syncopated rhythms sprinkled throughout.
Range/Tessitura	Not wide (c-sharp1–f-sharp2).
Vocal Articulation	Calls for good articulation and a sense of the dramatic.
Text Illustration	Ives uses syncopation in the vocal line to illustrate the parade as it passes—the color and small-town pageantry.

HARMONY

Texture	Very dense—as the song progresses, the texture thickens.
Tonality	Major. Harmonic deviations are found in the piano accompaniment figures.
Text Illustration	Dissonances for color. Ives liberally sprinkles some "wrong notes" in the chords, especially in the interludes, to musically illustrate the amateur small-town band—enthusiastic but seldom perfect.

RHYTHM

Rhythmic Patterns	Eclectic, with syncopations. Two prominent examples—"We boys dreamed 'bout big circus joys"; and "Cleopatra's on her throne; That golden hair is all her own."
Tempo	Sprightly march rhythms. Ives's marking: Moderato (In a half boasting and half wistful way; not too fast or too evenly). In quickstep time, half note = circa 132.

THE PIANO COMPONENT

Preludes/ Interludes/ Postludes	Short introduction (like a fanfare—the parade's about to begin!). Two interludes (1. before the last stanza, 2. before the repeat of the last stanza).

Texture	Dense; many piano figures. "Hear the trombones!" is marked under the octaves in the pianist's L.H. in the interlude preceding the final sung refrain. The pianist can shout it out, or the singer can, or it can remain a quirky little Ives-ian interpretive direction.
Use of Motives	No motives, but repeating stanzas.
FORM	Short introduction AA / BB / Interlude 1 / C / Interlude 2 / C

POEM/TEXT

The Circus Band   —Charles Ives

All summer long, we boys
dreamed 'bout big circus joys!
Down Main Street, comes the band,
Oh! "Ain't it a grand and a glorious noise."

Horses are prancing, knights advancing;
Helmets gleaming, pennants streaming,
Cleopatra's on her throne!
That golden hair is all her own.

Where is the lady all in pink?
Last year she waved to me I think
Can she have died? Can! that! rot!
She is passing but she sees me not.

Poet

Ives composed this song while attending Yale University. This poem captures the excitement of the annual visit of the circus to a small town, and the "big" parade that preceded the evening's performance, as seen through the eyes of a young boy.

Choice of text

Ives's wrote this text, based on a boyhood memory in a typical small town setting.

Prosody

Very good; any deviations of normal word stress are always deliberate.

STUDY SHEET 2:

Title: "Winter"
Composed: 1957
Composer: Dominick Argento (b. 1927)
Poet: William Shakespeare (1564–1616)

GENERAL

- Song belongs to Argento's cycle titled *Six Elizabethan Songs* (Spring, Sleep, Winter, Dirge, Diaphenia, Hymn).

- His second song cycle and one of his most performed works.

- Songs are called "Elizabethan" because texts were drawn from that period in literature.

- The cycle exists in two versions: the original, for tenor and piano, composed in Florence and dedicated to Nicolas Di Virgilio; and the second, with Baroque ensemble accompaniment (1962) for soprano Carolyn Bailey.

- High voice (soprano or tenor).

- Approximate performance time: 1:30.

MELODY

Melodic Contour/ Phrase Shape	Quick, staccato phrases, pointillistic and angular—almost conversational. Colorful vocal writing, also includes some very quick cantabile moments. Some sustained high notes.
Range/Tessitura	Fairly wide range; high tessitura (E1–A2).
Vocal Articulation	Demands facile, clear articulation and an excellent sense of rhythm for phrase shaping. Staccato phrases require flexibility and control.

| Text Illustration | Vocal line perfectly illustrates the teeth chattering, bone-chilling, biting cold. Colorful evocation of winter's cold seen in human terms and observed by the "staring owl." |

HARMONY

Texture	Busy, and fairly dense.
Key Scheme	Fluid tonal centers. Each new vocal phrase suggests a different direction.
Tonality	Very tonal despite chromatic touches and a feeling of shifting key direction throughout.
Text Illustration	Supple harmonies flow and change, adapting to poetic content.

RHYTHM

Rhythmic Patterns	Rapidly moving rhythmic patterns in voice and piano.
Tempo	Extremely rapid tempo. Argento: Allegro vivace con slancio.
Text Illustration	Subtle text painting with note values on the words "nipped," "foul," and the cry of the owl: "Tu-whit, tu-who," and "greasy Joan, skimming the pot."

THE PIANO COMPONENT

Preludes/ Interludes/ Postludes	No introduction. The two stanzas separated by a brief little interlude before the headlong pace resumes.
Texture	Toccata-like figures. Demands an excellent pianist. Extremely dense, animated texture. Accompaniment fashioned of three predominant figures and variants. Evocative writing that illustrates the text and complements the vocal line.
Shared Material with the Voice	Mirrored figures with the voice at times ("And milk comes frozen home in pail," "A merry note").

FORM

FORM	Strophic setting (2 stanzas)

POEM/TEXT

When icicles hang by the wall
—William Shakespeare

When icicles hang by the wall,
  And Dick the shepherd blows his nail
And Tom bears logs into the hall,
  And milk comes frozen home in pail,
When blood is nipped and ways be foul,
Then nightly sings the staring owl,
Tu-whit!
Tu-who!—a merry note,
While greasy Joan doth keel* the pot.

When all aloud the wind doth blow,
  And coughing drowns the parson's saw,
And birds sit brooding in the snow,
  And Marian's nose looks red and raw,
When roasted crabs** hiss in the bowl,
Then nightly sings the staring owl,
Tu-whit!
Tu-who!—a merry note,
While greasy Joan doth keel the pot.

*skim
**crab apples

Poet

The plays and poems of William Shakespeare have inspired a huge body of art song and other vocal works throughout music history.

Choice of text

Text is taken from Shakespeare's play *Love's Labour's Lost*, Act V, Scene 2.

This Shakespeare text also set by numerous composers, including Thomas Arne, Gerald Finzi, Roger Quilter, Ralph Vaughan Williams (2 settings), Ernest Moeran, and Charles Parry. Most of these are titled "When icicles hang by the wall," although Vaughan Williams, who set the text twice, also used "Winter" as one of his titles.

Prosody

Excellent sense of prosody.

STUDY SHEET 3:

Title: "Heart, we will forget him"
Composed: 1949–50
Composer: Aaron Copland (1900–1990)
Poet: Emily Dickinson (1830–1886)

GENERAL

- This song belongs to Copland's *Twelve Songs of Emily Dickinson* (Nature, the gentlest mother; There came a wind like a bugle; Why do they shut me out of Heaven?; The world feels dusty; Heart, we will forget him; Dear March, come in; Sleep is supposed to be; When they come back; I felt a funeral in my brain; I've heard an organ talk sometimes; Going to Heaven!; The Chariot).

- All the songs stand alone and can be sung separately; Copland preferred they be performed as a unit.

- At 28 minutes, the Dickinson songs are Copland's longest work for solo voice. About the cycle, Copland said: "It was my hope, to create a musical counterpart to Emily Dickinson's unique personality."[21]

- For high or medium voices. Texts more suited to womens' voices. Singers often find not all songs suit their voices, for timbre or range.

- Approximate performance time: 2:15.

MELODY

Melodic Contour/ Phrase Shape	Simple and lyric; intimate mood. A few larger intervals to highlight word stress (see below: "vocal articulation"). Some subtle angularities.
Range/Tessitura	(b-flat1–g2)
Vocal Articulation	Poem set syllabically with exception of "tonight," "warmth," and "haste."

HARMONY

Texture	Chords and linear melodic material, continuing without pause throughout the song.

| Tonality | Tonal, with some dissonance and chromaticism. |
| Text illustration | Subtle harmonic punctuations on key words: "light", "dim", and "him." Constantly moving harmonic/rhythmic patterns act as an emotional "subtext" for the narrator. |

RHYTHM

Rhythmic Patterns	(see above)
Tempo	Copland directions: "Very slowly" (dragging). Copious markings by Copland as to tempo, dynamics, timbre.
Text Illustration	Rhythmic patterns, combined with tempo gives a halting quality to the overall mood, illustrating the narrator's inner tumult.

THE PIANO COMPONENT

Texture	Linear melodic lines in R.H. of piano coupled with chordal figures.
Shared Material with the Voice	Piano and voice maintain their own independence.
Postlude	Tiny postlude commenting on text.

FORM

Modified strophic (2 stanzas)

POEM /TEXT

For comparison of a similar poetic concept, see Paul Heyse's translation from Italian folk poetry of "Heut Nacht erhob ich mich um Mitternacht," set by Hugo Wolf in his *Italienisches Liederbuch*, another poem in which the poet also directly addresses his heart.

Heart, we will forget him   —Emily Dickinson

Heart, we will forget him
You and I, tonight!
You may forget the warmth he gave,
I will forget the light.

When you have done, pray tell me,
That I my thoughts may dim;
Haste! lest while you're lagging,
I may remember him!

Poet

Emily Dickinson is recognized as one of America's most distinguished nineteenth-century poets. She chose to live a reclusive life with her parents and sister in the family home in Amherst, Massachusetts. Only ten of her poems were published during her lifetime. After her death 1,800 manuscript poems and fragments were found by her sister. Well over 2,000 musical settings of her verses by countless composers have been composed, published, and performed.

Choice of text

This Dickinson poem has also been set by John Duke, Arthur Farwell, Robert Baksa, and Richard Hundley.

Prosody

Not always fluid in the entire cycle; however, this song is beautifully shaped for word stress.

STUDY SHEET 4:
Title: "A Nun Takes the Veil (Heaven-Haven)"
Composed: 1937
Composer: Samuel Barber (1910–1981)
Poet: Gerard Manley Hopkins (1884–1889)

GENERAL

- From *Four Songs*, Op. 13 (A Nun Takes the Veil, The Secrets of the Old, Sure on this shining night, Nocturne).

- This song dedicated to English cellist Rohini Coomara, who shared Barber's interest in Hopkins's verse.

- This song's musical setting anticipates his *Hermit Songs*.

- Title, but not necessarily text, indicates women's voices (soprano or mezzo). Best for intermediate to advanced singers.

- Barber later arranged this song for a capella four-part chorus.

- Approximate performance time: 1:45.

MELODY

Melodic Contour/ Phrase Shape	Broad-lined, lyrical vocal phrases of longer note values. Stepwise movement for the most part—a few phrases where thirds and fourths occur in the line. Singer needs an excellent command of legato.
Range/Tessitura	High Key (g1–g2), Tessitura somewhat high.Low key (e-flat1–e-flat2), Original key.
Vocal Articulation	Vocal phrases set syllabically— a hymn-like soliloquy. Sense of movement provided by shifting chord tonalities of the accompaniment.
Text Illustration	Declamatory and dramatic vocal line reflects the nun's religious fervor.

HARMONY

Texture	Vibrant sound quality created by chord figures.
Tonality	No stable tonal center. Shifting chords control harmonic design.
Text Illustration	Changing chords provide shifting tone colors that illustrate the text.

RHYTHM

Rhythmic Patterns	Barber's marking: "Slow and sustained in exact rhythm."
Tempo	Broad, majestic; 3/4 (quarter note = 48). Text illustration, poetic mood captured by the tempo and the sweeping rhythmic arpeggios.

THE PIANO COMPONENT

Texture	Accompaniment texture is fashioned from two figures: a broad, arpeggiated piano figure and a simple chordal figure in half notes for the last six measures of each strophe. These two figures support and punctuate the vocal line for both verses.

Shared Material with the Voice	None. Voice and accompaniment maintain their own identities, but complement each other harmonically.
Text Illustration	Piano figurations recall a bardic harp, accompanying the nun's ecstatic soliloquy of her longing for spiritual union with God.

FORM	Two stanzas, modified strophic setting

POEM/TEXT

Barber's beautifully simple blend of writing for voice and piano perfectly captures the poem's deep intensity.

A Nun Takes the Veil —Gerard Manley Hopkins (Heaven-Haven)

> I have desired to go
> Where springs not fail,
> To fields where flies no sharp and sided hail
> And a few lilies blow.
>
> And I have asked to be
> Where no storms come,
> Where the green swell is in the havens dumb,
> And out of the swing of the sea.

Poet

Hopkins converted to Roman Catholicism in 1868 and destroyed most of his poetry. This poem survived. He later became a Jesuit priest and professor of Greek literature at University College in Dublin. After his death, his poetry became appreciated for its freedom of prosody and its vivid imagery. This is one of Hopkins's early poems.

Choice of text

Hopkins's poem title was "Heaven-Haven: A Nun Takes the Veil." It is from his *Lyra Sacra: A Book of Religious Verse*, published in 1895. This text was also set as an art song by Celius Dougherty and as a choral work by a number of other composers.

Prosody

Barber had an unerring sense of writing for the voice, and his feeling for vocal prosody was always excellent.

What does this exercise do for you as a performer? By delving deeper into the musical structure of the art song, you accumulate many details that you can internalize for your performance. For example: this process will enable you to make artistic choices about tone color and weight regarding single words and overall musical phrases; your sensitivity to the blend of word and tone will develop rapidly, and thus, your expressivity as an artistic singer will grow at a commensurate rate.

NOTES

1   John Dryden, From the Dedication to the Duke of Somerset of *The Prophetess, or the History of Dioclesian*, 1690 by Henry Purcell (this dedication was written for Purcell by Dryden). In *Composers on Music: An Anthology of Composers' Writings from Palestrina to Copland*, ed. Sam Morgenstern (New York: Pantheon, 1956), 33.

2   Glenda Maurice, "When Poetry Becomes Music," Lecture at the National Association of Teachers of Singing National Conference, Seattle, WA.,1996. Notes taken by the author.

3   Edward T. Cone, "Words into Music: The Composer's Approach to the Text," in *Music: A View from Delft: Selected Essays*, ed. Robert P. Morgan (Chicago: University of Chicago Press, 1989), 123.

4   Peter Laki, "On Songwriting: An interview with composer Lori Laitman," *Lyrica*: The Newsletter of the Lyrica Society for Word-Music Relations, Issue 29 (Fall 2007).

5   Ned Rorem,"Poetry of Music," in *Settling the Score: Essays on Music* (New York: Doubleday, 1988), 398.

6   Ned Rorem, "The NATS Bulletin Interviews Ned Rorem" *The NATS Bulletin*, (November/December 1982): 9–10.

7   Quoted in Keith W. Daniel, *Francis Poulenc: His artistic development and musical style* (Ann Arbor, MI: UMI Research Press, 1982), 249.

8   Scott Wheeler, "Composer Scott Wheeler Remembers Virgil Thomson," website, Norfolk Festival Neighborhood; www.music.yale.edu/norfolk/blog (accessed October 27, 2011).

9   Peter Laki, *Lyrica* newsletter 29 (Fall 2007).

10 Jeffrey Ryan, associate composer of the Canadian Music Centre VISI website (Vancouver International Song Institute, in partnership with the Canadian Music Centre, Vancouver British Columbia Creative Hub) www.artsonglab.com/Podcasts/Entries/2011/12/4_Jeffrey_Ryan%2C_composer.html (accessed February 6, 2012).

11 Lori Laitman, "Frequently Asked Questions," on her website, artsongs.com (accessed September 25, 2005).

12 Dana Gioia, "The Apple Orchard." Copyright 2003 by Dana Gioia. First published in *The Hudson Review* (Spring 2003 issue), used by permission of Dana Gioia.

13 Dana Gioia, in an e-mail to the author, April 23, 2009. Laitman's setting of "The Apple Orchard" may be heard on *Becoming a Redwood: Songs of Lori Laitman*, Albany Records, TROY865 (2006).

14 Marilyn Lerch, poet, podcast video, VISI Art Song Laboratory website, www.artsonglab. com/Podcasts/Entries/2011/12/24_Marilyn_Lerch_Poet.html (accessed February 5, 2012).

15 Donald Ivey, *Song: Anatomy, Imagery, and Styles* (New York: The Free Press, 1970), 96.

16 The material in this section was excerpted from, or based upon "Components of Style," Kimball, *Song*, 3–21. For more in-depth reading on each musical component, readers are directed to this chapter in *Song*, 3–16.

17 Don Michael Randel, ed., *The Harvard Concise Dictionary of Music and Musicians* (Cambridge, MA: The Belknap Press of Harvard University Press,1999), 237.

18 Erwin Stein, *Form and performance* (New York: Alfred A. Knopf, 1962), 14.

19 See "Developing Style Sheets," in Kimball, *Song*, 23–24. *See also* "Style Sheet Examples," 24–37.

20 Victoria Etnier Villamil, *A Singer's Guide to The American Art Song 1870-1980* (Metuchen, NJ: The Scarecrow Press, Inc., 1993), 227.

21 Quoted in Vivian Perlis, *Aaron Copland Since 1943* (New York: St. Martin's Press,1989),158.

Chapter 5

Working With Repertoire: Formatting Recitals

*Recitals offer personal expressivity,
the stylistic projection of the whole performer,
and an experience that is always real and stimulating.*[1]

—Shirlee Emmons and Stanley Sonntag

The Recital Template: Building Programs

*...there is no reason to program a dull, garden-variety recital
in a format that does not inspire a musical and interpretively
committed performance on the part of the singer, nor offer
some entertainment value for the audience.*

Creating a Cohesive Program

Good programs are the result of research and study. Planning a good program demands creativity coupled with a wide-ranging knowledge of song repertoire. Singers need to work to fill in the gaps in their database of repertoire. There are many references available in music libraries: song anthologies, song cycles, single songs. Look up a composer you do not know and look at the songs he or she has written. When you attend song recitals, if there is a song programmed that you especially connect with, make a note of it and look it up. Save programs for reference. Some will provide excellent format models, some will be instructive in what *not to do*.

You might give multiple recitals during your studies—a junior and senior recital, a masters recital, and if you work toward a doctoral degree, a number of doctoral recitals.

Get familiar with art song literature—a broad overview of some depth—not just contemporary songs, but also older art song repertoire. You can refer to Appendix 3 of Sample Programs to get ideas. It seems a formidable task, but every long journey begins with a few steps, and it seems to me that these should be:

- Read about song literature. There are a number of books available to serve as references for an overview of the literature. Space precludes my listing them here, but there is a good selection in the Bibliography section of this book, under these headings: General Studies of Song Repertoire and History; Texts and Translations, and Repertoire Studies and Style. Most of these are available in school libraries and for commercial purchase. If you are serious about learning about art song literature, you should add some of these to your personal bookshelf.

- If you are in a school that offers a Song Literature class, *enroll in it*—even if it is *not* required for your degree! (Again, see the Bibliography section at the back of this book to browse through some available repertoire books).

If at some point in your career, you find yourself teaching, you will be very glad you have some information to fall back on. I have seen *many* young teachers whose information about song literature was quite sketchy. Initially they are overwhelmed with the task of choosing suitable repertoire for their students. They usually fall back on what *they* studied—repertoire that *cannot* suit beginning singers, nor all voice types.

How many times have I heard a freshman or sophomore student sing Hugo Wolf or Richard Strauss before they have sung Robert Franz or some judiciously chosen Robert Schumann or Franz Schubert? This sort of repertoire "cherry picking" does not work for long. Young students will become frustrated because they are not allowed to succeed in their early, developmental stages of singing. If teachers are conversant with a broad spectrum of vocal repertoire, and stay current with up-to-date literature, the job of assigning and working with songs tailored to a student's vocal needs becomes so much easier.

Note to young teachers: The schedules of highly successful voice teachers leave little time for exploration and planning repertoire with their students. If one has multiple recitals coming from their studio in one semester, it is easy *and* comfortable to fall back on the tried and true repertoire. Often that repertoire does not suit young singers nor ignite their interest in exploring new and appealing repertoire. Instead, many of them use the myriad "helpers" available (CDs, videos, accompaniment CDs, already done translations, already transcribed IPA) to learn it faster. Our fast-paced culture does not perpetuate detailed research, but settles for what will achieve the desired results in the shortest amount of time.

Note to students: It is *not* good form to just cobble together all or most of the assigned repertoire from your voice teacher during several semesters of study into a program, grouping songs by language, and then consider it a finished job. You probably will not sing *every* song you study as part of any recital you perform. This does not mean that the time spent studying and singing that song was wasted.

This chapter is not meant to solve all the planning problems inherent in all recitals, but it is designed to offer ideas as a template or a pattern for beginning to build programs. It is designed to involve students in the process of planning their own recitals. It is meant to spark ideas and exploration on their part.

Some Parameters and Guidelines

There is no *one way* to format recitals. There are as many ways as there are imaginative minds; however, one thing should remain sacrosanct: the integrity of the art song repertoire. The uniqueness of a classical musical form that links an existing poem with a composer's vision for it should be respected and performed accordingly. The materials presented here are meant to serve as guidelines and food for thought.

- There are usually three groups in the first half of the recital, plus two groups in the second half; however, if there is a song cycle of considerable length programmed, this pattern may be varied.

- A good rule of thumb to begin with: twenty songs for a full recital, usually five groups (three in the first half and two in the second half), depending on length and the vocal/technical demands of the music.

• The first half should be longer than the second half.

In his classic book, *The Art of Accompanying and Coaching*, Kurt Adler offers guidelines for putting together song groups of varying lengths–or a varying number of composers: "If the group consists of 4 songs, the division should be 2 + 2 (for instance, 2 Fauré and 2 Poulenc songs). If the group consists of 5 or 6 songs, the relation should be 2 + 2 + 1, or 3 + 2, or 2 + 2 + 2." [2]

Composer Francis Poulenc placed great importance on the placement of songs in a recital group, comparing it to the presentation of paintings in an art museum: "It is all a question of 'the hanging,' as essential in music as in painting." [3] If we take Poulenc's statement as a guideline for putting together a recital group, then we need a strong song to build the group around. It might be the most intense emotionally, the most dramatic or colorful, or the longest. Build the group out from there toward the first song and then, on to the last. If the set is three songs, this central song is obviously flanked by one song on either side; if the set is four songs, it might be the third song. A five-song set needs two songs on each side of the central song, and so forth. Try and avoid putting two songs together and calling that "a group."

The overall format of the entire recital needs to have:

• BALANCE (Unity and Contrast)

• VARIETY (Differences of Color, Mood, Tempos)

• A MIXTURE OF LANGUAGES

The choice of repertoire needs to be thoughtfully planned, with songs that will give the audience a sense of enjoyment through the balances and contrasts of the entire recital. Attention should be paid to the length of the recital. For full recitals and half recitals, many schools dictate this time frame.

In planning recital groups and programming them in juxtaposition one with another, care should be taken so that the difficulty of repertoire is spaced thoughtfully so singer and pianist are not technically taxed for a long period of time, and the audience does not get tired as well.

Here are some guidelines for the traditional recital (5 groups).

Group 1: You want to plan a program that allows you to use many vocal colors, drawing a broad spectrum of sounds from the poetry you are singing. The first group should be repertoire that allows you to settle yourself and "warm up," although this is a misnomer. Of course you will be vocally "warmed up"; however, nerves need to be calmed and an onstage rhythm needs to be established. Choose something that will allow you to be comfortable on the stage. The first group is the first time the audience hears your voice. Do not choose repertoire that is too complex.

Good choices for this group are Mozart or Haydn songs; Bach, Handel, or Scarlatti arias from cantatas or Baroque operas; or Purcell, Campion, or Dowland lute songs. More advanced singers might program a Mozart concert aria here.

Group 2 is the "highlight" group. It should feature the repertoire you especially want to showcase. These songs might be the most difficult repertoire on the program, or the lengthiest. Here is where you would program a song cycle if you are singing one, or perhaps you might want to place a work with an obbligato instrument in this slot. If you are fortunate enough to be singing the first performance of a new work, this would also be the spot to program it.

Group 2 should be in a different language than Group 1. The languages used in the first two groups decide the languages of Groups 3, 4, and 5. You want to have at least three languages in total.

Group 3 is the group immediately before the intermission, if a full recital is being formatted. This could be a shorter group of songs in a different language than Group 2, or in the same language. Care should be taken to program songs that contrast with Group 2 and do not perpetuate the same sort of dramatic atmosphere.

This is a place to program a shorter group or a piece with an obbligato instrument, for example: Rebecca Clarke's *Three English Songs* (voice and violin) or her *Four Irish Songs* (voice and violin). If you have used instruments in Group 2, you might not want to repeat here.

At the conclusion of Group 3, given our format of approximately 20 pieces, this is a good place for an intermission or in the case of a Junior Recital (a half recital) or an abbreviated recital, this would be the ending group.

After the intermission, **Group 4** should be something lighter in character and mood, perhaps a group of three to four songs in another language. An American group of folksongs or art songs works well here, or a group of lighter Spanish songs, if you have already sung some American repertoire.

Finally, the last group (**Group 5**) can be a perfect place to put a group of "crossover" material (if you are programming this type repertoire), or lighter fare. A group of American songs by several composers (see Kurt Adler's admonition above), or musical theatre "arias" would be perfect here. The group is usually in English for the native-speaking American singer; otherwise, it should consist of songs in the native language of the singer. Folk song arrangements in English or contemporary American art songs work well in this spot.

Variety Is the Spice of Life

When an audience member leaves the concert hall, they should have the feeling of having spent a satisfying hour and a half. If a recital has been planned with a sense of proportion and balance, the audience need not be aware of the design—it simply results in an enjoyable musical experience.

Some years ago, in a conversation with a colleague, we talked about the need for a recital being designed with balance in mind, and agreed that if balance is planned, then satisfaction is built in. He said: "Every recital should be like a good meal: *Hors d'oeuvres*, then the *Soup*, then the *Grand plat, La salade, Le fromage, Le dessert—et puis— le digestif.*" [4] If you are planning five groups with two encores, this is not a bad template on which to build a recital!

Encore!

encore (Fr.) again; once more; once again

An *encore* is an additional performance added to the end of a concert. Encores originate spontaneously when audiences continue to applaud, demanding another performance from the artists after the recital has ended. In some academic situations, encores *are not done*.

In many instances today, encores have come to be expected, and if you are singing a full recital, it is a good rule of thumb to plan for them. Even though the singer may plan one or more encores, they are not listed on the printed program, but are announced from the stage.

The choice of repertoire for encores varies widely. Some singers opt to show off their artistry by singing fast, bravura pieces as encores; some choose to close the evening with quieter, calm songs to bring down the audience's energy. If more than one encore is offered, the two choices above could both be used, using the slower, calmer song at the end. Audiences are showing their appreciation of the talents of the singer and pianist, and simply want to enjoy another chance to listen.

Encores might be thought of as that "little something" after dinner—a delightful ender to an enjoyable evening. Just because an encore might be planned, you are not obliged to sing it. The singer should gauge the applause before turning around and bolting onto the stage again. Oftentimes, the audience is satisfied, and their applause—while warm and appreciative—will not call for an encore on the part of the artists.

If the recital is overly long, or overly taxing, the audience and artists should be content with several bows. One can tell by the applause level when the evening is over.

There are countless examples of art songs that can be used as encores. Any encore that the singer chooses should be one that is comfortable to perform after having sung a full recital. An encore can be of any length, but should not be too long nor too short. In many cases, the audience may be familiar with the art song, and hearing the singer sing it will be "a treat." Here are some attractive examples:

Virgil Thomson: Take, o take those lips away

Stephen Foster, arr. Ned Rorem: I Dream of Jeanie with the Light Brown Hair

Lee Hoiby: Where the music comes from

Richard Hundley: Come Ready and See Me

Ned Rorem: Rain in Spring

John Musto: Triolet

Charles Ives: The Things Our Fathers Loved

Madeleine Dring: Song of a Nightclub Proprietress

Rebecca Clarke: Down by the Salley Gardens

Benjamin Britten: Down by the Salley Gardens

Pauline Viardot: Haï luli!

Ernest Chausson: Le colibri

Claude Debussy: Mandoline

Erik Satie: La Diva de l'Empire

Pyotr Il'yich Tchaikovsky: Net, tol'ka tot, kto znal

Serge Rachmaninoff: Zdes' khorosho

Edvard Grieg: Jeg elsker dig

    Wilhelm Stenhammar: I skogen

    Arne Dørumsgaard: Pampano verde (Francisco de la Torre)

    Fernando Obradors: Del cabello más sutil

    Carlos Guastavino: La rosa y el sauce

    Jaime Ovalle: Azulão

    Lori Laitman: Dreaming (Soprano; also soprano/baritone, soprano/mezzo duets)

    Ben Moore: Sexy Lady (Mezzo; text directed for this voice type)

Choosing Repertoire

Be a Pro-active Planner

Students need to take charge of their own recitals! Do not wait to have your teacher recommend every piece of repertoire for you to sing on a recital. Take charge of your recital, and plan it with your teacher. If you are a graduate student, you should plan the entire program on your own and then get it approved. Be a *doer* and not an *onlooker*. The *doer* spends time making possible choices of repertoire, the *onlooker* will let the teacher choose the recital repertoire and then will learn and perform it, usually without doing too much more than learning the notes and memorizing the song. The fusion between musical setting and poem is left by the wayside.

Singers need to experiment with innovative, interesting programming that will feed their imaginations and develop their musical and dramatic skills. This is very much a "hands-on" experience. Each time you do this, it becomes an easier task. In going through many pieces of repertoire to find a cohesive program format, you will discard (for that program at least) many other pieces. These should be revisited at a later time and will probably become part of later programs. When you take charge of your own recital—planning and studying the repertoire—the experience makes the performance of that program richer and more rewarding.

Below are some examples of projects/assignments that will help you to begin researching song. All of them may be adapted for undergraduate, graduate, or non-traditional students.

- Paraphrasing texts

- Writing program notes for songs in groups or for a song cycle

- Designing song groups using texts by one poet set by different composers composers (example: Shakespeare, Dickinson, Goethe, Verlaine)

- Designing a song group with a theme or idea that links the songs in some way

- Designing a half recital in one language

Wise Choices for Your Voice

"One size fits all" is *not* a saying that applies to song literature. You have to search, locate, test drive, and then choose the literature that suits your particular voice, your vocal maturity, and experience. All of these will change with time, and so will your repertoire choices. First, find out what sort of repertoire choices suit you *now* and use *that* as a starting point.

Do not assume that because you can sing all the notes in a song that it is a song you can interpret in performance. The text may require emotional depth you have not yet attained; it may require communicative skills that are subtler than those you have mastered to this point. There is a huge gulf of artistic understanding between singing Samuel Barber's "The Daisies" and his "Nuvoletta." The second poem by James Joyce, is a difficult text to decipher and Barber has pointed out its lighthearted craziness using a complex rhythmic framework. On the other hand, "The Daisies" is an early Barber song, a charming setting without much vocal difficulty. Oftentimes, a complex poem will present interpretive problems just as a complex musical setting can present technical problems. Make wise choices for your voice.

We are living in a time where everything has to be spectacular. We cannot hope to compete with electronic entertainment. Recitals should be entertaining, but they should offer the audience an evening of storytelling—hopefully, one that will engage their intellects and feelings, and draw them into the moment. It may be an unfamiliar world to the listener, but if the singer has done his homework, then the experience will be a pleasurable one. *Live* music is always a special event.

Song literature is an amazing treasure house of music. There is no way we can explore or know all of it, yet I am always surprised at the number of singers and performers who rarely venture into American art song before they sing numerous pieces of German and French repertoire. When they choose French *mélodies* do they look beyond Fauré or Debussy? Do they explore German *Lieder* by composers who lived after Hugo Wolf? Are they acquainted with some Russian *romans*, some Spanish repertoire, or some Scandinavian *romanser*?

A *Caveat* for Recital Planners

Caveat: A warning or word of caution.
Literarally, "may he beware."

There ought to be a list of *caveats* to read before starting to design song recitals. Many singers make unwise choices of repertoire. The fatal flaw in programming is choosing a song because "this music 'shows me off'." Wrong! It may have the potential to "trip you up." You do not want *anything* on your recital that has musical pitfalls that might create problems for you. Instead, you want to make wise and thoughtful choices that suit your instrument and your natural strengths as a performer. Choose music that fulfills you as an artist by offering interesting challenges—technical, musical, intellectual, artistic. Challenges are what drive good performances. If you can successfully meet the challenges of the repertoire you choose to program, then you have chosen wisely.

What will you be missing if you do not prepare and plan for your recital in this manner? You will be singing a public performance of song repertoire without having examined the emotional meaning of the poem, its imagery, and the music inherent in the framework the composer has created for it. Your performance, therefore, is assured of being one-dimentional. You will be missing going beyond the pronunciation of the word to the emotional content and color of the word. You will be missing the exhilaration of really getting "inside the song" and communicating it to a listener who then can experience your joy by being involved in your performance.

A Word on Gender-Specific Texts

Some poems are defintely gender specific. Can women sing men's texts? Can men sing women's texts? There really is no definitive answer to this question, except to say that if your comfort zone allows you to sing it, and the work in question does not make the audience uncomfortable to hear you singing it, then perhaps . . .

One test for suitability: look in the publication. If the composer has marked "for baritone and piano" or "for soprano and piano" then we can presume *that* is the voice type the composer had in mind when he set the poetry. If the music is marked "High voice" or "Medium voice" or "Low voice" then the gender specificity of the poem needs to guide you.

The second thing to think about is "*Why* do I want to sing this?" The art song repertoire is so vast, can you find something else to sing? There are a number of important song cycles that are normally heard sung by a male voice that female singers have recorded—namely, Schumann's *Dichterliebe* and Schubert's *Winterreise*.

I have a wonderful DVD of soprano Barbara Bonney singing Schumann's *Dichterliebe* and admittedly, I purchased the DVD in great part out of curiosity. Ms. Bonney, a gifted recitalist, gave a memorable performance, meticulously nuanced and marvelously shaped, both musically and dramatically. Mezzo soprano Brigitte Fassbänder, another excellent recitalist, has recorded Schubert's *Winterreise*, and her performance has all the artistry we have come to expect from all her performances.

Does that give you permission to sing anything you want? I don't think so. Obviously, there are some texts that are intensely gender-specific. I do not ever want to hear a man perform Schumann's *Frauen-liebe und -leben*, and it would be more than a stretch of the imagination to hear a mezzo soprano sing Fauré's *L'Horizon chimérique*, yet Ravel's Greek songs seem to work for both male and female singers (three of the songs have gender references). There are many songs for which a good case could be made for their appropriateness for male *and* female voices. Caveat: For complicated social issues, men singing womens' texts is riskier than vice versa.

One *does* have to take into account that when a woman sings a man's texts (soprano for tenor, mezzo for baritone) and vice versa, you have the octave displacement of the voice to deal with and many times that just does not work very well. When asked about women singing men's texts, distinguished pedagogue Pierre Bernac said "Well, I suppose so. If they did not sing *some* of them, they would have nothing to sing!" (this punctuated by a typical Gallic shrug and a knowing smile). [5]

A Word on Transpositions

Another thorny problem is that of transposing an art song up or down from the original key the composer chose when he set the poem.

Many composers do not object to singers transposing their songs, but there *are* those who do, and you had better know before you "just decide" to transpose a work to suit your particular voice. If the music you have chosen is not published in two keys, there might be a problem. You need to do some research on this one.

As a general rule, the original key when possible, is the preferred one for song literature. Thomas Grubb's classic book *Singing in French*, includes a guide to French song and opera repertoire, and some words from the author on transposition:

> The singer should make it a general practice to sing songs in their original keys and include this as a factor in his selection of repertoire. Just because a song is printed in different keys does not condone its being sung in a transposed key. Each vocal tessitura has its own color and power to evoke an atmosphere. The composer usually chooses a certain tessitura for a song because it offers a specific tonal climate and dictates a vocal type and quality appropriate to its text. Also to be considered here is the piano. A transposition can completely alter the tonal aura of an accompaniment and occasionally render its execution unnecessarily difficult and at times almost impossible. [6]

Arias on Recitals?

This is always a good debate, but a song recital is just that—a *song* recital. Frequently, early Baroque arias are used to begin a song recital, but it is not a rule. Arias by Handel, Scarlatti, Vivaldi, and cantata arias by J.S. Bach fall into this category and work well. When they were composed, those arias were part of operas which today are no longer staged, and we do not hear Bach's church cantatas in their entirety on a regular basis.

Furthermore, if you are attending a recital by a celebrated singer, known for their career in opera, you will probably hear an aria or two during the evening. These singers are usually excellent art song interpreters, but the public (and they buy the tickets) expects to hear an aria from these artists during the evening's performance. Artists such as Frederica von Stade, Leontyne Price, Dmitri Hrvostovsky, or Jonas Kaufmann program arias on their recitals. These are artists known for their performances on the operatic stage, and audiences look forward to hearing them sing an aria or two live and in person.

What would be *your* reason for programming an operatic arias on your recital? Because you like it? Because you sing it better than any of the artists listed above? Because you like it better than any of the art songs you are singing? If your answer to any of these auestions is "yes," then you need to rethink your repertoire.

There is just too much art song repertoire in the world from which to choose when putting together an art song recital. Many schools have strict guidelines about what type of repertoire may be programmed on degree recitals. Arias are not usually a part of the list, but often they are allowed. This is a decision you need to make with your teacher.

Repertoire Checklist

In choosing the overall design for your recital, you need to observe the following general parameters:

- Balance

- Different musical styles (variety/color/mood)

- A mixture of languages

- Reasonable length

The second tier of criteria deals with observing the following about the repertoire you have chosen:

- Range—comfortable for your voice at this moment in your development

- Key—see above

- Level of technical difficulty

- Musical challenges

- Sophistication of text

- Diction problems

Creating Song Groups

There are many ways to build song groups. The familiar and all-too-predictable program of song groups by one composer or in one language needs a little shaking up. The list below contains assorted subjects that will serve as exercises or springboards to explore different formats. Try putting together a group of songs that fit under these headings:

- Settings of one poet by different composers.
- Settings of one or two poems by different composers.
- Songs with a common theme or topic.
- Songs that refer to, or come from a specific historical period.
- Songs by women composers and/or women poets.
- Songs whose texts contain the same character, similar characters, or characters from a specific group.

In designing a group of songs, be careful that you have variety in key, tempos, mood; differences in rhythmic structure, texture, and piano figures. Pianist Graham Johnson: "Rhythm and tempo are absolutely crucial. They provide <u>atmosphere</u>, allow <u>technique</u>, and <u>time</u> to hear the text. One tempo sets one mood, another sets another mood." [7] You do not want an entire group of slow songs, nor songs in one tempo or key, nor do you want to juxtapose songs in the same key.

Below is a well-ordered group of *Lieder* by Richard Strauss. It has variety of tempos, moods, vocal and piano writing. Songs 1 and 3 share an affinity of calm musical tempo, Songs 2 and 4 share similarities in their vibrant pianism and dramatic storytelling.

Breit' über mein Haupt	Richard Strauss
Ich schwebe	(1864–1949)
Allerseelen	
Schlectes Wetter	

A Weaker Group:

Below is another German group with little cohesion as to musical style or historical linking:

Widmung	Robert Schumann
Al Luise die Briefe ihres ungetreuen	
	Wolfgang Amadeus Mozart
Zueignung	Richard Strauss

There are many Schumann *Lieder* that could have filled out an all-Schumann group. This group would also have been more effective with two Mozart plus two Schumann songs. Putting Richard Strauss into the mix after Mozart is a bit of a stylistic jolt to the listener.

Opening Groups

For some reason, choosing an opening group often seems to pose a problem when planning a recital. We want the song group to be just right, not too difficult, not too easy—something that will allow us to sing and settle into the ambience onstage. Here are some ideas for opening groups.

EXAMPLES OF OPENING RECITAL GROUPS:

Example 1: Early Baroque (Italian)

Early art song groups, some of which are more properly called arias, make effective opening groups for a recital. This is an opening group of early Italian Baroque arias, arranged by Arne Dørumsgaard. They are not a cycle; the heading is to group them together as pieces from a musical period. By not italicizing the heading, a cycle is not indicated.

Arie Italiane Barocche	**arr. Arne Dørumsgaard**
Son ancor pargoletta	Cavalli
O dolcissima speranza	A. Scarlatti
Apra il suo verde seno	Quagliato
Toglietemi la vita ancor	A. Scarlatti

More early Italian works arranged by Dørumsgaard were chosen by French baritone, Gérard Souzay, who programmed four of them as the opening group for his recital given at the Bing Theatre at the University of Southern California. [8]

O miei giorni fugaci	Peri
Apre il suo verde seno	Quagliati
Ferma, Dorinda mia	Calestani
Toglietemi, la vita ancor	A. Scarlatti

Example 2: Italian opening group, 19th century

The songs of Donizetti, Rossini, and Bellini provide good choices for opening groups. Their bel canto lyricism and graceful phrasing make them effective openers. Here are three Bellini songs that opened a faculty recital, followed by a longer (seven song) Schubert group. [9]

Malinconia, ninfa gentile	Vincenzo Bellini
Ma rendi pur contento	
Vanne, o rosa fortunata	

Example 3: *An opening group in English*

If English is preferred as an opening group, there are many good choices from the Lutenist period by Campion, Dowland, and/or Purcell.

Here is a group I used once, which was sung with harpsichord and cello as continuo. If you have a lute player handy, all the better.

If thou long'st so much to learn	Thomas Campion
Never love unless you can	Thomas Campion
Music for a while	Henry Purcell
If music be the food of love	Henry Purcell

The opening song is quick in tempo, and the words are sly and attention-grabbing. It is followed by another lively song, one whose words link easily with the first song, in which the girl invites intimacy. In the second song, she pronounces her mocking verdict of men in general. The two Purcell songs are linked by "music": the first, for its beautiful melody over a ground bass, and the second, quicker in tempo, exultant in its praise of the sensual blend of music and love. Another option for programming this group would be to reverse the two pairs of songs, beginning with the Purcell, followed by the Campion.

Example 4: *An opening group of early Spanish songs*

Opening a recital does not mandate repertoire in Italian. Early Spanish songs offer another option.

Songs of the Spanish Renaissance
arr. Arne Dørumsgaard

Con amores, la mí madre	Juan de Anchieta
Pampano verde, racimo albar	Francisco de la Torre
De Antequera sale el Moro	Cristobal de Morales
A la caza, sus, a caza	Mena Gabriel

EXAMPLES OF WEAKER GROUPS:

Example 1 : *A three song group that needs "tweaking"*

Un moto di gioia	Wolfgang Amadeus Mozart
Das Veilchen	
Oiseaux, si tous les ans	

Comments:

While all these Mozart art songs are charming, they also have a "sameness" about them, in regards to tempos, note values in musical phrases, and general musical atmosphere/texture/color. The only song less "bouncy" than the others in mood is Mozart's masterpiece, "Das Veilchen," but even that's not enough to save the day. It would have been nice if a slower tempo song had been inserted after "Un moto di gioia," such as "Ridente la calma," or "Abendempfindung," to make the group work more effectively.

Example 2: A three song Purcell that could be re-ordered

Here is a three song Purcell group used as an opening group.

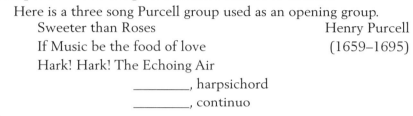

Sweeter than Roses	Henry Purcell
If Music be the food of love	(1659–1695)
Hark! Hark! The Echoing Air	
_____, harpsichord	
_____, continuo	

Comments:

A better order might have been to begin with "If Music be the food of love," since the tempo is fluid and flowing, and the text is particularly appropriate for the first song on a program. "Sweeter than Roses" is much longer song, and calls for more vocal control, so it might have been better placed as the middle song in the group. "Hark! Hark! The Echoing Air" is a good closer.

Example 3: A "hodge-podge" group

El paño moruno	Manuel de Falla
from *Siete canciones populares españolas*	
Va! laisse couler mes larmes	Jules Massenet
from *Werther*	
Hence, Iris, Hence Away	G. F. Händel
from *Semele*	

Comments:

Here is an actual group that appeared on a student recital. It juxtaposes one song excerpted from a collection of seven; one aria from a nineteenth-century French opera; and a Handel opera aria in English. It only remains to say: "Don't do this."

Song Choices for Different Occasions

What about choosing repertoire for those occasions that are not recitals—where you have been asked to sing—that church group social, ladies' club luncheon, dinner honoring a community leader, and so on? This is not the time for a group of songs from Schubert's *Win-*

terreise. Opt for musical theatre selections, or lighter fare from art song composers. Choose songs that are tuneful, or arias with melodies that are very familiar to the listening audience, even if they don't know the aria's title or its operatic context (example: "Quando m'en vo" from *La Bohème*; "Habanera" from *Carmen;* "Largo al factotum" from *Il barbiere di Siviglia*, or "Una furtiva lagrima" from *L'elisir d'amore*.") Below are some ideas, although the choices out there are almost limitless, but you do not want to program all foreign language selections. Try to find songs in English (see the list of musical theatre "arias" below).

Since you will probably not have a program or program notes, plan on announcing your selections and saying a little something about them. Keep it short and informal. Your verbal delivery and performing persona will carry the day.

Below are some selections that might spark some ideas for your choices.

Arias that might fit the occasion (depending on your technical level):
Georges Bizet: Habanera (*Carmen*), mezzo soprano
Wolfgang Amadeus Mozart: Voi, che sapete (*Le nozze di Figaro*), mezzo soprano
Friedrich von Flotow: M'appari (*Martha*), tenor
Gaetano Donizetti: Una furtiva lagrima (*L'elisir d'amore*), tenor
Giacomo Puccini: Quando m'en vo (*La Bohème*), soprano
George Gershwin: Summertime (*Porgy and Bess*), soprano
George Gershwin: I Got Plenty o' Nuttin (*Porgy and Bess*), baritone
George Gershwin: It Ain't Necessarily So (*Porgy and Bess*), tenor/baritone

Some art songs that might be apropos:
Georges Bizet: Ouvre ton cœur
Erik Satie: La diva de l'Empire
Erik Satie: Je te veux
Reynaldo Hahn: Si mes vers avaient des ailes
Stephen Foster, arr. Ned Rorem: Jeanie with the Light Brown Hair
Ned Rorem: Early in the Morning
Benjamin Britten: The Salley Gardens
Francis Poulenc: Les chemins de l'amour
Johann-Paul Martini: Plaisir d'amour
Madeleine Dring: Song of a Nightclub Proprietress

Francesco Paolo Tosti: Selected songs (La serenata, Mattinata)
Stefano Donaudy: O del mio amato ben
Fernando Obradors: Del cabello más sutil
Lee Hoiby: The Serpent
Richard Hundley: Come Ready and See Me
William Bolcom: Selections from *Cabaret Songs* or *MiniCabs*
Ralph Vaughan Williams: Linden Lea

Crossover material, such as songs by Cole Porter, Jerome Kern, Richard Rodgers/Lorenz Hart, Richard Rodgers/Oscar Hammerstein II, Harold Arlen, Kurt Weill, Leonard Bernstein, and Stephen Sondheim are also viable options as repertoire to sing at the aforementioned occasions.

Examples of musical theatre selections that are "aria-like" in style:*
Soprano:
And This is My Beloved (*Kismet*)
Art Is Calling for Me (*The Enchantress*)
Moonfall (*The Mystery of Edwin Drood*)
Somebody, Somewhere (*The Most Happy Fella*)
Think of Me (*The Phantom of the Opera*)
So in Love (*Kiss Me, Kate*)

Mezzo Soprano:
Can't Help Lovin' Dat Man (*Show Boat*)
Falling in Love With Love (*The Boys from Syracuse*)
You'll Never Walk Alone (*Carousel*)
My Ship (*Lady in the Dark*)
Something Wonderful (*The King and I*)
To Keep My Love Alive (*A Connecticut Yankee*)

Tenor:
Maria (*West Side Story*)
Fanny (*Fanny*)
On the Street Where You Live (*My Fair Lady*)
Stranger In Paradise (*Kismet*)
Lonely House (*Street Scene*)
Tschaikowsky (and other Russians) (*Lady in the Dark*)

Baritone/Bass:

If Ever I Would Leave You (*Camelot*)

They Call the Wind Maria (*Paint Your Wagon*)

The Man of La Mancha (I, Don Quixote) (*The Man of La Mancha*)

Where is the Life That Late I Led (*Kiss Me, Kate*)

With So Little to Be Sure Of (*Anyone Can Whistle*)

Joey, Joey, Joey (*The Most Happy Fella*)

*The selections above were chosen from the series *Musical Theatre for Classical Singers*, musical theatre "aria collections," with repertoire chosen for the classical voice. Each album, Soprano; Mezzo Soprano; Tenor; Baritone/Bass, offers a wide variety of literature from operetta to Broadway (Milwaukee, WI: Hal Leonard Corp., 2010).

Ramping Up the Recital: Thinking Outside the Box

Making Imaginative Choices

The trick in building successful recital programs is choosing repertoire that is musically viable for the singer, and varied in style and language—a program that offers students music that suits their level of vocal possibilities, but also offers musical and interpretive challenges for growth. Then lastly, to put it together into a design that connects the singer's persona with the audience they sing to. This requires research, imagination, and creativity.

Imagination should lead singers in the choice of their recital repertoire, just as it should lead them in working with the words that they sing.

On the final page of *Opera News* magazine is a feature titled "Coda." In October 2006, Brian Kellow wrote the following about recital programs: "I think it would be a good thing if more singers remembered to keep the audience in mind . . . We mustn't forget that exhilaration is, or should be, part of the concert-going experience." He went on to say: "A recital should never seem drab and dutiful. I recently heard a gifted young mezzo make her New York recital debut in an evening of works that seemed purposely chosen to *conceal* her greatest musical gifts. It was *utterly lacking* in that most prized of qualities—*imagination*." [10]

Song Groups With Different Design

One Poet: Song Settings of William Shakespeare

The plays and sonnets of William Shakespeare are a treasure trove for finding interesting song repertoire. As students begin to research musical settings of the same poetry, they begin to see many other design possibilities for song groups. Below is a partial list of song settings of Shakespeare by various composers, and this is only the tip of the iceberg.

To avoid too much of a good thing, try choosing *two* poems and build your group using two settings of each poem for a total of four songs, or depending on song length, use three settings of one poem and two settings of the other for a total of five songs.

Some Art Song Settings of William Shakespeare

Song Title	Composer(s)
Blow, blow thou winter wind	Madeleine Dring, Erich Korngold, Roger Quilter
Winter	Dominick Argento
It was a lover and his lass	Gerald Finzi
Pretty ring time (see above)	Peter Warlock, Madeleine Dring, Gerald Finzi, Roger Quilter, Richard Faith, Mervyn Horder, Rebecca Clarke
When birds do sing (see above)	Erich Korngold
Take, o take those lips away	Virgil Thomson, Peter Warlock, Amy Beach, Madeleine Dring, Roger Quilter, Rebecca Clarke, David Amram
Tell me where is fancy bred?	Virgil Thomson
Fancy (see above)	Francis Poulenc (in English)
Come away, death	Erich Korngold, Ralph Vaughan Williams, Gerald Finzi, Roger Quilter, Jacques Leguerney (in English)

Fear no more the heat o' the sun	Gerald Finzi, Roger Quilter, Charles Parry
If music be the food of love, play on	Lee Hoiby, Henry Purcell
Orpheus with his lute	William Schuman, Ralph Vaughan Williams, Roger Quilter, Arthur Sullivan
When Orpheus played (see above)	Richard Hundley
Orpheus (see above)	Thomas Pasatieri, Marc Blitzstein, Ivor Gurney
Sigh no more, ladies	Virgil Thomson, Geoffrey Bush, Peter Warlock, Mario Castelnuovo-Tedesco

More One-Poet Groups

Designing groups is a simpler way to start to think about one-poet texts. This can also grow into a full recital using the poems of one poet. There are many poets whose words have provided many musical settings—William Shakespeare, Emily Dickinson and Walt Whitman, for example. Below are two groups using poems by one poet, one using musical settings by one composer, one using musical settings by several composers. For a full recital of art songs using one poet (e.e. cummings, Johann Wolfgang von Goethe), see Appendix 3.

Example 1: One poet/one composer group –
An all-Verlaine group by Debussy

| CLAUDE DEBUSSY (1862–1918) | *Poèmes de Paul Verlaine* Il pleure dans mon cœur Green En sourdine Mandoline |

Comments:

Nice transition from *mélodie* to *mélodie*. First selection, fluid movement in piano, broadly lyric vocal line; second song, thicker textures and expansive vocal phrases; third song, an intimate, atmospheric scene; and finally, Debussy's fast tempo, whirling "Mandoline." Appending a title to the group ("Poèmes de Paul Verlaine") is slightly misleading since this is not a cycle nor are these published as a group. Another way to handle this is to use: "Poems by Paul Verlaine" without italics, in English, or just omit the title completely.

Example 2: One poet /several composers group – Poems by Goethe

Here is an example of a group of songs by one poet, Johann Wolfgang von Goethe. Because a number of composers have set the Suleika poems of Goethe, the group is arranged to feature three of these.

Text settings from the *West-östlicher Divan*
(Johann Wolfgang von Goethe)

Suleika I (Was bedeutet alle Bewegung?)	
	Franz Schubert
Suleika (Ach um deine feuchten Schwingen)	
	Fanny Mendelssohn Hensel
Als ich auf dem Euphrat schiffte	Hugo Wolf
Hoch beglückt in deiner Liebe	Hugo Wolf

Song Groups Using One Poem, Different Musical Settings

Finally, here is a group using one *poem* with different musical settings. There are many countless instances of composers setting the same text. A little research on the part of the singer will yield numerous songs to choose from.

This group features the poem "Gretchen am Spinnrade" (Gretchen at the Spinning Wheel) from Goethe's *Faust*. These are three very different settings, but feature one character, one poem (one in Italian translation). To break the "sameness" of hearing the text two times in a row, place the Italian text in the middle to separate them.

Gretchen am Spinnrade	Richard Wagner
Perduta ho la pace	Giuseppe Verdi
Gretchen am Spinnrade	Franz Schubert

More ideas: Art songs using the poems of Paul Verlaine, set by Gabriel Fauré, Claude Debussy, and others.

Song Groups That Feature One Character or Linked Characters

Choosing a character or characters linked by some common thread is another interesting way to begin to build a group of songs. The *Commedia dell'Arte* that began in Europe in the sixteenth century was improvised comedy. It also became known as the "Comedy of Masks" because most of the characters appeared masked, an invention that created fixed type characters. The players finally became known as the Italian Comedy (or simply "the Comedy") since the form was created and developed almost exclusively by Italian comedians.

Some of these stock *Commedia* characters appear in several poems of Paul Verlaine's *Fêtes galantes*, published in 1869. Composers were drawn to Verlaine's delicate but evocative images and their elegant, fluid verses. We often see a "comparison" group of Verlaine settings by Fauré and Debussy programmed, but if the Verlaine poems are narrowed to include only those with *Commedia* characters, the field of composers expands. Here are some musical settings:*

* Song titles are italicized instead of in quotation marks for ease of reading

EXAMPLE 8: Commedia dell'arte characters

Composer	Song Title	*Commedia del arte* characters in the poem
Gabriel Fauré	*Mandoline*	Tircis/Aminte, Clitander, Damis
Claude Debussy	*Mandoline*	(same as above)
	Pierrot	Pierrot, Clitander, Colombine
	Pantomime	Colombine, Pierrot, Clitander, Cassander, Harlequin
	Fantoches	2 buffoons: Scaramouche, Pulcinella/Polichinelle Colombine (not mentioned by name, only described), Doctor from Bologna, The Captain (Spanish pirate)
Jósef Szulc	*Mandoline*	(see Fauré and Debussy)
Reynaldo Hahn	*Fêtes galantes*	Hahn's title for "Mandoline" (see Fauré and Debussy)
Poldowski (Lady Dean Paul)	*Colombine*	Colombine, Leander, Cassander, Pierrot, Harlequin

Adding Instruments to the Mix

Single songs with an obbligato instrument, or multiple songs in a collection or cycle with one or more instruments, add variety of tonal color and mood to a recital. A young performer or novice recitalist may not yet have the command of color and nuance to keep a full recital musically vibrant for the audience. Adding another sound color to the mix offers variety and a change of pace and gives young instrumentalists an opportunity to perform without having to present an entire recital. It's a win-win for everyone.

The list below seems overweighted with female voices; however, a good number of the soprano listings could also be sung by tenor. Be sure and check the texts and of course, the music. Also, this is only the tip of the iceberg. Singers would do well to check the solo cantatas and the church cantatas of Johann Sebastian Bach for solos with obbligato instruments. Some research into this particular art song literature will yield a number of works that are suitable for your voice.

A Selected List of Vocal Works With Instruments

Voice/Flute or Violin:

Adolphe Adam: Ah, vous dirai-je maman (Variations on a theme attributed to Mozart) (coloratura soprano, flute, piano)

André Caplet: Viens! Une flûte invisible (voice, flute, piano)

André Caplet: Écoute, mon cœur . . . (voice, flute)

André Caplet: Corbeille de fruits (voice, flute)

André Caplet: *Deux mélodies* (voice, flute, piano)

Cécile Chaminade: Portrait Valse Chantée (soprano, flute, piano)

Luigi Cortese: Due Canti Persiani (mezzo soprano, flute, piano)

Henry Cowell: Vocalise (voice, flute)

Leo Delibes: Le Rossignol (soprano, flute, piano)

Richard Faith: The Solitary Reaper (voice, flute, piano)

Daron Hagen: Dear Youth (soprano, flute, piano)

George Frideric Handel: Neun Deutsche Arien (voice, violin or flute, piano)

Georges Hüe: Soir Païen (soprano, flute, piano)

Jacques Ibert: Deux steles orientées (voice, flute)

Jacques Ibert: Aria (soprano, flute, piano)

Lori Laitman: The Silver Swan (mezzo soprano, flute, piano)

Libby Larsen: Righty 1966 (soprano, flute, piano)

Frank Martin: Trois chants de Noël (soprano, flute, piano)

Joseph Marx: Pan trauert um Syrinx (Eine mythologische Szene) (soprano, flute)

W. A. Mozart: L'amero, saro costante (soprano, flute or violin, piano)

André Previn: Two Remembrances (soprano, alto flute, piano)

Jean-Philippe Rameau: Rossignols amoureux (*Hippolyte et Aricie*) (soprano, flute, piano)

Maurice Ravel: La flûte enchantée [from Shéhérazade] (soprano or mezzo, flute, piano)

Joaquín Rodrigo: Dos Poemas de Juan Ramón Jiménez (2 songs for voice, flute)

Albert Roussel: Deux poèmes de Ronsard (soprano, flute)

Camille Saint-Saëns: Une flûte invisible (voice, flute, piano)

Alessandro Scarlatti: Cantata "Solitudine Avvenne" (voice, flute, continuo)

Scott Wheeler: At Home on Staten Island (soprano, violin)

Eric Whitacre: Five Hebrew Love Songs (soprano, violin, tambourine, piano)

Voice/Violin, Viola, Cello

Amy Beach: Chanson d'amour, Op. 21, No. 1 (mezzo soprano, cello, piano)

Johannes Brahms: Zwei Gesänge, Op. 91 (mezzo soprano, viola, piano)

Tom Cipullo: The Cove (soprano, viola [or cello], piano)

Rebecca Clarke: Three English Songs (voice, violin)

Rebecca Clarke: Four Irish Country Songs (voice, violin)

Alexander Dargomïzhsky: Elegy (med. high voice, viola, piano)

Richard Faith: Chant (voice, cello, piano)

Richard Faith: Ships (voice, cello, piano) trans. from the French (de Mirmont: "Vaisseaux, nous vous aurons aimés")

Richard Faith: I have embarked (voice, cello, piano) trans. from the French (de Mirmont:"Je me suis embarqué")

Charles Gounod: Evening Song (med. high voice, viola, piano)

Roy Harris: Abraham Lincoln Walks at Midnight (mezzo soprano, violin, cello, piano)

Jake Heggie: My True Love Hath My Heart (soprano, cello, piano)

Jake Heggie: Before the Storm (mezzo soprano, cello, piano)

Gustav Holst: Four Songs with Violin (voice, violin)

Lori Laitman: Long Pond Revisited (baritone, cello)

Lori Laitman: The Love Poems of Marichiko (soprano, cello)

Libby Larsen: Sifting Through the Ruins (mezzo soprano, viola, piano)

Charles Loeffler: Quatre poèmes, Op. 5 (medium voice, viola, piano)

Daniel Pinkham: Heaven-Haven (tenor or baritone, viola)

Dmitri Shostakovich: Seven Romances on Poems of Alexander Blok, Op. 127 (soprano,violin, cello, piano)

Alan L. Smith: Four Folksongs (soprano, viola, piano)

Alan L. Smith: Vignettes: Covered Wagon Woman (mezzo soprano, violin, cello, piano)

Voice/Oboe, Bassoon

Ralph Vaughan Williams: Ten Blake Songs (soprano or tenor, oboe)

Judith Cloud: The Poet's Pen (tenor, oboe, piano)

Libby Larsen: Saints Without Tears (soprano, flute, bassoon)

Ernest Chausson: L'invitation au voyage (voice, bassoon, piano)

Poldowski: Soir (medium voice, oboe d'amore, piano)

Voice/Clarinet
Dominick Argento; To Be Sung Upon the Water (high voice, clarinet, piano)
Gordon Jacob: Three Songs (alto, clarinet in A)
Franz Schubert: Air from Rosemunde (voice, clarinet, piano)
Franz Schubert: Der Hirt auf dem Felsen (soprano, clarinet, piano)
Louis Spohr: Sechs Deutche Lieder, Op. 103 (soprano, clarinet, piano)
Virgil Thomson: Four Songs of Thomas Campion (med. voice, clarinet, viola, piano)
Judith Cloud: Three Songs from "Gleanings" (soprano, clarinet, piano)

Voice/Saxophone
Lori Laitman: I Never Saw Another Butterfly (Soprano/alto saxophone; also soprano/
  clarinet; soprano/bassoon)

Voice/Horn
Simon Sargon: Huntsman, What Quarry? (soprano, horn, piano)
Franz Schubert: Auf dem Flusse (tenor, horn, piano)

Voice/Harp
Mario Castelnuovo-Tedesco: *Three Sephardic Songs* (voice and harp)

Voice/Guitar
Dominick Argento: Letters from Composers (high voice, guitar)
Benjamin Britten: Folksong Arrangements, Volume VI (voice, guitar)
Judith Cloud: The Waking (medium voice, guitar)
Judith Cloud: Songs of Need and Desire (soprano, guitar)
Libby Larsen: Three Rilke Songs (high voice, guitar)
Joaquín Rodrigo: Canciónes españolas (3 songs for voice, guitar)
Joaquín Rodrigo: Villancicos (3 songs for voice, guitar)

Voice/Three or More Instruments
Dominick Argento: Six Elizabethan Songs (soprano, oboe, harpsichord, violin, cello)
Jean Berger: Five Songs of Mary Stuart (mezzo soprano, flute, viola, cello)
Tom Cipullo: The Ecuadorian Sailors (mezzo soprano, flute, viola, harp)
Tom Cipullo: Rain (tenor, flute, violin, viola, cello, percussion, harp, piano)
Jake Heggie: From Emily's Garden (soprano, flute, violin, cello, piano)
Jake Heggie: Camille Claudel "Into the Fire" (mezzo soprano, string quartet)
Jake Heggie: Friendly Persuasions: Homage to Poulenc
  (high voice, flute, cello, oboe, harpsichord, piano)
Jake Heggie: Some Times of Day (mezzo soprano, violin, cello, piano)
Libby Larsen: Selected Poems of Rainer Maria Rilke (soprano, flute, guitar, harp)
Frank Martin: Quatre Sonnets à Cassandre
  (mezzo soprano/baritone, flute, viola, cello)
Francis Poulenc: Le Bal masqué (baritone, oboe, clarinet, bassoon, cornet, violin, cello,
  percussion). and a conductor
Maurice Ravel: *Chansons madécasses* (mezzo soprano/baritone, flute, cello, piano)

Ottorino Respighi: Il Tramonto (mezzo soprano, string quartet)
Ned Rorem: *The Santa Fe Songs* (mezzo-soprano, violin, viola, cello, piano)
Richard Pearson Thomas: *At last, to be identified!* (soprano, violin, cello, piano)

Women Poets / Women Composers

Here is an eclectic list of some women poets. Explore their poetry and peruse the song settings of their texts.

Margaret Atwood (b. 1939)
Elizabeth Bishop (1911–1979)
Louise Bogan (1897–1970)
Gwendolyn Brooks (1917–2000)
Elizabeth Barrett Browning (1806–1861)
Emily Dickinson (1830–1856)
H. D. (Hilda Doolittle) (1886–1961)
Rita Dove (b. 1952)
Alice Fulton (b. 1952)
Alice Wirth Gray (1934–2008)
Denise Levertov (1923–1997)
Marianne Moore (1887–1972)
Linda Pastan (b. 1932)
Mary Oliver (b. 1935)
Kathleen Raine (1908–2003)
Christina Rossetti (1830–1894)
Anne Sexton (1928–1974)
Barbara Strozzi (1619–1664)
Edna St. Vincent Millay (1892–1950)
Gertrude Stein (1874–1946)
May Swenson (1913–1989)
Sara Teasdale (1884–1933)
Louise de Vilmorin (1902–1969)
Elinor Wylie (1885–1928)

Women Composers

Here is a doctoral recital formatted to highlight the work of women composers. Using the topics of women poets and women composers offers many design options—formatting recitals of all women composers, all women poets, or a combination of the two.

PROGRAM

Barbara Strozzi (1619–1677)	Con male nuove, non si puo cantare Pensaci ben mio core
Fanny Mendelssohn Hensel (1805–1847)	Warum sind denn die Rosen so blass Morgenständchen Nachtwanderer Frühling

Poldowski (1879–1932)	Five Paul Verlaine Songs
	    Colombine
	    Spleen
	    Cythère
	    Crépuscule du soir mystique
	    Danson la gigue

INTERMISSION

Amy Marcy Beach (1867–1944)	Three Shakespeare Songs, Op. 37
	    O Mistress Mine
	    Take, O take those lips away
	    Fairy Lullaby

Lori Laitman (b. 1955)	Four Dickinson Songs
	    Will There Really Be a Morning
	    I'm Nobody
	    She died
	    If I . . .

Lin-Ning Chen (b. 1968)	Gone . . .
Jian-Fen Gu (b. 1935)	It Is Me

More Design Topics on the Subject of Women

This topic of "women" has other format possibilities beyond women poets and women composers. You might design a group of songs whose titles are <u>womens' names</u>, or musical settings <u>sung by women</u> in various emotional states, for example, Poulenc's "Fleurs." Keep the scope of the texts *focused* so the intent of the group remains clear. Song groups may be in various languages, or in one language. There are hundreds of possibilities! Some of these are listed below, grouped by language. Many of these songs are suitable for a male voice, too.

Example 1:

Some Songs with Womens' Names in the Title

Gabriel Fauré: Nell, Lydia

Ernest Chausson: Hébé

Reynaldo Hahn: A Chloris

Jules Massenet: Si tu veux, Mignonne

Cécile Chaminade: Mignonne

Richard Wagner: Mignonne

Erik Satie: Sylvie

Maurice Ravel: *Deux épigrammes de Clément Marot*

> D'Anne qui me jecta de la neige
>
> D'Anne jouant de l'espinette

Arthur Honegger: *Petit cours de morale*

> Jeanne
>
> Adèle
>
> Cécile
>
> Irène
>
> Rosemunde

Henri Duparc: Phidylé

Charles Gounod: Mignon

George Enescu: Estrene à Anne (*Sept chansons de Clément Marot*)

Ludwig van Beethoven: Adelaide

Hugo Wolf: Mignon

Franz Schubert: An Silvia

Johannes Brahms: Therese

Giulio Caccini: Amarilli, mia bella

Ned Rorem: Upon Julia's Clothes (*Flight for Heaven*)

Richard Faith: To Celia (Drink to me only with thine eyes)
 (*Four Elizabethan Songs*)
Dominick Argento: Diaphenia (*Six Elizabethan Songs*)
Richard Hundley: Ballad on Queen Anne's Death
Theodore Chanler: from *Eight Epitaphs*
   Alice Rodd
   Susannah Fry
   Three Sisters
   Ann Poverty
Stephen Foster, arr. Ned Rorem: Jeanie With the
         Light Brown Hair
Frederick Delius: Irmelin Rose
Gerald Finzi: Who is Silvia? (*Let Us Garlands Bring*)
Peter Warlock: Jillian of Berry
Virgil Thomson: Rose-cheek'd Laura, come

Example 2:
Songs with a Text Sung by a Woman

Wolfgang Amadeus Mozart: Als Luise die Briefe . . .
Hugo Wolf: Die verlassene Mägdlein (*Möricke Lieder*)
Hugo Wolf: Die Spröde, Die Bekehrte (*Goethe Lieder*)
Hugo Wolf: Mein Liebster singt (*Italienisches Liederbuch*)
Hugo Wolf: Ich hab in Penna (*Italienisches Liederbuch*)
Robert Schumann: *Frauenliebe und –leben*
Robert Schumann: Die Kartenlegerin
Robert Schumann: Singet nicht in Trauertönen
Franz Schubert: Die junge Nonne
Franz Schubert: Gretchen am Spinnrade
Franz Schubert: Suleika I
Fanny Mendelssohn Hensel: Suleika
Richard Wagner: Gretchen am Spinnrade
Kurt Weill: Nanna's Lied
Gioachino Rossini: La pastorella delle Alpi
Gioachino Rossini: *La regata veneziana*
    Anzoleta avanti la regata
    Anzoleta co passa la regata
    Anzoleta dopo la regata
Giuseppe Verdi: Perduta ho la pace
Albert Roussel: Réponse d'une épouse sage

Claude Debussy: *Chansons de Bilitis*
          La Flûte de Pan
          La Chevelure
          Le Tombeau des Naïades
Francis Poulenc: *Fiançailles pour rire*
          La Dame d'André
          Dans l'herbe
          Il vole
          Mon cadavre est doux comme un gant
          Violon
          Fleurs
Madeleine Dring: Song of a Nightclub Proprietress
Leonard Bernstein: *I Hate Music!*
          My name is Barbara
          Jupiter has seven moons
          I hate music!
          A big Indian and a little Indian (Riddle Song)
          I'm a person too
Dominick Argento: *From the Diary of Virginia Woolf*
          The Diary
          Anxiety
          Fancy
          Hardy's Funeral
          Rome
          War
          Parents
          Last Entry
Dominick Argento: *Miss Manners on Music*
          Prologue
          Manners at a Concert
          Manners at the Ballet
          Manners for Contemporary Music
          Manners at a Church Recital
          Manners at the Opera
          Envoi
Libby Larsen: *Love after 1950*
          Boy's Lips (A Blues)
          Blond Men (A Torch Song)

Big Sister Says (A Honky-Tonk)
Empty Song (A Tango)
I Make My Magic (Isadora's Dance)
Libby Larsen: *Try Me, Good King* :
Last Words of the Wives of Henry VIII
Katherine of Aragon
Anne Boleyn
Jane Seymour
Anne of Cleves
Katherine Howard
Lori Laitman: Eloise at Yaddo
Enrique Granados: La maja dolorosa, Nos. 1, 2, 3 (Tonadillas)
Richard Strauss: Schlectes Wetter

Theme Recitals

Do not format a theme recital unless it is *interesting, well-thought out*, and *well-programmed*. Putting together a recital and slapping a title on it is *not* a theme recital. On the other hand, choosing a "theme" and picking repertoire that fits that subject has the advantage of not being tied to grouping songs in one language, or composers in one chronological period.

Another option is to have an idea or "theme" in mind, but simply plan a well-organized, formatted program. If your audience is paying attention, they will see immediately that you have programmed songs that fit into a category, mood, or atmosphere, and form a cohesive idea. In this case, it is not even necessary to give the recital a thematic "title."

Considerable care should be taken in repertoire choices and order when putting together a recital with a "theme." Otherwise, stick to simply putting together a well-planned recital with a balanced, variety of repertoire.

Theme recitals are perhaps not appropriate for undergraduate recitals. They are most usually the domain of graduate and doctoral recitals, although there is nothing to prevent formatting *a song group* with a central idea (see below). Undergraduate students should be thoroughly conversant with the more "generic" repertoire in a number of languages.

As an example, here is a group of songs that was put together without using a header giving a theme title. By reading titles, texts/translations, and/or program notes, the audience will become aware that these single songs share a mood or a subject.

Franz Schubert   Im Frühling
                  Frühlingsglaube
                  Gott im Frühling
                  Der Schmetterling
                  Das Lied in Grünen [11]

Example:
Some Themes That Might Be Used in Planning a Recital:
The Children's Hour
A Little Night Music
In the Forest
Sorcerers, Witches, and Magic
American Scenes
A Grand Tour

The idea of formatting song groups and entire recitals using a mood, poet, or place was pioneered by The Songmakers Almanac, formed in 1976 by pianist Graham Johnson to provide an alternative to conventional recitals. There were four singers in the original group: Felicity Lott, Ann Murray, Anthony Rolfe Johnson, and Richard Jackson.

Graham Johnson's knowledge of vocal repertoire is inexhaustible, and it results in exciting recital designs, many of which are recorded. The CD: *My Garden: An Anthology of Flower Songs* (Hyperion CDA66937, 1997), with soprano Felicity Lott is a case in point. The origin of the word *anthology* derives from the mid-seventeenth century Greek *anthologia, anthos* "flower" + *logia* "collection" (from *legein* "to gather"). From this word Johnson has fashioned a recorded recital of songs about gardens and flowers featuring German, French, British, and American art songs. Unity, contrast, and variety exist in the selection of repertoire and its overall design. Critic John Steane referred to the programs of Songmaker's Almanac as "works of art in themselves." [12] Readers are encouraged to research the Songmakers Almanac and to seek out their recorded programs (particularly see Souvenirs de Venise).

Crossovers in the Concert Hall

In 1993 I presented a lecture-recital in San Diego for a national summer workshop sponsored by the National Association of Teachers of Singing. I called it "Crossovers in the Concert Hall." My lecture was punctuated by performances of songs that could be combined into groups and performed on a song recital. At that time, the "formal" recital design plan was fairly traditional, but the lines of demarcation between different kinds of repertoire were beginning to strain at the seams.

Today, musical theatre songs are appearing more frequently on recitals, usually as a last group, or somewhere in the second half of the recital. I should caution you that some of this repertoire *may not be acceptable* in academic situations.

If musical theatre repertoire is to be programmed on an art song recital, there is some repertoire which fits the heading of sung poems better than others. The sophistication of certain songs by Cole Porter, George Gershwin, Kurt Weill, Leonard Bernstein, Richard Rodgers, Stephen Sondheim, Marc Blitzstein, and Harold Arlen offer a vast selection of songs that can be programmed on art song recitals.

Example 1: Kurt Weill Song Groups

A. Nanna's Lied	Kurt Weill
Berlin im Licht-Song	(1900–1950)
Und was bekam des Soldaten Weib?	
Der Abschiedsbrief	

Comments:

Here are two Weill groups which I programmed at various times. The songs in Group A are taken from the publication *The Unknown Kurt Weill* (2005). They are cabaret style, each different, and each dramatic in a different way: a young prostitute, hommage to the city of Berlin, the soldier's wife who receives a gift from each place he is stationed, and a "Dear John" letter from a hardened, disillusioned lady.

B. Four Songs from *The Threepenny Opera*	Kurt Weill
The Barbara Song	(1900–1950)
Solomon Song	
Pirate Jenny	
The Ballad of Sexual Dependency	

Comments:

This is another Weill group from *The Threepenny Opera*, sung by different characters in the work. Programming them together in this manner offers the singer a wide emotional and dramatic range. This group was sung in English translation. "The Barbara Song" had to be transposed down. Not all singers will be able to negotiate the tessitura of these songs together as a group; for instance, Mrs. Peachum's "The Ballad of Sexual Dependency" is quite low and differs markedly from Polly Peachum's "The Barbara Song." Nonetheless, these make an arresting group and give the singer a chance to explore the facets of these characters.

C. September Song (*Knickerbocker Holiday*)   Kurt Weill
    Speak Low (*One Touch of Venus*)   (1900–1950)
    What Good Would the Moon Be? (*Street Scene*)
    Sing Me Not a Ballad (*The Firebrand of Florence*)

Comments:

Finally, here is a Weill group featuring song selections from three of his musical theatre works as well as his opera *Street Scene*. This group closed the program from which it was excerpted.

Example 2: A Group of George Gershwin Songs

    In the Mandarin's Orchid Garden   George Gershwin
    But Not for Me   (1898–1937)
    Just Another Rhumba
    Love is Here to Stay
    By Strauss

Comments:

Here is one of my George Gershwin groups—five songs. Numbers 1, 3, and 5 are less familiar than Numbers 2 and 4, and so balance between the songs is created. This group followed a Kurt Weill group in German (see Example 1A) and the two groups made up the second half of the program. The German language Weill paved the way for a second half of "crossover" repertoire. The Gershwin closed the recital; the inclusion of its three unfamiliar songs complemented and balanced the Weill.

Example 3: Another Cross-Over Closing Group

My House (*Peter Pan*)	Leonard Bernstein
Who am I? (*Peter Pan*)	(1918–1990)
I Am Easily Assimilated (*Candide*)	
I Can Cook, Too (*On the Town*)	

Comments:

This Bernstein group is a good program closer for a mezzo soprano or a soprano with a very strong middle and low range. It pairs two of the four Bernstein songs written for *Peter Pan* (a play with music) with the Old Lady's solo from *Candide*, and Hildy's hilarious jitterbug, "I Can Cook, Too" from *On the Town*. If the last selection proves unworkable vocally, then the group works by using all four of the Bernstein songs from *Peter Pan* and cutting the selections from *Candide* and *On the Town*.

Example 4: Another Closing Group by Stephen Sondheim

Stephen Sondheim is one of the most important composer-lyricists in musical theatre today. His works for the musical theatre are wide-ranging, diverse, and brilliant. To sing Sondheim is always exhilarating for the performer—the lyrics are alive, dramatic and charged with energy. This group closed the recital, and was preceded by Erik Satie's mini-cycle *Ludions* and "La Diva de l'Empire."

Songs by Sondheim	Stephen Sondheim
I Remember . . . (*Evening Primrose*)	(b. 1930)
Could I Leave You? (*Follies*)	
Losing My Mind (*Follies*)	
With So Little to Be Sure Of (*Anyone Can Whistle*)	

What do you want the audience to remember?

You *should* want them to remember the totality of the songs you sang, with some of the images that registered most vividly during their listening experience. Poetry is a satisfying musical experience; it nourishes the listening ear when we read it, and coupled with a musical setting, its images are doubly potent. *This* is what the singer should aim for: the listener's capacity to hear the images you communicate through your performance—color, nuance, and shape.

Adding props, costumes, or staging to the art song

Careful with this! The more you add to a piece that is already complete in its union of poetry and music, the more you subtract from one of the real joys of listening to art song—that is, having the singer communicate through their face, their voice with all its colors, and their understanding of what they have internalized through studying poem and music. The minute you put on a hat, or use a walking stick or boa, or dress in the historical period style of the work being sung, the audience's focus is distracted from the words, how the composer has set them, and how you sing them.

This warning does not apply to presentations that are dramatic monologues in which a singer portrays a composer or other personage from a historical period and through the monologue, sings art songs specific to that period, while giving information about the person and the time he/she lived. This is a fascinating and enjoyable production, but it is not an art song recital.

We are living in a world where everything is expected to be entertaining. We have become a very visual society, to the exclusion of taking time to study, internalize, read, and prepare with the *word* rather than with the *picture*. We are used to pushing a button, tapping a screen, moving a mouse, and seeing a picture. The advent of YouTube allows us to watch singers, and often not *listen* to them.

Why then, are recitals allowed to "just happen?" Why are students content to let teachers do most of the work in choosing repertoire and in designing the program? It should be a collaborative effort with the student being pro-active in choosing the repertoire. Of course, teachers have veto power over unsuitable choices, but the idea of involving students in planning their own recital yields a more involved musical performance, one in which they leave what a colleague of mine calls "*singerland*" (a place where only technique is on their mind). Suddenly, students are singing poems and not just vowel sounds and words. They are "ringing the *ring of words*." [13]

NOTES

1 Shirlee Emmons and Stanley Sonntag, *The Art of the Song Recital* (New York: Schirmer Books, 1979), 6.

2 Kurt Adler, *The Art of Accompanying and Coaching* (Minneapolis, MN: University of Minnesota Press, 1965), 176.

3 Francis Poulenc, *Diary of My Songs (Journal de mes mélodies)*, trans. by Winifred Radford (London: Victor Gollancz, Ltd., 1985), 79.

4   Thomas Grubb, in conversation with the author. Mr. Grubb teaches French Vocal
     Repertoire and Diction at The Juilliard School and coaches at New York City Opera. He
     is the author of *Singing in French*.

5   Pierre Bernac, in his series of master classes, Blossom Festival, Kent State University, Kent,
     Ohio. Summer, 1970. Author's private tapes and notes.

6   Thomas Grubb, *Singing in French: A Manual of French Diction and French Vocal
     Repertoire* (New York: Schirmer Books, 1979),142–143.

7   Graham Johnson, Masterclass at Songfest, Chapman University, Summer 2002. From the
     author's notes. Underlining by the author.

8   Gérard Souzay, baritone; Dalton Baldwin, piano. Artist Recital, USC Bing Theater, June 19
     1977. University of Southern California, School of Performing Arts, School of Music.

9   Jerold Siena, tenor; Paula Fan, piano. Faculty Recital. Crowder Hall, September 17, 1979.
     University of Arizona, School of Music.

10 Brian Kellow, "Coda: Razzle Dazzle 'Em," *Opera News* 71, no. 4 (October 2006), 84.

11 Artist Recital. Elly Ameling, soprano, with Dalton Baldwin, piano. University of Wisconsin,
     Milwaukee's International Festival of the Art Song, UWM School of Fine Arts, July 10,
     1981. UWM Fine Arts Theatre.

12 John Steane, Passing Notes: "Going for a Song": *The Songmakers Almanac: 20 Years of
     Song Recitals in London* (London: Thames Publishing,1996). In *Gramophone*, July 1997,
     29. (accessed April 31, 2012).

13 From "Bright is the Ring of Words" by Robert Louis Stevenson. *"Bright is the ring of words
     / When the right man rings them / Fair the fall of songs / When the singer sings them."*

Chapter 6

The Performance
of Art Song

*There is no one right way to perform any piece;
there are as many right ways as there are true performers,
and the notion of rightness shifts every generation,
even within the composer himself.* [1]

—Ned Rorem

Is there such a thing as a definitive interpretation? The very definition of the word "interpret" begs a negative answer: Dictionaries make clear that the subjective factor inherent in the definition cannot be ignored: "To perform or render according to one's understanding or sensitivity" (*The Random House Dictionary*); "To find the meaning of something; to establish or explain the meaning or significance of something"; "To make or bring out the meaning of a creative work" (*The Pocket Oxford Dictionary*); "To perform something in a particular way; to perform something such as a play or piece of music in a way that conveys particular ideas or feelings about it" (*Encarta World English Dictionary*); "To understand in one's own way; to show one's understanding by the way one performs it (especially, a piece of music)"; or "To conceive in the light of individual belief, judgement, or circumstance" (*Langenscheidt's New College Merriam-Webster English Dictionary*).

In the light of these definitions, there can be no single definitive interpretation, only performances which can serve as exemplary models of style through a performer's understanding of the interaction between all the musical and poetic elements in a musical work.

The Artistic Quest

Students often give very bland performances. Why? They could be unsure of their repertoire—they have not attained complete control of the blueprint on the musical page. Expressive interpretation cannot happen until this level of competency has been reached, and solid mastery has been completed.

Integrity as an artist is nurtured by discipline. *Discipline* has to happen before *freedom* is attained. For the singer: What did the composer really mean when he wrote a certain passage in a particular way? This requires a subjective answer, but it *must* be answered by the singer, who should ask "What script is the composer giving me?" Every performer must make a sincere effort to find out the answer to that question. This is what guides interpretation. The answers that derive from solving the "why" of the musical score are bound up with imagination.

What Do You Put First? Yourself or the Music?

There are those who let the art serve them,
and those who serve the art. [2]

—Henri Sauguet

Jane Bathori (1877–1970) was a fascinating personality of her time—the era which saw the full flowering of the genre known as the *mélodie française moderne*. Bathori was a composer's dream—she could sight-read anything, singing and playing the piano simultaneously, and by all accounts, grasp the emotional and poetic sense of the work at once. Totally dedicated to promoting new works of the day, she threw her energies into the artistic activities of one of the most exciting eras of French vocal music. During her lifetime she gave over 100 first performances of songs, and had approximately 60 dedicated to her.

Bathori's writings and speeches indicate she believed the act of artistic creation was based on shaping the musical material; to her, the coherence, clarity and distinction of musical details had tremendous impact on the work as a whole.

She firmly believed that "one must have taste and must not want to substitute one's own personality for that of the composer . . . The role of the interpreter must be above all one of understanding and of humility."[3] Jane Bathori's "*simplicité*" allowed the music to take center stage. She was extremely sensitive to poetry, the beauty of language, and to style, and this was her great strength. Georges Jean Aubry wrote of Bathori: "In listening to her it is not of herself or of her voice that we think, but of what she suggests through the music."[4]

Jane Bathori's interpretive credo remained unchanged throughout her career: "*Ayez de la spontanéité et de l'humilité.* (Be spontaneous, but be humble)."[5] Sadly, this is not always what we get in performances today, but it is food for thought.

The Singer as a Conduit

No music passes directly from the composer to the listener;
it must pass through the interpreter;
if he betrays the composer the work is destroyed.[6]

—Claire Croiza

In the art of music, it is the interpreter's performance
which we come to regard as the work itself.[7]

—Pierre Bernac

The singer who is an artistic interpreter is one who puts aside thoughts of self and becomes a channel for the composer and poet. Every performer's interpretation will be unique, based on their understanding of the poem and the music, and the personal choices they make while performing.

By some mysterious alchemy, the best of performers give the impression of being "in the moment" and having something spontaneous happening as they sing. It is as if they are creating the song "on the spot." The singer needs to build an internal world filled with the information they have researched about the poem and music, practiced technically, and finally—let *that* world be reflected out to their listening audience. It is this inner intensity that radiates out to the listeners in the most natural way and draws them into the world of the art song.

Perception occurs simultaneously with *reception* as we listen to a song. We hear words; words produce meanings and/or images; images create an awareness (perception) based on our stored experiences and personalities.

You have heard singers say "What a wonderful audience!," meaning that the inner energy they send out is received by, and is sent back from the audience in the form of encouragement or confirmation. It is a palpable connection that happens when artistry is being telegraphed from the platform. Harry Plunket Greene calls it "a gossamer thread over which passes that nameless current which stirs the singer to his depths and holds his audience thrilled and still . . . Its application is unconscious and spontaneous . . . It is the greatest gift the singer can have, for its possession means power." [8]

If you have sincerely applied yourself to working with the poem you are singing, and then thoroughly explored the musical re-creation of that poem by the composer, you are poised to bring *your* honest re-creation to your listening audience. You are, in effect, channeling the *composer and the* poet in a completely impulsive performance based on painstaking preparation. When singers achieve this inner energy, their pianist senses it, and the collaborative process kicks into high gear.

Francis Poulenc, speaking of his song cycle *La Fraîcheur et le feu*, wrote: "The technical side must be perfected with cold precision, then, sure of oneself, one should forget everything and give an impression of improvising, listening only to one's instinct." [9]

The Final Goal: An Organic Performance

Ours is a complex art. A singer should be so identified with the material that you don't notice they're singing...a complete organic expression—musical, poetic, led by the imagination . . . [10]

—Phyllis Curtin

When we speak of an "organic performance," we are describing a presentation in which all of the elements which make up the work have a relationship that perfectly and harmoniously fits together as necessary parts of the complete entity. When performing an art song, the preparatory work should already have been done with all the poetic and musical details. Now, as the singer enters the interpretive level, the song must be thought of as *a whole*.

Here are some components needed for a performance which could be termed to be *organic*:

- Excellent, solid musicianship

- Secure vocal technique, capable of flexibility and a sizeable range of vocal colors

- A solid background study of the song: poem, music, and how their musical fusion works

- An understanding of the musical style of each piece of repertoire you are singing

- Sufficient preparation and rehearsal time with your pianist

- A close artistic relationship with your pianist that results in each performer being attuned to the musical instincts of the other

- A sense of dramatic imagination capable of creating the ambience necessary for your repertoire

- A charismatic personality that communicates with your audience

- Humility—the ability to give yourself over to the music and its message and communicating that to your audience

Interpretation and Individuality

The interpreter is for the composer what light is for the painter. [11]

—Claire Croiza

One of the things I love about the human voice is that it is different every time, every take. I love it when singers bring a whole new world of experience and personality to my music. Great singers will always bring something unexpected to a performance and will ask lots of questions about the music to help them to personalise their interpretation. Less brilliant singers will just sing the notes on the page. [12]

—Jake Heggie

Interpretation is an elusive term and one that defies precise parameters, but it might be described as the performance of a musical work with the performer adding his musical understanding, experience, and personality to the composer's musical score. It is an artistic merger in which the performer seeks to communicate his ideas about a piece of music, forged through studying and assimilating music, poem, and characterization. Harry Plunket Greene writes that interpretation is the highest branch of the singer's art and the interpretive act itself is essentially individual, since "every singer's response to the combination of words and music is emotional and subjective, and depends on his temperament, intelligence, and equipment. It is well that it is so, for if it became stereotyped there would be no scope for personality; imagination would count for nothing and originality would be a dead letter. Individuality is the singer's greatest asset." [13]

Imagination is justly synonymous with creativity and originality, especially when referring to the production of an artistic work. To remove the performer's individuality from a performance would result in a loss of differing levels and details of communication. Ultimately, it implies the loss of the uniqueness of each singer and all that term encompasses. It would reduce all performance to a state of computerized replays.

Just to muddy the interpretive waters a bit further, changing ideas of what constitutes beautiful sound and expressive performance have made systematic investigations of the details of performing imprecise, if not impossible. Aesthetic comparisons of sound quality, vocal color, and poetic response are plainly unscientific activities and are not easily quantifiable. Gender, vocal classification, tessitura, ensemble between singer and pianist, and recording techiques, to name a few, are variables that fluctuate and evolve, and the subjective factor is difficult to separate out of the multiple parameters that make up a perfomance.

Imagination and Creativity

Creativity is rooted in imagination;
imagination in singing is rooted in the word…
Poetry, in fact, is the vocabulary of imagination. [14]

—Richard Sjoerdsma

Imagination is an essential prerequisite of singing—
not an optional extra. [15]

—Thomas Hemsley

Synonyms for *creativity* include *imagination, innovation, originality, individuality, artistry, inspiration, vision, initiative, resourcefulness.* Any of these provide a starting place for thinking about interpretive concerns in performing a specific piece of art song repertoire.

Imagination is "Square 1" for making interpretive choices. We have seen that we form images when reading a poem, and we also form images when we hear poetry set as an art song. In performance, the singer makes creative choices based in large part on his reaction to these images. There are some song texts that have a built-in character or characters just waiting to be exhumed and translated into vocal sound by the singer; there are also song texts that are full of exquisite images formed by the union of words with music. A world of color and nuance lies waiting within the lines of every text set to music as an art song.

Every artist is unique and original as far as musicianship, experience, and emotional makeup is concerned. Distinguished pianist Martha Argerich states:

"Everyone has a different sound, even on the same piano." [16] Every singer has a unique vocal timbre and different ways of looking at the same poem. Every composer has a different approach in setting the same poem, since each has his own reaction to the words.

Speaking of interpretation, baritone Gérard Souzay said: "Style may have yet another meaning, which is hard to explain—something like charm, grace, things that simply exist (or don't) but remain invisible . . . Each composer, each work, has its own style; to bring the whole to life, one requires that sense of recreating at the moment, which I can only call inspiration." [17]

Another distinguished French singer and one of Souzay's early teachers, Claire Croiza, also emphasized that the text must join musicality and sensitivity in creating an interpretation:

> In the theater, costumes and make-up help the actor sketch his character; in concerts, it is completely different . . . The singer must depend only on himself when on stage in order to interpret the song. His art is simpler, and he must reach a truth and intensity of expression possible only through his musicality, pronunciation, and extreme sensitivity. Here, more often than in the theater, the word becomes an element of choice with the fullness of sound, sense, and the beauty of the syllable . . . [18]

In Chapter 3, we observed that we make choices as to how we speak words when we are reading a poem. Even in our everyday speech, we make choices as to the how we *say* words—their rhythm (smooth or rough), tempo (fast or slow), inflection (high or low), and weight (light or heavy). We make these choices instinctively, often based on emotional issues or immediate situations.

We make similar choices as to how words are sung. In singing, when we shape musical phrases, these same elements come into play, coupled with the musical setting in which the composer has framed the poem. The poem and the components that combined to create the poem's texture have been absorbed into the totality of the art song. All the components of the poem's texture have been subtly altered by their new framework.

Shaping Phrases Creatively

One facet of creativity is bound up with the manner in which singers shape phrases. Shape is created by *inflection*, which springs from patterns of rhythm and sound used in poetry called *prosody*. The prosody of any language is part and parcel of the stress and intonation of that language. Some composers have a superb "sense of prosody"; their art songs are somehow easier to sing than those of a composer who does not feel the stresses of a language as keenly.

Even when we sing a structured phrase of musical pitches, we add inflection in the form of *weight* and *color*. These can be used to give a *vocal* shape to the phrase that becomes part of our interpretation.

The composer has created a shape in musical terms by specific pitches, note values, and rhythms, but the singer adds another layer to the vocal texture, and that is *inflection*—born of study and preparation, an inflection of weight and color that stems from assimilating the text plus the *sine qua non*, imagination.

The rich sound texture produced by the addition of these subtle nuances and vocal colors creates a unique interpretation and enhances the communicative experience for the listener.

Performance Is a Collaborative Effort

The word *collaborate* comes from the nineteenth-century word *collaborat* (worked with), from the word *collaborare*, from (*col-* "together" plus *laborare-* "to work"). One definition: to work jointly on an activity; to produce or create something.

The singer of art song is only half of the equation. The other half is the pianist, and the performing duo should be termed collaborative, since like poetry and music, one without the other does not result in an art song performance. The minute a creative project involves collaboration, the equation changes. Control is supplanted by collaboration. The implications inherent in "letting go" do not always sit easily with creative personalities and yet this is exactly what must happen in order for you and your pianist to establish a comfortable "wave length" upon which you can both make joint decisions, talk about your individual feelings about poem and music, and establish firm performing strategies which can adapt to the repertoire being presented.

The Singer-Pianist Duo

I have never (well, almost never) stepped onto a stage or even into a rehearsal without being able to sing the soloist's music and play my own part simultaneously. [19]

—Martin Katz

The best collaborations between singer and pianist or indeed, between any performing musicians are those in which both parties are flexible and courteous, have respect for the talents of the other, and generosity towards working out any musical issues that may arise during the collaboration on the work.

The term *duo* is the operant word here. Singers should not consider that the pianist is their accompanist, but a full-fledged partner in creating the art song. It is always a joy to work with a collaborative artist who is just that—a real collaborator. It is not by chance that many artists team with the same pianist for years. The collaborative bond that is forged by the elation of creating something profoundly artistic is not a partnership to be taken lightly or neglected once the performance is finished.

If the artistic singer is one who really sings poems, then the pianist is the poet of the keyboard. Distinguished pianist Martin Katz, whose excellent book on the collaborative pianist should be required reading by singers as well as collaborative pianists, recounts a compliment paid to him that he has savored throughout the years: "Oh, Mr. Katz, I just loved your performance. You really played the *words!*" [20]

It is not just the singer who needs to work with the words of the poem. The pianist should be responsible for working with the poetry as well. All the excellent pianists who are true collaborators with all that the word implies, have done their homework. The listener can immediately tell when they are being nourished by images emanating from the totality of the fusion of word *and tone, voice and piano.*

Like Martin Katz, renowned pianist Graham Johnson is another superb artist-collaborator. Speaking in a master class, he admonished pianists: "The third stave with the singer's words should remain in the mind *always*. If you can't hear a poem as you play—you can't *really* play it." To singers: "The inner *conductor* of every singer is what has to be cultivated." [21]

The musical and emotional parameters of an art song offer unique possibilities for collaboration between singer and pianist. Each needs to walk a mile in the other's shoes. If the pianist needs to know every word of the poem and every note of the singer's part, this is a sword that cuts both ways. If singers want a close-knit collaboartive experience with their pianist, they should consider that the pianist's accompaniment needs to be studied as much as their vocal line. For example, in extended interludes or postludes, singers need to keep the text energized in their minds so that they are not simply "waiting their turn" to sing. Both singer and pianist need to consider that they are only halves of the whole art song. Making sure that all the details of words and music fit together is what makes the process of teamwork so invigorating. Putting the performance puzzle together with the other half of the team is not only good music-making, but it also creates vivid performances.

Working With the Composer

Not all singers have the chance to work one-on-one with the composer of the art song(s) they are performing. It should be said, however, that *both* singer and pianist "collaborate" with the composer every time they perform an art song, by the very nature of the act. Student singers sometimes have access to a composer, but generally do not. Interactions with composers can happen in master classes, question-and-answer sessions/lectures, or private coachings. Not every composer is a coach, or enjoys that activity.

Preparing a work with the composer is a special experience not offered every performer. It might be a piece composed for that singer's voice, and the preparation—coaching, if you will—with the composer could be for a public performance or for a recording.

Artistic interaction between composer and interpeter is a subject not fully researched. Aesthetic experience does not lend itself easily to objective studies. You truly cannot quantify the creative process, yet the subject remains fascinating. Timbre and text, nuance and phrasing, tempo and emotion are all parameters that can fluctuate broadly and offer countless options to composers and as many possibilities to performers as well.

Artistic interaction between composer and performer must always involve a sense of balance, but it should be said that *what the composer intended is what you should try and do.* Such interactions are much better witnessed than learned about second-hand. Very often sound recordings document the end result of such collaborations, and therefore can assume a somewhat definitive quality. When a composer accompanies a singer in a performance of his art songs on a recording, does that create artistic limits for future performers? Yes and no. We often come to regard an interpreter's performance as the work itself, but to embrace this notion in its entirety negates the idea of interpretation with all the attendant musical and personal factors inherent in that word. We should not consider such recordings as a set of performance restrictions, but an indispensable record of the style and essence of each work, and as such, a valuable research tool for future singers and pianists.

When speaking with composer Daron Hagen about preparing his art song cycle *Larkin Songs* for recording with baritone Paul Krieder, he described the give-and-take between singer and composer. In recording the Larkin songs, Hagen was quick to praise the artistic generosity of his collaborator: "Paul was willing to go where I wanted him to—interpretively and musically." [22]

Their teamwork resulted in some changes to the music; in one instance, changing a pitch that Hagen had thought would be easier to sing back to the original, more difficult interval; in another place, creating symmetry by changing the beginning of the song to match the closing measure. Kreider acknowledged Hagen's advice in working with Larkin's poetry, which did not yield its secrets easily: "Daron was really helpful in getting through the progression of what Larkin was saying in these poems—all Daron's opinions—and [all] very helpful."[23]

In her dissertation study, Linda Laurent labels singers whose exceptional abilities inspire the composer to write for their voices "performer-catalysts." [24] These artists have the specific privilege of having works created for their particular instruments and temperament, and the satisfaction of working closely with the composer and providing a definitive interpretation with him. In such instances, the performer's gifts may shape the composer's ideas directly or subliminally and actually make a difference in what the composer writes.

Collaborations such as this may result in changes to the musical score (changing pitches or adapting word stress to accommodate the singer), or the poetry may take on new imagery when discussed between the performers. When the singer is totally prepared as to the music and poetry, it is possible to be more spontaneous in such a collaboration.

Very often the composer-singer collaboration happens because the work was written for or commissioned by a specific singer. In such a case, the composer often tailors the musical material for the strengths of the singer's voice . . . the material takes on a unique intimacy because of that.

How much daring, color, and spontaneity can a performer add to the performance without infringing on the composer's domain? In preparation for performance, the singer must make certain interpretive choices, including understanding and carefully gauging where it is important *not* to do something and the places where it is possible to be more spontaneous.

Matters of Style

It is perhaps style that singers lack the most—however, it is an indispensable element to sing well...One must first have the discipline to respect the musical text. This is the first step to take, to penetrate the meaning of the words, because they all have extreme importance. Musicality can and must help interpretation, but it does not suffice: taste is also necessary. [25]

—Jane Bathori

The concept of musical style is used principally to compare works or performances with one another, and to reference the musical components that make up the piece. It also refers to features that characterize music of a certain historical period, country, genre, specific composer or performer. Style also refers to the component parts of a piece of music and how the composer has used them in his music.

Singers need to know about musical style. You do not approach a Schubert *lied* like a Debussy *mélodie*. You cannot sing Purcell in the same way you sing Richard Strauss. Some twentieth-century art songs have certain vocal "gestures" that call for a different sort of vocalism.

Art songs belong to the historical period in which they were written, and as such, they have in their musical makeup many of the stylistic conventions of that time. Singers need to be aware of this so they can make informed decisions about all the vocal aspects that are brought into play during the performance of that piece.

Singers need to seek out information about the composers, the culture in which they composed, other repertoire that was being written and performed during that period, and any stylistic conventions that were in use at that time; for example: ornamentation, rubato, portamento, tempo, articulation, etc. A very helpful book to begin your search for stylistic aspects of vocal music is Martha Elliott's *Singing in Style: A Guide to Vocal Performance Practices* (see Bibliography). This book focuses on art songs, sacred music, and chamber music of stylistic periods from the Baroque to the present. In addition to chapters on each historical period, an excellent bibliography "For Further Reading" serves as a resource and/or starting point for learning about historical musical style.

Other books about national periods and composers may be found in the Bibliography of this book.

The Art Song Recital: Art or Entertainment?

To pander to the audience in a way that draws focus away from the words and music being performed is to cheapen your performance. We are living in a world where everything is expected to have a certain "entertainment" quality about it, and that quality is more often than not, visual. Our world today and we who live in it are visually oriented, and our attention spans have shrunk considerably. When the blatantly visual is subtracted from the moment, then our hearing is required to shift into high gear, and create images from what we hear.

Entertainment is a pleasurable sensation which, by itself, generally does not last long past the moment. It is an enjoyable diversion, but it is *not* creative and imaginative artistry. The art song recital should offer the audience an evening of well sung, imaginative storytelling—hopefully, one that will engage their intellect and feelings, and draw them into the moment. It may be an unfamiliar world to the listener, but if the singer has done his homework, it will become an enjoyable experience for both performer(s) and audience.

Overstating the text of a song shows a lack of confidence in yourself *and* in your audience. It also shows a disregard for the worth of the repertoire you are performing. In a recital, artistic singing establishes a firm mood in a song, and then sustains it—it creates a moment in which a poem and its musical setting can come to life again.

How Much Is Too Much?—
Some Thoughts on Dramatization

Interpretation is not a matter of standing in front of a mirror and practicing gestures and facial expressions while you sing. This exercise has no basis in an organic performance. There has to be in your communication with the audience an open and candid connection—one that emanates naturally from your singing. When a singer is honest with the repertoire he sings, an audience immediately senses it, and is drawn into the experience.

Creating a character in an art song does not mandate that you "act out" a song. The character and his or her personality is always a part of the poem you are singing. The same is true of creating atmosphere or mood. It does not take gestures or body poses that have no basis in the poem you are singing. The unfocused gesture is the most common culprit in this category. Hands and arms can suddenly draw the attention from what you are singing to some stiff pose that is completely unnatural, and has no basis in being a part of the poem and/or mood you are trying to create vocally.

If you have prepared the poem and the music, the text will be on your face as you sing and the words will be colored by your vocal nuances. Jane Bathori wrote that it was like "theatre in miniature… watching a little story as it unfolds before your eyes" [26]

Le bon gout?

In a vocal repertory recital in a university setting, I witnessed an over-zealous singer offer Ravel's "Chanson à boire," the third *mélodie* of the *Don Quichotte à Dulcinée* songs, lounging like an inebriate at a bar, clinging to the piano, and actually falling on the floor at the conclusion of the song! This tasteless burlesque of a brilliant song was an astounding breach of respect for the repertoire.

In his master classes, distinguished artist and master teacher Pierre Bernac made it quite clear that Don Quichotte is a nobleman and *always* remains so; even in a drunken state, he retains his dignity. [27] The music *does* have a Ravellian "hiccup," (after "Je bois" and "Lorsque j'ai") and if the singer has *taste*, he will *not* make a lurching bodily movement at that point, but will simply reflect the movement on his face. Cheap effects at the expense of any song have no place on the recital stage. A singer who resorts to such travesty has no real regard for Ravel's work, other than it serves to accompany his juvenile antics.

Another *mélodie* that falls into the "easy prey" category for deliberate over-elaboration is Francis Poulenc's "Violon," the fifth song in his cycle *Fiançailles pour rire*. This song often finds the singer deliberately "getting into the mood" by weaving tipsily into the crook of the piano, and then striking a seductive pose before beginning the song. Here, instead of intoxicated body language, the text can be telegraphed through vocal *glissandos* at specific places in the song, and by subtle vocal nuances. The character singing this song is an elegant woman. Collapsing into, or rolling around in the crook of the piano is *not* what is called for.

Other songs that carry caveats about distasteful embellishment of musical details are those involving the animal kingdom. Descriptive texts about animals, birds, fish, and insects tempt the singer to add just a little extra "drama" for the audience. A singer is not obliged to "waddle" while singing Chabrier's "Villanelle des petits canards," or use elaborate hand gestures that telegraph the motions of Ravel's little cricket ("Le Grillon") in the *Histoires naturelles*. If such dramatic mime was needed in these sort of texts, then at the conclusion of William Bolcom's "The Fish" (*I Will Breathe A Mountain*) the singer would indeed be exhausted.

The drama, atmosphere and emotion is *all in the music*. Be very careful about adding overt actions as you sing. If you always feel compelled to manufacture drama in order to perform the art song, then you have a poor opinion of the repertoire you are singing, and are probably unsure of your own talents as well.

EXAMPLE: Ravel's *Histoires naturelles,* on prose texts by Jules Renard

Maurice Ravel once claimed that he did not want his music to be interpreted, but merely performed. He also characterized Jules Renard's texts as "delicate and rhythmic, but rhythmic in a completely different way from classical music."[28]

This is confusing to a performer researching this work. The music demands technical precision from singer and pianist, but the witty words require a vocal approach that judiciously mixes lyricism with conversational articulation.

Singers are tempted to paint the text in broad comic strokes that transform Renard's charming portraits of the peacock, cricket, swan, kingfisher and guinea hen into cartoon characters. The five creatures need to remain in their musical habitats, and speak to the listeners through Renard's witty texts and Ravel's delightful musical settings, not leap out of the texts as though shot from a cannon.

Unfortunately, in texts involving stories about animals, fish, and fowl the temptation is there to actually dramatize the text in movement or over-exaggerate the story in facial expressions. Show restraint. The humor is built into the song as a whole, and need not be embellished further by you.

Does this mean nothing shows on the face? Indeed not! But the expressions on a singer's face are an outward manifestation of the inner instincts of what has been learned by study and preparation. This also applies to gestures. If a hand or arm gesture happens unconsciously from a singer's coloring a word or shaping a phrase, it will not seem contrived. It should be almost involuntary, however, and then it is likely to be natural and unaffected.

In private coachings, two distinguished French baritones spoke of interpreting Ravel's cycle *Histoires naturelles*. Some of their observations are printed here.

Regarding the performance of the *Histoires*, celebrated French baritone Gérard Souzay affirms the "less is more" approach to be the correct one, dubbing Renard's prose as "poetic":

> You must follow the story with your eyes. The public will follow you, because your eyes and your face must absolutely "live" the story. You can't do much interpretively. It's a remote kind of cycle. It's not a cycle in which you should exaggerate. I think it's a poetic cycle altogether. There are moments of drama but not so many. It's not something you can explode with. Many people tend to be funny all the time, which is completely wrong. [29]

The eminent Ravel interpreter, baritone Martial Singher acknowledged that Renard's witty text must be heard and understood, but cautioned that the singer must find the right interpretive balance in the vocal line:

But you see, there is *some* kind of interpretation which cannot be avoided. If you sing "Le Paon" you have to feel like the Paon himself, you see (he sings the first phrase) . . . and it must be pompous. The fact that you introduce some pomposity in your voice is already an interpretation. It cannot be just an enunciation. If it is *just an enunciation*, I don't think that the song will be as interesting as it should be.

In songs like these . . . there are several sides to the song. On the one hand, it is essential to make the text by Renard—which is very witty—to be heard and understood. Second, it is essential to be able vocally to follow the musical line by Ravel—but the person who sings this is at the same time the peacock, the witness to the activities of the peacock, and a person who has an opinion about it. So when you are singing this, you are seeing what you say, you are feeling the wit in it, and you are delighted with it by yourself.

[Singher reads the first part of the text.] So you see, the intonation I give to the words is personal. Somebody else would say it completely differently. Even when singing the music I can have these inflections . . . But nobody else will do it like me. It's my right to do it this way, you see? That's all interpretation is. [30]

Are You a Good Storyteller?

Imagination can only enrich interpretation if it is backed by an intimate assimilation of the text. [31]

—Claire Croiza

An art song recital is essentially an evening of storytelling. The singer and pianist sing and play stories for the listening audience. It is akin to a magical journey of "time travel," that takes the listener to many different places, through many diverse emotions and myriad experiences.

When someone reads or tells a story, they make numerous vocal inflections to help bring the story's words to life; the modulations of their voice colors the details of the story as it unfolds.

When singing an art song, if a composer has used a specific harmony to color the meaning of the words, then the imagination of the singer reacts to that stimulus by adding another vocal color or a subtle weight of vocal stress to further enhance and communicate the image.

The more singers know and understand about the literary elements of any song they perform, the more they will understand the work and the richer their communication will be. Researching a poem in detail will uncover hidden nuances of words, images, and emotional content which will help shape the musical phrases with weight and color as they are sung.

The ability to layer ideas onto a text takes imagination and creativity; a creative mind works hand in hand with imagination. This cannot be taught, but it can be cultivated through a commitment to studying poems and musical settings to plumb the meaning of both—separately and together. The ability to recognize which word in a musical phrase needs a different color or a bit more vocal weight is part and parcel of an inspired imagination at work.

Writing about the late mezzo soprano Lorraine Hunt Lieberson, William R. Braun said: "One of the manifestations of the depth of her artistry was the variety of ideas she could impart to a single line of text." [32]

Interpretation is essentially rooted in each individual singer. Every performance is different. All singers have to one degree or another, natural musical intelligence and intuition. Your communication with your audience must be an open and candid sort of connection—one that springs directly from the process of internalizing text and music into *your* persona. Because individuality is our greatest asset, we actually *own* every song we sing.

You will never sing any given song like *any other* singer, and you will never sing a song the *same* way the *next* time you sing it.

When we return to a song we have performed before, we will probably see it in a different way. But if one never loses the feeling that it is a new piece, that there is more to learn from performing it, then it remains ever new, unmarked by old habits, unsullied by previous opinions. We are constantly evolving, and so we continue to find new surprises in the repertoire we sing. This is the delight of performing, and *this is why we sing songs.*

Some Thoughts on Interpretation

Here are some thoughts about interpretation gleaned from distingished composers, performers, and teachers. Their words may prove inspirational, or offer a new way of looking at the final piece of the puzzle—the performance itself.

Music does not exist in a vacuum.. It does not exist until it is performed. The magic comes only with the sounding of the music... [and can] be said to consist of just the music that is not in the score . . . [33]

—Benjamin Britten

I think the first duty of an interpreter is to be, as Stravinsky has said, a flawless executant, that is, perform the music exactly as it is written. This is the basis. Beyond this, if you can add something of yourself without compromising the music, then you are an artist. If not, you are just a performer like all the other performers. [34]

—Pierre Bernac

The act of artistic creation consists in the shaping of the material. The state in which the composer delivers his work is not the final state. [35]

—Erwin Stein

*In the final analysis, all the precise elements of any interpretation
build up to one goal: to express. The inspired mind and the
sensitive heart of a good interpreter find in the shape of the phrase,
the inflection of the words, the right rhythm, the true nuance, the
rare color, the changes of pace, the silences, all they need to convey
to the audience ...* [36]

—Martial Singher

*Being a singer and musician is one of life's rarest and most
precious privileges. It also brings with it exacting responsibilities,
which can be both exhilarating and humbling...To be a fit channel
for this wonderful but awesome task requires that you do all
you can to nurture and sustain your emotional, spiritual, and
intellectual lives. A vital part of your musical discipline is this
readiness to communicate the caring for human values that give
substance and understanding to your musical emotions.* [37]

—Jan De Gaetani

*No virtuosos are sure of themselves...their electricity comes from
the sense of risk being run...The interpreter's voyage exists in time
so he is prey to more perils than the creator.* [38]

—Ned Rorem

*There is no such thing as a definite interpretation. An
interpretation cannot be the same twice, even for the same artist...
To be an interpreter is fundamentally a paradoxical situation:
you place yourself at the author's service without giving up your
identity. Both creator and performer must be reflected in an
interpretation. If one of the two is missing, everything is lost.* [39]

—Gérard Souzay

*Interpretation is the forgetfulness of self... Although the interpreter
leaves fewer traces than other artists, his task is a magnificent
one, for me the most beautiful of all: to serve and not to consider
one's self any more...Once our word has carried the poet's word,
once our voice has sung the music of the composer, we have only to
disappear, and our work is accomplished.* [40]

—Claire Croiza

*Someone once said of poets: the poet speaks to himself and the
world overhears. I believe this is the most important point a singer
can emphasize in performance of songs: the singer sings only for
himself or herself and the audience is permitted to eavesdrop.
When this happens, we best serve the composer—the song remains
private, unaffected, intimate, moving and truthful.* [41]

—Dominick Argento

*One is not expected to do anything that is not on the written
page, but given that discipline, there is always bound to be a
certain freedom with a great piece of music. You do exactly
what the composer has written, as nearly as you possibly can,*

and one spends a lifetime searching out just that. But within this very severe framework there is always this exciting thing of the individual contribution...An essence is going out of you if you're doing your job properly. It's the very deepest part of your personality and your life that is being presented to those strangers, in order that you can carry the far more important message of the sound or of the piece of music. Nothing less than this outpouring of one's deepest self is permissible. [42]

—*Dame Janet Baker*

Some Models of Artistry in Recital Performance

Below is a subjective list of singers who have devoted a good part of their careers to recitals, or have carved a niche for themselves as outstanding recitalists with recorded art song discographies.

Each singer represents honesty in presentation, and artistry in communication. Thanks to today's technology, we may access their performances on the Internet, on CDs, DVDs, YouTube, and even vinyl recordings. In watching performances available on video, it is clear that communicating the union of text and music is uppermost in the minds of these artists. In many cases, videos of live performances are not available but *listening to a recording with a musical score* confirms their mastery of the texts they are singing, as well as their abilities to shade and color their vocal sound to shape the poetry and music to the fullest.

Their interpretations of art songs are not to be copied, nor their voices imitated. Instead, theirs is a level to which art song performers can aspire.

SOPRANOS

Elly Ameling	(Dutch)
Arleen Auger	(British)
Isabel Bayrakdarian	(Lebanese-Canadian)
Barbara Bonney	(American)
Régine Crespin	(French)
Claire Croiza	(French)

Renée Fleming	(American)
Veronique Gens	(French)
Barbara Hendricks	(American)
Solveig Kringelborn	(Norwegian)
Felicity Lott	(British)
Karita Mattila	(Swedish)
Dora Ohrenstein	(American)
Lucia Popp	(Slovakian)
Leontyne Price	(American)
Margaret Price	(Welsh)
Christine Schäfer	(German)
Elisabeth Schwarzkopf	(Austrian)
Elisabeth Söderström	(Swedish)
Dawn Upshaw	(American)
Benita Valente	(American)

MEZZO SOPRANOS

Janet Baker	(British)
Teresa Berganza	(Spanish)
Grace Bumbry	(American)
Sarah Connolly	(British)
Jan DeGaetani	(American)
Joyce Di Donato	(American)
Bernarda Fink	(Argentinean)
Susan Graham	(American)
Marilyn Horne	(American)
Angelika Kirchschlager	(Austrian)
Irma Kolassi	(Greek-French)
Jennifer Larmore	(American)
Marie-Nicole Lemieux	(French)
Lorraine Hunt Lieberson	(American)
Christa Ludwig	(German)
Nan Merriman	(American)
Susanne Mentzer	(American)
Ann Murray	(British)
Tatiana Troyanos	(American)
Jennie Tourel	(Russian-American)
Anne Sofie von Otter	(Swedish)
Frederica von Stade	(American)

| Shirley Verrett | (American) |
| Sarah Walker | (British) |

CONTRALTOS

Brigitte Fassbaender	(German)
Maureen Forrester	(Canadian)
Nathalie Stutzmann	(French)

TENORS

Ian Bostridge	(British)
Nicolai Gedda	(Swedish)
Jonas Kaufmann	(German)
Alfredo Kraus	(Spanish)
Peter Pears	(British)
Peter Schreier	(German)
Michael Schade	(Canadian-German)
Paul Sperry	(American)

BARITONES

Thomas Allen	(British)
Pierre Bernac	(French)
Gerald Finley	(Canadian)
Dietrich Fischer-Dieskau	(German)
Matthew Goerne	(German)
Nathan Gunn	(American)
Håkan Hagegård	(Swedish)
Thomas Hampson	(American)
Wolfgang Holzmair	(Austrian)
Dmitri Hvorostovsky	(Russian)
Bernard Kruysen	(Dutch)
Hermann Prey	(German)
Martial Singher	(French/American)
William Sharp	(American)
Bo Skovhus	(Danish)
Gérard Souzay	(French)
Bryn Terfel	(Welsh)
José Van Dam	(Belgian)

Envoi . . .

And so, we have come to the end of the performer's journey. It is a demanding one, for there is much to live up to, much to learn, and much to do. In embarking on this journey, we continue the long lineage of artistry that has been handed down to us from our artist teachers, and their teachers, and their teachers from generation to generation. This is not to be taken lightly, for it demands the best efforts we can give to our art.

Interpretation in singing is a question of preparation, intelligence, imagination, and taste. It demands a great deal from us. It requires that we let go the part of our ego that demands adulation, and cultivate the part that works tirelessly to be the best we can be. We need to work continually to enrich ourselves as singers by taking our places in that long continuum of artists who led the way for us.

Singers should always strive to reach that transcendent moment when they abandon thoughts of self and submerge their entire being in the act of communicating word and tone to a listening audience. That moment equals artistry.

It only remains to end with a quotation from baritone Dietrich Fiescher-Dieskau, a singer whose artistry spanned nearly five decades, and whose performances of art song have inspired and guided generations of recitalists. In his long and distinguished career he established himself as perhaps the finest modern interpreter of German Lieder. His dedication to, and advocacy for, the art song has led countless others to follow his example:

> *Music and poetry have a common domain, from which they draw inspiration and in which they operate: the landscape of the soul. Together, they have the power to lend intellectual form to what is sensed and felt, to transmute both into a language that no other art can express. The magic power that dwells inmusic and poetry has the ability ceaselessly to transform us.* [43]
>
> —Dietrich Fischer-Dieskau

NOTES

1 Ned Rorem, "The NATS Bulletin Interviews Ned Rorem," *The NATS Bulletin* 39, no.2 (November/December, 1982), 16.

2 Henri Sauguet, *Hommage à Jane Bathori/*, O.R.T.F. Paris, France, sur France-Culture. February 23, 1970. This is a compilation of numerous radio transmissions and live broadcasts, after Bathori's death. A recorded copy of this two hour program in the author's personal files.

3 Jane Bathori, "Style." Typewritten article in the Bathori archives, Bibliothèque Nationale, Paris, France (accessed March, 1986). This was probably a copy of one of her numerous radio transmissions.

4 Georges Jean-Aubrey, trans. Edwin Evans, "Jane Bathori," *Recorded Sound* 1, no. 4 (1961), 102.

5 Jane Bathori, "*Les Musiciens que j'ai connus*," The Mayer Lectures II, trans. Felix Aprahamian, *Recorded Sound*, 1, no. 6 (Spring 1963), 176.

6 Betty Bannerman, ed. and trans., *The Singer as Interpreter: Claire Croiza's Master Classes* (London: Victor Gollancz, 1989), 42.

7 Pierre Bernac, *The Interpretation of French Song* (New York: W.W. Norton Co., 1978), 1.

8 Harry Plunket Greene, *Interpretation in Song* (New York: Da Capo Press,1979), 9.

9 Pierre Bernac, *Francis Poulenc: The Man and His Songs*, trans. Winifred Radford (New York: W.W. Norton, 1997), 49.

10 Phyllis Curtin, Keynote address, National Association of Teachers of Singing National Conference. Boston, Massachusetts, July, 1992.

11 Betty Bannerman, 36.

12 James McCarthy, "Interview with Jake Heggie," *Gramophone* (Awards issue, 2010), 107.

13 Harry Plunket Greene, *Interpretation in Song* (London: Macmillan, 1966), 3.

14 Richard Sjoerdsma, "Creativity and Imagination," Editor's Commentary, *Journal of Singing* 67, no.5 (May/June 2011), 500.

15 Thomas Hemsley, *Singing and Imagination: A human approach to a great musical tradition* (Oxford, UK: Oxford University Press, 1998), 111.

16 Martha Argerich, quoted in Jessica Duchen, "First Among Equals," *BBC Music Magazine* (June 2011), 33.

17 Gérard Souzay, quoted in Shirlee Emmons, "Voices from the past, " *The NATS Journal* (November/December, 1982), 33.

18 Claire Croiza, *Exposition catalogue*. Paris: Bibliothèque Nationale, 1984, no. 95: 35. Quotation from a paper "L'art lyrique et l'interprétation," given by Croiza to the 2ème Congrès International d'Esthétique et de Science de l'Art, Paris, France, 1937.

19 Martin Katz, *The Complete Collaborator: the pianist as partner* (New York: Oxford University Press, 2009), 7.

20 Ibid., 21.

21 Graham Johnson, at SongFest. Chapman University, Summer, 2002. Commentary from his master classes. Author's notes.

22 Daron Hagen, Interview with Carol Kimball for liner notes to *Four Composers: One Voice*, Arsis Recordings, CD 142, 2002.

23 Paul Kreider, interview with Carol Kimball, March, 2001. *Larkin Songs* were commissioned by the University of Nevada, Las Vegas, Department of Music and premiered there by Kreider and Hagen, February 18, 2001.

24 Linda Cuneo-Laurent, "The Performer as Catalyst: The Role of the Singer Jane Bathori (1877-1970) in the Careers of Debussy, Ravel, 'Les Six,' and their Contemporaries in Paris 1904–1926." Ph.D. dissertation, New York University, 1982, 175.

25 Jane Bathori, "Style."

26 Jane Bathori archives, R.T.F. (Radio-Téléphone France)1957. Six cours consacrées a la mélodie française.

27 Pierre Bernac, master classes at Blossom Music Festival, Kent State University, Kent, Ohio, June–July, 1970. Author's notes.

28 Quoted in Arbie Orenstein, A Ravel Reader (New York: Columbia University Press, 1990), 339.

29 Gérard Souzay. Private coaching of Ravel's Histoires naturelles, Paris, France (April 2, 1986).

30 Martial Singher. Personal interview and coaching of Ravel's Histoires naturelles and Debussy's Chansons de Bilitis. Santa Barbara, California (January 22, 1985).

31 Hommage à Claire Croiza: Département de la musique, 15 juin-1er septembre 1984 (Paris, France: Bibliothèque Nationale, 1984) French edition. Out of print.

32 William R. Braun, "Pieces of Time," Opera News 75, no. 5 (November 2010), 38.

33 Quoted in Aksel Schiøtz, The Singer and His Art (New York: Harper & Row, 1970), 109.

34 John Ardoin, "Bernac's Wisdom Shared at SMU," World of Music, Dallas Morning News, 4C. Sunday edition,1973.

35 Erwin Stein, Form and Performance (N.Y.: Alfred A. Knopf, 1962), 17.

36 Martial Singher, An Interpretive Guide to Operatic Arias (University Park, PA: Pennsylvania State University Press, 1983), Introduction.

37 Barbara Saropoli, SSU, "If You Encounter a Great Teacher," The NATS Journal 50, no.2 (November/December,1993), 29.

38 Ned Rorem, "Song and Singer," in Setting the Tone: Essays and a Diary (New York: Limelight Editions,1984), 314.

39 Gérard Souzay, "The Mystery of Performing." Opera News 32, no. 5 (November 25, 1967).

40 Betty Bannerman, 70–72.

41 Dominick Argento, Keynote address, National Association of Teachers of Singing National Conference. Philadelphia, Pennsylvania. December, 1976.

42 Stephen Wadsworth, "Sense and Sensibility," an interview with Dame Janet Baker. Opera News 42, no.1 (July 1977).

43 Dietrich Fischer-Dieskau, The Fischer-Dieskau Book of Lieder, chosen and introduced by Dietrich Fischer-Dieskau, with English trans. by George Bird and Richard Stokes (New York: Limelight Editions, 1984), 28.

Chapter 7

A Selected List of Vocal Literature for Collegiate Voice Majors
(Undergraduates)

Building an Art Song Library

The totality of art song repertoire is so vast that choosing a place to begin study is often daunting. To begin, your music library should have some mainstays in it. The easiest starting point in building your library is with song anthologies. You will not sing every song in every anthology you own, but you will gain knowledge about the body of art song literature in specific national areas. In your music library there should be art song anthologies of:

- 17th–18th century Italian songs and early arias

- Art songs by American and/or British composers

- French art songs (*mélodies*)

- German art songs (*Lieder*)

After working with the songs assigned by your teacher as study pieces, it is good to do a little exploration into other examples of art song literature. This exploration can begin on any number of paths: the admiration for the work of a specific composer; curiosity about a body of national song literature or interest in the songs of a particular historical period; poems by a favorite poet that have been set as songs, and so on. The journey may be joined as a result of listening to a CD of a favorite artist or singing repertoire that invites a search about its composer or poet.

As you work, you will discover that your "song searches" often branch off into areas of peripheral study. Everything you discover and study becomes part of a collection of knowledge from which you can draw as you work with songs. This is your private art song archive. Keep the information organized by composer, poet, historical period, musical style, language, or any other heading that will make it easy to access. Your database may take on a life of its own, but keeping it organized and up-to-date will save time when you are designing song groups or recitals.

Criteria for Choices

Below are some lists of song literature, organized by country/language, suggested for undergraduate collegiate students or vocal students in the first four years of study. The lists are by no means all-inclusive, and as with any list of this sort, <u>they are subjective</u>. There are countless other songs that could be added, but this should provide a "jumping off" place for further research and study. The songs were selected with the following criteria in mind:

- technical demands that are not excessive, but in some instances, offer challenges
- opportunities for development in:

    –vocal quality/color

    –diction practice (English and foreign languages)

    –challenging emotional and/or interpretive concerns

- not excessive in length
- for the most part, piano accompaniments are manageable

Some songs require a more mature interpretive/emotional approach; some require more advanced levels of vocal technique. As with any suggested list, the voice teacher is the final expert in assessing the vocal/technical level of each of their students.

It is important that singers coming to song repertoire in a foreign language for the first time choose songs that will allow them to *work* with the language *and* also to absorb the style of the repertoire.

In performing *any* song in *any* language, we need to make the poems *sing*.

Here is a selected list of art songs suitable for study during the first years of vocal study at the university level. Some composers have written songs in languages other than their own. Those selections are listed under the composer's national area.

AMERICAN ART SONG

The name of the poet appears in parentheses after the song title.

STEPHEN FOSTER (1826–1864)

Gentle Annie (Stephen Foster)
A lyrical, romantic parlor song. Not difficult, but effective. Male voices.

Ah! May the Red Rose Live Always! (Stephen Foster)
One of Foster's finest early songs. Poem reflects the popular topics in mid-Victorian America: innocent beauty, sentimental longing, mortality. Three strophic verses in 6/8 time.

If You've Only Got a Moustache (Stephen Foster)
A humorous song about the allure of the moustache in romance.

I Dream of Jeanie with the Light Brown Hair (Stephen Foster)
One of Foster's best-known songs, a prime example of the originality, beauty, and simplicity of his melodies.

ARTHUR FARWELL (1872–1952)

The Level Bee (Emily Dickinson)
Farwell's settings of Dickinson show his deep sensitivity to her poems.

The Grass So Little Has To Do (Emily Dickinson)
A fresh, pastoral mood pervades this energetic song.

CHARLES IVES (1874–1954)

At the River (Robert Lowry)
The venerable hymn tune with some rhythmic and harmonic Ivesian twists.

Memories, A- Very Pleasant, B- Rather Sad (Charles Ives)
Two contrasting sections, each a short song in itself: the excitement of two children at a theatrical show, and a nostalgic, poignant character study composed in parlor song style.

The Things Our Fathers Loved (Charles Ives)
A recollection of childhood. Emotional, patriotic text with musical quotations from American songs, among them "Dixie," "My Old Kentucky Home," and "The Sweet Bye and Bye."

Charlie Rutlage (D.J. O'Malley)
A great country-western art song. Rhythmic, rugged musical style, with some spoken dialogue. Text graphically describes a cowpuncher who meets his death during a spring roundup. A capsulized Western *scena*.

When the Stars are in the Quiet Skies (Edward Bulwer-Lytton)
One of Ives's early songs. Text about love, with beautiful melody, and understated accompaniment. Almost hymn-like in style.

The Circus Band (Charles Ives)
Nostalgic boyhood memory of when the circus came to small American towns, and the populace turned out for the circus parade. Colorful but thick piano textures. Male voices.

Tom Sails Away (Charles Ives)
A cluster of childhood memories, viewed introspectively. Piano textures create a misty "recall." Piano and vocal lines create an impressionistic feeling of free-floating meter. Polyrhythms and polyharmonies give a feeling of passing time. A poignant and beautiful song, with some rhythmic challenges for the voice.

The Children's Hour (Henry Wadsworth Longfellow)
Nostalgic and familiar Longfellow poem is set in a lyric, intimate musical style by Ives. Works well in a group with the following song…

Two Little Flowers (Charles Ives)
Ives's own poem about two of his daughters, Edith and Susanna. Charming short song. Works well as an inner song in a group.

In the Alley (Charles Ives)
Has the jaunty rhythm and mood of an Irish folk tune. Not difficult. Good as a first Ives song. Male voices.

VIRGIL THOMSON (1896–1989)

Take, o take those lips away (William Shakespeare)
A beautiful, languid melodic line dominates this song. The arpeggiated accompaniment is reminiscent of a guitar. Male voices.

A Prayer to St. Catherine (Kenneth Koch)
Simple vocal line, declamatory in style. A heartfelt entreaty to St. Catherine of Siena to cure the singer of chronic shyness and heartache. All voices.

Sigh no more, ladies (William Shakespeare)
A lively setting of Shakespeare using rhythms of the Spanish *fandango* and figures like the Spanish guitar. A rousing setting, most suited to male voices, although the poem could also be sung by a woman.

If Thou a Reason Dost Desire to Know (Sir Francis Kynaston)
Poem is suited to a male voice. Begins in linear fashion, textures thicken as harmonic tension builds. Sophisticated poetic content. Thomson's unerring prosody and classic sense of form always present. A beautifully crafted song.

ROY HARRIS (1898–1979)

Fog (Carl Sandburg)
Sandburg's metaphorical little poem is given an effective, atmospheric setting by Harris. This song is effective when programmed as an interior song in an American song group. Medium voices.

ERNST BACON (1898–1990)

It's All I Have to Bring (from *Five Poems of Emily Dickinson*)
Uncomplicated setting, warm, heartfelt vocal line. Probably Bacon's best known song.

One Thought Ever at the Fore (Walt Whitman)
Reminiscent of a church chorale. Melody is exalted and solemn. Melodic outline is like the Doxology. A most expressive setting.

To Make a Prairie (Emily Dickinson)
A Dickinson miniature, only 25 measures long. Vocal lines image the darting playful bee of the poem.

Omaha (Carl Sandburg)
Bursts with jazzy color and energy. Vocal lines declamatory and rhythmically driven. Piano figures mirror the poetic imagery. Baritones.

Fond Affection (Anonymous)
Very much a folk tune in character…3 strophes, broken chord accompaniment. Sophisticated harmonic treatment does not detract from the simple vocal line.

JOHN DUKE (1899–1984)

i carry your heart (e.e. cummings)
A wonderfully attractive setting—flowing vocal lines, romantic tonal textures. All voices.

Loveliest of Trees (A.E. Housman)
One of Duke's most familiar songs to Housman's equally familiar poem. Lyric and singable. Fine for beginners. All voices.

Richard Corey (Edwin Arlington Robinson)
Poem depicts a young man who on the surface, has everything. Vocal phrases are speech-like in articulation; piano figures are jaunty and self-assured. The first three stanzas describe Corey in detail. In the fourth, everything halts abruptly before the last shocking line. Effective, dramatic song. Male voices.

I Can't Be Talkin' of Love (Esther Mathews)
Rhythmically driven, folk-like setting. Charming and effective. Women's voices.

Morning in Paris (Robert Hillyer)
Duke's treatment of Hillyer's poem "Early in the Morning." Duke's setting is effusive and bright, full of hopeful

expectancy. Swift tempo, broad lyric vocal lines. Compare with Ned Rorem's setting. Poem best suited to male voices.

Heart, we will forget him (Emily Dickinson)
In contrast to Aaron Copland's setting, Duke sets this poem in a passionate, fast moving tempo. High tessitura. More advanced women's voices. See Copland's setting for comparison.

AARON COPLAND (1900–1990)
from *Old American Songs* (Sets 1 and 2)
Long Time Ago (Set 1)
Folk-like setting. Sentimental melody.

The Little Horses (Set 2)
A children's lullaby from the southern states. Lyric, languid melody.

Zion's Walls (Set 2)
Revivalist song set in a rhythmic piano texture.

At the River (Set 2)
The familiar hymn tune, given a stately piano texture that becomes more dense as the song unfolds. All voices

from *Twelve Poems of Emily Dickinson*
Heart, we will forget him
A quiet, romantic love song. Compare with John Duke's setting. Women's voices

Why do they shut me out of Heaven?
A charming but petulant soliloquy. Some challenging angular phrases. Poetic content allows some dramatic leeway with the character. Women's voices.

THEODORE CHANLER (1902–1961)
Eight Epitaphs (Walter de la Mare)

Alice Rodd	Susannah Fry
Three Sisters	Thomas Logge
A Midget	No Voice to Scold
Ann Poverty	Be Very Quiet Now

More advanced repertoire. Skillfully crafted interaction between voice and piano. Calls for a competent pianist. Settings of imaginary epitaphs.

O mistress mine (William Shakespeare)

Chanler sets this with a shimmering Fauréan-like accompaniment, An elegant and romantic treatment of the words.

CELIUS DOUGHERTY (1902–1986)

The K'e (seventh century B.C. Chinese poem)

Slow tempo. A song of love lost. Dougherty's harmonic treatment gives an oriental touch to the overall mood. Women's voices.

Across the Western Ocean

Dougherty's setting of the old sea chantey. Male voices.

SAMUEL BARBER (1910–1981)

Sure on this shining night (James Agee)

One of the most beautiful art songs ever written. Demands good legato singing through some long-lined phrases. All voices.

The Crucifixion from *Hermit Songs* (Irish texts, 8th–13th centuries)

Lyric, intensely emotional setting depicting the crucifixion of Jesus.

The Daisies (James Stephens)

A short and charming early song. Vocal line is almost pointillistic, but always lyric. All voices.

A Nun Takes the Veil (Gerard Manley Hopkins)

For the more experienced singer. Womens' voices.

The Monk and His Cat from *Hermit Songs* (Irish texts, 8th–13th centuries)

A scholar and cat amiably pass the time with their own duties. Padding cat-like figures in the piano depict the cat. Rhythmic challenges for the voice in spots.

A Slumber Song of the Madonna (Alfred Noyes)

Early Barber song, charming and not musically difficult.

A Green Lowland of Pianos (Jerzy Harasymowicz, trans. C. Milosz)

A humorous and effective piece that draws comparisons between grand pianos and cows.

PAUL BOWLES (1910–1999)

Blue Mountain Ballads (Tennessee Williams)
> Heavenly Grass
> Lonesome Man
> Cabin
> Sugar in the Cane

Bowles's best-known and most-performed songs. Four disparate scenes from an imaginary Mississippi town. The songs are by turn, lyric, rhythmic, languid, and jazzy.

Three (Tennessee Williams)
Bowles's poignant song, meter in 3, is a diminutive *sarabande* resembling a small *gymnopédié*.

VINCENT PERSICHETTI (1915–1987)

Emily Dickinson Songs, Op. 77
> The Grass
> I'm Nobody
> When the Hills Do
> Out of the Morning

These Dickinson miniatures are simply but beautifully realized by Persichetti. Not difficult musically. Effective as a group.

LEONARD BERNSTEIN (1918–1990) (see Crossover)

Four Songs from *Peter Pan*
> Who am I?
> My House
> Peter, Peter
> Dream with Me

Incidental songs to the play *Peter Pan*. Charming and expressive. The last song was not a part of the original group of "Pan" songs, but was added later. Can be sung with a cello obbligato. Beautiful, flowing melody.

I Hate Music! (A Cycle of Five Kid Songs)
> My name is Barbara
> Jupiter has seven moons
> I hate music!
> A big Indian and a little Indian (Riddle Song)
> I'm a person too

Bernstein's first song cycle. The protagonist is a ten-year-old girl named Barbara. The singer must take care not to be too overly dramatic and cloying with Barbara's personality in these songs. Some tricky intervals and rhythms. Female voices.

So Pretty (Comden and Green)
A political anti-war statement. Musical theatre style popular setting. Effective song.

NED ROREM (b. 1923)
The Lordly Hudson (Paul Goodman)
This early Rorem song is still classic and beautiful—an elegant and heartfelt paean to New York and the stately Hudson River. Good practice for legato phrasing. All voices, except high, light.

Early in the morning (Robert Hillyer)
Delightful, folk-like quality in this well-known Rorem song. A young man enjoys the atmosphere of an outdoor Parisian café.

Rain in Spring (Paul Goodman)
Another Rorem vignette about a soft spring rain. Languid vocal phrases match the falling rain in a falling piano melody of double-dotted rhythms.

Jeanie with the Light Brown Hair (Stephen Foster, arr. Rorem)
Rorem pays homage to Foster's lovely melody by giving it new and evocative harmonic textures.

Love (Thomas Lodge)
Voice and piano lines intertwine, creating a fluid rhythmic texture of question-answer that perfectly fits the poetic construction.

O you whom I often and silently come (Walt Whitman)
Only 14 bars long, this intimate avowal of love glides calmly to the end. Declamatory setting. Not difficult. Good for practicing articulation in legato phrasing.

Ferry me across the water (Christina Rossetti)
A lovely, succinct song, ending on a sustained high G#. The singer needs to be able to manage this without problems. A wonderfully crafted song with a folk-like mood, but elegant throughout. Sopranos.

Flight for Heaven (Robert Herrick)
  To Music, to becalm his Fever
  Cherrie-ripe
  Upon Julia's Clothes
  To Daisies, not to shut so Soon
  Epitaph upon a Child that died
  Another Epitaph
  To the Willow-tree
  Comfort to a Youth that had lost his Love
  To Anthea, who may command him Any thing

  Rorem's first published cycle is wonderfully effective in recital.
  Herrick's sophisticated and elegantly nuanced poetry, filled
  with evocative images, is given an equally sophisticated and
  stylish musical treatment by Rorem. Written for a bass, but
  baritones can sing this also. Check the song ranges, however.
  Advanced singers.

LEE HOIBY (1926–2011)
  ### Lady of the Harbor (Emma Lazarus)
  This song, with Lazarus's stirring words inscribed at the base of
  the Statue of Liberty makes an appealing addition to a recital.
  Works well in an American group or in an all-Hoiby group.
  Begins softly, builds in intensity to extended phrases at the
  finish. All voices.

  ### Where the Music Comes From (Lee Hoiby)
  A lilting melody in a flowing texture, overall feeling of a
  popular song. All voices. A very popular Hoiby song.

  ### Jabberwocky (Lewis Carroll)
  Humorous, colorful setting of this familiar poem. A bizarre
  story, imaged in both piano and voice. This is like a little
  operatic *scena*. Good practice in vocal storytelling.

  ### The Serpent (Theodore Roethke)
  Another humorous poem, with play on the serpent's hissing
  [s] sounds. Very rhythmic, demands vocal flexibility for the
  wide-range vocal line. Fairly lengthy, dramatic changes at each
  section.

DOMINICK ARGENTO (b. 1927)

Six Elizabethan Songs

Spring (Thomas Nash)
Sleep (Samuel Daniel)
Winter (William Shakespeare)
Dirge (William Shakespeare)
Diaphenia (Henry Constable)
Hymn (Ben Jonson)

This is Argento's most popular and most performed cycle. Strongly lyric, with texts from the Elizabethan period that lend themselves to formal structures, mostly two and three-part sections, varied slightly. Piano and voice are integrated, but not to the extent found in *From the Diary of Virginia Woolf*. The faster tempo songs (Spring, Winter, Diaphenia) demand facile articulation and a strong rhythmic sense. Some challenging intervals and rhythms. Intermediate to advanced. Soprano or tenor voice. Also exists in a Baroque ensemble version (see Chapter 5).

RICHARD HUNDLEY (b. 1931)

The Astronomers (based on an epitaph found in Allegheny, Pennsylvania)

Hundley's evocative setting of a four-line epitaph is almost more about the piano writing. Two-page song. The last vocal phrase calls for excellent breath support and a sustained final note. There is an extended postlude. Use this as an interior song in a group. All voices, intermediate to advanced.

Sweet Suffolk Owl (Anon. Elizabethan verse, 1619)

A witty verse. Vocal line has dotted rhythms and syncopations, piano has a pompous, buoyant chordal texture. Charming song. All voices.

Come ready and see me (James Purdy)

This song has become one of Hundley's most popular. It is a simple, lyric melody that should be sung simply and gracefully, with a hint of popular song style. All voices.

Ballad on Queen Anne's Death (Anon.)

Fluctuates between 3/8, 5/8, and 6/8 time. Piano figures are like an Elizabethan lute. This is like a lovely improvised ballad. All voices.

WILLIAM BOLCOM (b. 1938)

Nevermore Will the Wind from *I Will Breathe a Mountain* (H.D. [Hilda Doolittle])

This song, from Bolcom's cycle of settings of American women poets, is less complex than some of the songs. A wistful and touching elegy. Intermediate to advanced. Low voices.

Cabaret Songs

Bolcom's cabaret songs are a skillful blend of popular and classical idioms. The 23 songs present a number of character portraits and diverse scenes, etched in highly entertaining snapshots.

LIBBY LARSEN (b. 1950)

Three Cowboy Songs
Bucking bronco (Belle Starr)
Lift me into heaven slowly (Robert Creeley)
Billy the Kid (Anonymous)

Effective, colorful settings of poems about the "Wild West" and cowboys. Excellent short cycle. Diverse moods. Female voices.

Love After 1950
Boy's Lips (Rita Dove)
Blonde Men (Julie Kane)
Big Sister Says (Kathryn Daniels)
Empty Song (Liz Lochhead)
I Make My Magic (Muriel Rukeyser)

The poems in this short cycle suggested a dance group to Larsen. She subtitled each song with a dance or music style and used it for her musical approach: blues, torch song, honky-tonk, tango, Isadora's dance. More advanced female singers.

JUDITH CLOUD (b. 1954)

Quatre mélodies de Ronsard

Ronsard in four very different moods. Piano figures act as unifying elements throughout the songs. All the songs are lyric and expressive. Originally for a baritone, but mezzos may also sing this. More sophisticated emotionally for the poetry.

Quand je te vois, seule, assise

Ronsard muses about his love, seated and alone, far from him physically and mentally. An idealized soliloquy.

Bonjour, mon cœur

Ebullient tempo, bright and impulsive setting. A litany of "good mornings" to the beloved.

A sa guitare

Simple, lyric line, some angularity. Easy, syncopated accompaniment that emulates the strumming of a guitar.

Je suis homme, né pour mourir

The finality of man's progress toward death. Magnificent poem.

JOHN MUSTO (b. 1954)

Recuerdo (Edna St. Vincent Millay)

A vignette about a couple who has spent the night riding back and forth on the Staten Island Ferry. Vocal lines demand flexibility. Bluesy, ragtime style. Singer needs dramatic insight. Delightful setting. Advanced. All voices.

Triolet (Eugene O'Neill)

A rose, the flower of love, on the beloved's breast, symbolizes the poet's desire. (It's like an American "Le spectre de la rose" à la Berlioz's "Les Nuits d'été"). Musto's setting features an imaginative piano accompaniment, rhythmically and harmonically.

LORI LAITMAN (b. 1955)

Echo (Christina Rossetti)

Fluid, musical textures that match the contemplative nature of the poem. Theme of lost love. Simple ABA structure. Published in several keys. All voices.

The Apple Orchard (Dana Gioia)

For tenor or soprano, although the text is gender-specific. Simplicity of style. Beautiful and evocative poem describes a *carpe diem* moment.

The Silver Swan (Orlando Gibbons)

Laitman's beautiful setting of Gibbons's famous poem. There is also a version for voice, flute, and piano. All voices. Touching setting of the words, effective in recital.

Last Night the Rain Spoke to Me (*Early Snow*) (Mary Oliver)

Calm, flowing vocal lines. Falling figures in the piano image the rain. Singer's line is broadly lyrical. Two unaccompanied measures divide the song's two sections—in the second, the night sky is revealed, dotted with stars and the final measures bring the song to a close in a mood of hushed wonder.

The Metropolitan Tower (Sara Teasdale)

Laitman's first song and one of her best-known. Strongly lyric and expressive.

TOM CIPULLO (b. 1956)

Deer in Mist with Almonds (Alice Wirth Gray)

Beautiful setting of Gray's poem High sustained notes needed. For more advanced singers.

RICKY IAN GORDON (b. 1956)

Ricky Ian Gordon's musical compositions for the voice are prolific; many are for more advanced singers. His settings blend the classical art song with idioms from the Broadway stage. They are always tonal, and have a lyrical grace about them, even when clothed in distinctive rhythmic patterns. He especially catches the directness of the poetic voice of Langston Hughes, and is at home with the rhythmic complexities of Emily Dickinson and Edna St. Vincent Millay. *Genius Child* is a collection of 10 songs, and they may be excerpted for single performance. Intermediate to Advanced.

Genius Child (Langston Hughes)
Winter Moon
Genius Child
Kid in the Park
To be somebody
Troubled Woman
Strange Hurt
Prayer
Border Line
My people
Joy

Song for a Dark Girl (Langston Hughes)
Heaven (Langston Hughes)
Too Few the Mornings Be (Emily Dickinson)
Soprano

Will There Really be a Morning? (Emily Dickinson)
Soprano

Souvenir (Edna St. Vincent Millay)
Soprano

Recuerdo (Edna St. Vincent Millay)
Soprano or tenor. Comparison settings: John Musto, Mario Castelnuovo-Tedesco.

DARON HAGEN (b. 1961)

Congedo from *Love in a Life* (Nuar Alsadir)
Love in a Life is a collection of 7 songs, arranged in a vocal cycle in 1998. Intensely lyric vocal lines. Begins with an unaccompanied phrase.

Ample make this bed from *Love in a Life* (Emily Dickinson)
Touchingly simple, almost hymn-like tune.

Deer in Mist and Amonds from *Figments* (Alice Wirth Gray)
Figments features the wildly humorous poetry of Alice Wirth Gray. Two songs are less comical. "Deer in Mist and Almonds" is one of those. Fluid vocal phrases, atmospheric piano figures. Has a 3/4 section that is reminiscent of a Satie *gymnopédie*.

The Poetry of Sausages: Morcilla from *Figments*
(Alice Wirth Gray)

Earthy, comical setting marked "Cooking Joyously, quarter note = 160." Note: *Figments* is a charming cycle, but is for more advanced singers.

JAKE HEGGIE (b. 1961)

In the Beginning from *Of Gods and Cats*
(Gavin Geoffrey Dillard)

"In the beginning was the cat/ And the cat was without purr." So begins Gavin Dillard's delightful poem. Heggie's "cycle" consists of only two songs. This one is jazzy and popular and references Barber's "The Monk and His Cat" in its clustered seconds mirroring the cat's stealthy footsteps. Intermediate to advanced singers. Good group ender.

GERMAN *LIEDER*

WOLFGANG AMADEUS MOZART (1756–1791)

Als Luise die Briefe . . . (Gabriele von Baumberg)

Luise burns the letters of her faithless lover, but his memory will burn in her heart. Dramatic and passionate little *scena* for mezzos or sopranos. Best for heavier voices.

Das Veilchen (Johann Wolfgang von Goethe)

Mozart's famous early lied, the poem beautifully realized in voice and piano. A violet pines for love, but is trampled underfoot by the unfeeling shepherdess. Needs a sense of graceful, lyric phrasing. Best for sopranos.

Abendempfindung (Joachim Heinrich Campe)

Evening thoughts. Italianate, long lines, needs good breath management. Advanced singers. Sopranos, tenors, mezzos. One of Mozart's most beautiful songs, reminiscent of his arias.

Der Zauberer (Christian Weisse)

Delightful cautionary poem about a young man whose charms are so irresistible, he must be a magician! Strophic, tricky German. Female voices.

Dans un bois solitaire et sombre (Antoine Ferrand)

French elegance and style abound in this wonderful little *scena*, quasi-operatic in style. Quintessentially Mozart in little operatic devices used tastefully and scaled to miniature form. Sopranos, tenors, mezzos. Intermediate to advanced singers. Needs facile French.

Ridente la calma (Anonymous)

Composed in Salzburg, in his teens. ABA form, vocal phrases long, spun-out, emotionally expressive. Sopranos, tenors.

Warnung (Anonymous)

Slightly off-color text. Small range, Brief phrases that convey the "warning" of the title: Fathers, lock up your sugar cookies (daughters). All voices.

LUDWIG VAN BEETHOVEN (1770–1827)

Adelaide (Friedrich von Matthisson)

Italianate in style. Extended length. In 3 sections. More advanced male singers. Like a concert aria.

Der Kuss (Christian Wiesse)

A charming *ariette*. Flirtatious scene between a boy and a girl over a kiss. Male voices.

An die ferne Geliebte (Aloys Jeitteles)

This is thought of as the first song cycle, six songs connected by musical materials in piano interludes. A good first German cycle. Male voices.

Mailied (Johann Wolfgang von Goethe)

Lovely, flowing song. Demands good articulation and flexibility. Lighter voices best.

Mignon (Kennst du das Land) (Johann Wolfgang von Goethe)

Legato phrasing, interspersed with contrasting faster sections. Sophisticated poetry. Interesting to contrast with Schubert, Wolf, Schumann, Liszt.

Neue Liebe, neues Leben (Johann Wolfgang von Goethe)

Vibrant and lively. Needs facile articulation and good sense of rhythm. Effective song. All except heavier lower voices. Also set by Hensel, Spohr, Reichardt, among others.

FRANZ SCHUBERT (1797–1828)

Die Forelle (Christian Friedrich Daniel Schubart)

Schubert's gift of creating atmosphere with the piano part is nowhere more apparent than the quicksilver piano figures illustrating the playful trout in the stream. Famous Schubert song, but performed well, it never gets old. Fine for young singers.

An die Musik (Franz Schober)

Schubert sets Schober's hymn to music in strophic form. Phrases of breadth and nobility create a sense of exaltation. A wonderful lied that is always a gift to sing. Intermediate difficulty. All voices.

Die Musensohn (Johann Wolfgang von Goethe)

The Son of the Muses needs facile German and good dramatic instincts to perform this lied. Best for medium or low voices.

Im Frühling (Ernst Schulze)

Schubert uses a theme and variation format for this lovely song. Voice and piano have separate melodic material. The piano part is given the variation theme; the voice has variants of the piano's opening phrases from stanza to stanza. All voices.

Der Jüngling an der Quelle (Johann Gaudenz von Salis-Seewis)

Schubert's penchant for water figures in the piano is seen in this setting. Sustained phrases, but graceful and delicate. All voices.

An dem Mond, D. 259 (Johann Wolfgang von Goethe)

Schubert set this text twice. The first setting is strophic in form, this setting is more complex and searching. Good for shaping phrases, All voices.

An Silvia (William Shakespeare, translated by Eduard von Bauernfeld)

(from *Two Gentlemen from Verona*) Three verses, set strophically. An exuberant and joyous, yet sustained homage to Sylvia. All voices.

An die Leier (Franz von Bruchmann)

Wonderful song, unjustly neglected. Combination of dramatic recitative with long-lined *cantilena*. The bard would sing of

Greek heroes, but his lyre can only sing of love. Best for heavier voices. Intermediate to advanced difficulty.

Nachtviolen (Johann Mayrhofer)
This lovely *Lied* is set almost entirely syllabically. Schubert's beautiful melodic gift shines throughout. Simple rhythms. Good for shaping phrases, and working with subtle word nuances. All voices.

Liebhaber in allen Gestalten (Johann Wolfgang von Goethe)
A delightful humorous song of four verses, set strophically, in which the singer wishes to become several things—a fish, gold, a lamb—in order to be closer to his beloved and please her. This song, like all strophic settings, offers a chance to work with word color and weight within phrases. All voices.

Blondel zu Marien (poet unknown)
This lovely melody is ornamented in the style of eighteenth century arias, It is a Schubert lied that is not heard often. Its two verses are a love song of Blondel (King Richard the Lionhearted's minstrel) to Mary. All voices.

FANNY MENDELSSOHN HENSEL (1805–1847)
Frühling (Joseph von Eichendorff)
Animated, sparkling setting. Needs graceful phrase shaping, buoyancy of tone. Sopranos, tenors.

Suleika (Marianne von Wellemer)
The passionate mood of the text is skillfully captured by Hensel. Suleika's breathless plea to the West wind has also been set by Schubert, Felix Mendelssohn, and Karl Zelter. Woman's text.

Nachtwanderer (Joseph von Eichendorff)
A beautiful nocturne setting of Eichendorff's poem, full of typical Romantic themes: nature, moonlight, mystery. Voice and piano freely exchange melodic materials. All voices.

Du bist die Ruh (Friedrich Rückert)
Beautiful but rather simple treatment of this intimate poem, better known in Schubert's setting. Two stanzas. All voices.

FELIX MENDELSSOHN (1808–1847)

Nachtlied (Joseph von Eichendorff)
One of his finest songs. It is an evening soliloquy of great beauty and dignity. Form: AAB with a tiny codetta. The last stanza is exultantly dramatic, with expressive, expansive vocal lines. All voices.

Neue Liebe (Heinrich Heine)
Very rapid tempo, recounting the moonlight revels of elves. Vibrant images in poetry, translated into musical images with dotted rhythm patterns and staccato passages in the voice. Calls for facile articulation. Lighter voices best.

Auf Flügeln des Gesanges (Heinrich Heine)
One of his best-known, popular songs, typical of Mendelssohn's graceful melodic style. Beautiful melody, three strophes; piano interlude between the second and third stanzas. All voices.

ROBERT SCHUMANN (1810–1856)

Waldesgespräch (*Liederkreis*) (Joseph von Eichendorff)
The famous witch Lorelei appears on land to a huntsman riding through the forest and tells him in an incantation-like phrase that he will never leave the forest. Calls for dramatic interpretation. Intermediate to advanced difficulty. All voices.

Widmung (*Myrthen*) (Friedrich Rückert)
Exuberant declaration of love. Good for work in the middle voice. Form: ABA, with recapitulation slightly varied. All voices.

Die Lotosblume (*Myrthen*) (Heinrich Heine)
Beautifully descriptive nature setting. Sustained, legato phrasing. Piano texture changes with poetic elements as the lotus flower turns her face to her lover, blossoming in ecstasy. All voices.

In der Fremde (*Liederkreis*) (Joseph von Eichendorff)
Through-composed setting. Simple, but with subtle harmonic touches reinforcing the text. Chromaticism in the piano illustrates mood of the singer. All voices.

Die beiden Grenadiere (Heinrich Heine)

A great dramatic song that never fails to stir an audience. Chronicles the dialogue of two soldiers, making their way home to France after the defeat of Napoleon's Grand Army. Demands a singer with dramatic flair. Men's voices. See also Richard Wagner's setting.

Volksliedchen (Friedrich Rückert)

A charming, fresh verse in a simple setting, ABA'. Some subtle chromatic touches. Not difficult. All voices.

Der Nussbaum (*Myrthen*) (Julius Mosen)

One of Schumann's most-performed songs. Charming and tender. A young girl dreams beneath the walnut tree, its leaves whispering. An extraordinary little masterpiece in which voice and piano share musical shapes in a delicate texture. All voices.

Mein schöner Stern! (Friedrich Rückert)

Designated for tenor voice, this beautiful supplication to the evening star has arching phrases over the piano's repeated chord patterns. Two verses, set strophically.

Der arme Peter (Heinrich Heine)

I. Der Hans und die Grete tanzen herum

II. In meiner Brust da sitz ein Weh

III. Der arme Peter wankt vorbei

Three Heine poems constitute this small cycle, set continuously, as was Beethoven's *An die ferne Geliebte*. Less than five minutes in length, this is an effective recital piece, and can be combined with another Schumann song. Poor Peter watches his sweetheart marry another, and the pain he suffers causes him to find a final resting place. Men's voices.

Frauenliebe und –leben (Adalbert von Chamisso)

Seit ich ihn gesehen
Er, der Herrlichste von Allen
Ich kann's nicht fassen, nicht glauben
Du Ring an meinem Finger
Helft mir, ihr Schwestern
Süsser Freund

An meinen Herzen, an meiner Brust
Nun hast du mir den ersten Schmerz getan

This cycle is interpretively difficult, but for more advanced singers, it is a wonderful challenge. We follow a young woman from love at first sight through marriage, children, and death of her husband. Dramatically challenging. Women's voices.

Liebeslied (Johann Wolfgang von Goethe)
A neglected Schumann song. An exquisite lyric melody in which voice and piano overlap phrases that become more integrated and tightly knit as the song progresses. Through-composed. The embodiment of Romantic expression. All voices.

Singet nicht in Trauertönen (Johann Wolfgang von Goethe)
Quicksilver song of Philine, the actress in Goethe's play *Wilhelm Meister*. This lied calls for very good German diction and musicality. More advanced singers. A very effective little *tour de force*.

FRANZ LISZT (1811–1886)
S'il est un charmant gazon (Victor Hugo)
Charming graceful song, also set by Fauré (titled "Rêve d'amour"), César Franck, Camille Saint-Saëns. All voices.

O quand je dors (Victor Hugo)
Languorous, romantic long-lined phrases. An exquisite love song with a sophisticated text. Very sustained, needs command of soft dynamic in high voice. Advanced singers.

Comment disaient-ils (Victor Hugo)
This text set has been set by a dozen or so composers, including Bizet, Massenet, Lalo, and Saint-Saëns. Spanish rhythms accompany Hugo's famous poem. All voices.

Enfant, si j'étais roi (Victor Hugo)
Effusive reiteration of what the poet would give for the love of the beloved and for a kiss. Piano part thick, repeated chords in right hand, and strong melody in bass. A closing section changes mood and becomes beautifully lyrical. Advanced singers. All voices.

RICHARD WAGNER (1813–1883)

Mignonne (Pierre de Ronsard)

One of Wagner's forays into setting French poetry, written during his short stay in France.

Les deux Grenadiers (François-Adolphe Loeve-Veimar, translated from the German of Heinrich Heine)

Fascinating study in Wagner's early vocal writing. Quotes the "Marseillaise" in the piano part in closing measures. Schumann did this later in his setting, but gave the anthem to the voice instead of the piano.

ROBERT FRANZ (1815–1892)

Franz wrote over 300 songs, usually strophic in form and designed on a small scale. His melodies are simple, most of them in a moderate range, generally set syllabically. He used German folk songs and hymns as his patterns. These songs are excellent beginning songs to introduce young singers to the German language without having to deal with complex musical issues. Two examples are given below, but there are hundreds to choose from.

Widmung (Friedrich Rückert)

His most beloved song. Set like a hymn tune. Two stanzas. Piano doubles voice. Good beginning song.

Es hat die Rose sich beklagt (Von Bodenstedt from the Persian of Mirza-Schaffy)

The rose complains her perfume will fade all too soon. Six line poem that Franz has divided into two sets of three lines each, setting them strophically. Poem has some of the exoticism of the Orient.

CLARA WIECK SCHUMANN (1819–1896)

Er ist gekommen in Sturm und Regen (Friedrich Rückert)

Brilliant piano part dominates. Vocal line lyric in contrast, but each integrated skillfully into overall texture. Two stanzas in through-composed form. Effective as the last song in a group, for the dazzling overall movement and sparkling finish. Women's voices.

Liebst du um Schönheit (Friedrich Rückert)
Simple melody and rhythms, yet finely crafted. Intimacy of the poetry captured beautifully. Inner voices in the piano provide changing harmonic colors. Range not wide. Compare with Gustav Mahler's setting. All voices.

Lorelei (Heinrich Heine)
The Lorelei sits upon a rock high above the river, singing a song that lures sailors to their death. Vocal phrases are dramatic, breathless, underscored with a racing accompaniment. Exciting story. All voices, except very light.

Ihr Bildnis (Heinrich Heine)
This text, set by six other composers, also captivated Clara Schumann, who set it twice. This setting has an astonishing unresolved ending in the vocal line and the tension of delayed resolution in the piano postlude that underscores the anguish of the text. All voices.

JOHANNES BRAHMS (1833–1897)

Meine Liebe ist grün (Felix Schumann)
Glorious setting of a poem by Brahms's godson, Felix Schumann, son of Robert and Clara Schumann. Mood is effusive, full of youthful, ardent emotion. Two strophes with harmonic fluctuations. Thick texture.

Wie Melodien zieht es (Klaus Groth)
One of Brahms's most-performed songs. Broadly lyric melodies. Good for legato and rubato phrasing. All voices.

Vergebliches Ständchen (Lower Rhine folk song)
A delightful dialogue song in four verses. A boy stands beneath his beloved's window, imploring her to let him in. The piano part is varied for each verse. Will she? Won't she? All voices.

Auf dem Kirchhofe (Detlev von Liliencron)
Notable for many harmonic and rhythmic changes during a fairly short song. Text painting of power, strength. Last stanza features an unexpected, beautiful Bach chorale texture. Needs voices with some heft and good breath management. Best for mezzos and baritones.

Feldeinsamkeit (Hermann Allmers)

High tessitura, challenging for the the breath. Long phrases, needs good command of legato. Advanced students. Original key is for baritones/mezzos, but high key for sopranos/tenors fine also.

Therese (Gottfried Keller)

Women's poem. Simple, uncomplicated melody and rhythms. Soprano or mezzo.

Wenn du nur zuweilen lächelst (Georg Friedrich Daumer)

Graceful melodic lines. Good for legato work. Long-lined vocal phrases. All voices.

Der Schmied (Johann Ludwig Uhland)

Fine for beginning students. Woman's text ("My love is a blacksmith"). Two verses. Strophic.

Ophelia-Lieder (Shakespeare, trans. Schlegel and Ludwig Tieck)

Wie erkenn' ich dem Treulieb?
Sein Leichenhemd weiss wie Schnee
Auf morgen ist Sankt Valentins Tag
Sie trugen ihn auf der Bahre bloß
Und kommt er nicht mehr zurück?

Charming miniatures. This little "cycle" of Ophelia's songs deserves more recital outings. Simplicity of presentation in voice and piano. Very accessible for young voices.

GUSTAV MAHLER (1860–1911)

Wer hat dies Liedlein erdacht? (Brentano von Arnim, *Lieder aus Der Knaben Wunderhorn*)

This charming folk-like song has wide intervals, and melismas in several spots. Sounds best for soprano or tenor, but lyric baritones and lyric mezzos can sing it also. Best for more advanced singers.

Liebst du um Schönheit (Friedrich Rückert)

Mahler's love song to his wife, Alma. Better in low key (baritones/mezzos). Unisex poem. Compare with Clara Schumann's setting.

Ich atmet' einen linden Duft' (Friedrich Rückert)

Not for beginners. Slow tempo, sophisticated poetry that creates an atmosphere of wonder and calm. All voices, but best in the high key for soprano or tenor.

HUGO WOLF (1860–1903)

The *Lieder* of Hugo Wolf may certainly be termed "organic." All the elements of word and tone blend together as parts of a harmonious whole. Selections from Wolf's "poet" songbooks are listed here. His Spanish and Italian songbooks have selections that might be on the list, but these two songbooks should be performed by advanced singers for their highly challenging compression of musical and poetic materials and overall sophisticated subtleties between voice and piano.

Das verlassene Mägdlein (Eduard Möricke)

One rhythm glues the song together, both in voice line and piano texture. A grief-stricken servant girl stares without seeing into the hearth-fire, recalling her dream of her faithless lover. Masterful simplicity throughout. Compare with Robert Schumann's setting. Intermediate to advanced. Soprano or mezzo.

Auf ein altes Bild (Eduard Möricke)

Möricke's poem of six lines describes a painting of a summery green landscape. On the canvas, the Christ child plays happily on the Virgin's lap. In the background of the beautiful forest grows the tree for the cross. Contrary motion in close intervals between voice and piano perpetuates a solemn mood. Intermediate to advanced. All voices.

Verborgenheit (Eduard Möricke)

One of Wolf's most-performed songs. Broad vocal phrases, strong piano figures. Nobility of mood fitting poem's content. All voices.

Der Gärtner (Eduard Möricke)

Fresh and enchanting, fairytale-like story. A princess, astride a prancing horse, passes an adoring gardener who hopes for a feather from her hat. Lyric vocal lines, dotted rhythms in the piano emulate the horse's gait. Intermediate. A light soprano voice best.

Anakreons Grab (Johann Wolfgang von Goethe)

Anacreon was a Greek lyric poet of the sixth century B.C. Musical setting of simplicity and lyric feeling. Delicate piano figures paint the natural beauty surrounding the grave of the poet. Good for legato and shaping phrases. Intermediate to advanced. Low voices.

Der Musikant (Joseph von Eichendorff)

The figure of the wandering minstrel is seen in this poem. Four stanzas. Some chromaticism and harmonic subtleties. Advanced. Male voices.

RICHARD STRAUSS (1864–1949)

Allerseelen (Hermann von Gilm)

Composed when Strauss was 18, in his first collection of songs, Opus 10. Warmly romantic style. Long phrases, sophisticated poetry. Not for lighter voices. More advanced singers.

Breit über mein Haupt (A.F. von Schack)

Perhaps more appropriate for a tenor (for the text), though it is marked "high voice," and sopranos find this a very grateful song to sing. Peaceful and serene mood. For more advanced singers, and larger voices. Brief song.

Die Zeitlose (Hermann von Gilm)

Very brief song, one page. Early Strauss. Suitable for all voices, but not a beginner's song.

Zueignung (Hermann von Gilm)

One of his most familiar songs, composed at age 18. He wrote this for tenor voice, although all voices sing this with great pleasure. Broad vocal phrases, underlined with a piano texture of octaves and triplets.

Die Nacht (Hermann von Gilm)

Belongs to same opus as "Allerseelen" and "Zueignung." Gentle poetic mood, overall lean texture. Night's stealthy approach is announced by a single repeated note in the piano, and gathers weight with each measure. Manipulation of harmonic changes is subtle and skillfully integrated in the piano. All voices

Drei Liebeslieder
Rote Rosen
Die erwachte Rose
Begegnung

Early songs of Strauss (composed 1883, 1880, 1880). Very accessible for young voices. Lovely examples in which one hears the musical seeds that were to flourish and bloom very soon afterward.

ALMA SCHINDLER MAHLER (1879–1964)

Alma Mahler's songs represent Viennese turn-of-the-century music, a blend of late romanticism and early modernism. Discouraged from composing by her husband, Gustav Mahler, she composed only a small number of songs, but they are interesting and rewarding to sing, for intermediate singers. The songs below are a sampling from Alma Mahler's song catalog.

Bei dir ist es traut (Rainer Maria Rilke)
Laue Sommernacht (Gustav Falke)
Ich wandle unter Blumen (Heinrich Heine)

ERICH KORNGOLD (1897–1957)

Das Ständchen (Joseph von Eichendorff)

Composed at age 14. A young student stands singing beneath the window of his sweetheart. Ardent in mood, opening vocal phrase doubled by the piano. Three sections. Influences of Richard Strauss heard. Male voices.

The next two songs below were part of Korngold's Op. 9, composed at age sixteen.

Sommer (Siegfried Trebitsch)

A hymn to nature, richly flavored with the brash, romantic spirit of youth and the ambience of turn-of-the-century Vienna. The warbling blackbird in the text is introduced in the piano prelude, which features Mahler-like "nature" figures in the texture. The song concludes with an extended piano postlude. All voices.

Das Heldengrab am Pruth (Heinrich Kipper)

Harmonic materials take center stage in this song. Polytonality creates the detached, otherworldly feeling of the cemetery in the poet's garden. It is always springtime in the garden because the fallen hero rests there. All voices.

Come away, death (William Shakespeare)

Korngold's masterful sense of melody highlighted here. Vocal lines are a graceful, flowing lament. Simple accompaniment often doubles the voice. A mixture of major and minor intervals at places adds spice to the vocal line. Intermediate difficulty. All voices.

Nachtwanderer (Joseph von Eichendorff)

Eichendorff's dramatic verse describes Night, astride a charging horse, riding throughout the countryside until the cock crows at daybreak. Atmospheric song. Piano figures change and thicken as horse and rider race toward the final measures, where, exhausted the traveler sinks into the grave that his horse has pawed out for him. As the rooster crows, Korngold combines B minor and B major. Intermediate to advanced. Low voices.

KURT WEILL (1900–1950)

Nanna's Lied (Bertolt Brecht)

The poignant soliloquy of a young prostitute. Strophic variations with refrain, with a spoken sentence leading into each strophe. Women's voices. Touching, bitter text. Written for Lotte Lenya.

Youkali: Tango Habanera (Roger Fernay)

French text. Weill composed it in Paris. Nostalgic, languid text that yearns for the land where cares disappear, love is shared, and promises are kept . . . Youkali, the hope in all human hearts, is only a dream. Hypnotic song, quite effective. Sopranos, tenors.

FRENCH *MÉLODIE*

To perform any of these songs well, a singer must be able to sing with precision and clarity and produce a variety of vocal colors within a highly lyric vocal line.

JEAN-PHILIPPE RAMEAU (1683–1764)
Le Grillon (Béranger)
Strophic song. Delightfully melodious, not difficult musically. Allows work with textual nuance—found in one of the volumes of *Echos de France*, collections of eighteenth-century French arias. Finding this might require some searching, but it is worth the effort.

JOHANN-PAUL MARTINI (1741–1816)
Plaisir d'amour (Jean-Pierre Claris de Florian)
The quintessential *romance*. Graceful, expressive vocal phrases. Good beginning French song. All voices.

HECTOR BERLIOZ (1803–1869)
Villanelle (Théophile Gautier) [*Les Nuits d'été*]
This is the first song in Berlioz's orchestral cycle, and works well extracted from the cycle. Melodic, flexible vocal phrases, strophic form with subtle variations.

CHARLES GOUNOD (1818–1893)
O ma belle rebelle (Antoine de Baïf)
Undulating graceful vocal phrases. Excellent practice in French diction and breath management. Male text.

Venise (Alfred de Musset)
A strophic gem of lyricism and proportion. Tessitura remains on the high side throughout.

Viens! les gazons sont verts (Jules Barbier)
Light, delicate. Good practice in quick, light articulation.

PAULINE VIARDOT (1821–1910)
Haï luli! (Xavier de Maistre)
Lovely, lyric vocal line with a folk-like quality. Feminine text—a French "Gretchen am Spinnrade." Three stanzas, varied by harmonic changes.

Bonjour mon cœur (Pierre de Ronsard)

A brief song with a simple, delicate vocal line. French not difficult.

J. B. (JEAN-BAPTISTE) WECKERLIN (1821–1910), collector and arranger

Bergerettes (Pastoral Ditties): Twenty Romances and Songs of the Eighteenth Century

This collection contains good examples of songs that are not musically difficult, but many demand facile diction, and thus serve as useful practice pieces. This old and venerable publication, originally published in 1860, is worth searching out. A recital group of Weckerlin's charming settings of pastoral folk songs would be a good beginning French group.

GEORGES BIZET (1838–1875)

Guitare (Victor Hugo)

Lively tempo, florid vocal lines in a colorful setting. Calls for a sense of drama and vocal facility in melismatic passages. Women's voices.

Adieux de l'hôtesse d'Arabe (Victor Hugo)

Feminine text—the goodbye of a native Arab girl to her lover. Dance-like, sinuous vocal phrases punctuated with melismas. Bizet's fascination with the exotic plus dramatic situation makes this an effective song. Not for very light voices. Think *Carmen*.

Absence (Théophile Gautier)

We are used to hearing Berlioz's "Absence," from his larger work *Les nuits d'été*. Bizet reacted quite differently to the poetry, opting for a faster tempo and a flexible vocal line, supported with lovely melodic fragments and triplets in the piano. Bizet set six stanzas of the original text. All voices, except very light.

EMMANUEL CHABRIER (1841–1894)

Villanelle des petits canards (Rosemond Gérard)

A comical portrait of a line of little ducks, waddling along on their way. Needs energetic vocal articulation and crisp diction. Strophic form. All voices.

Ballade des gros dindons (Edmond Rostand)

Another in Chabrier's "barnyard" suite of songs, describing the pompous, deliberate gait of a flock of turkeys. Each stanza is separated by a *ritornello* in very quick tempo, quoting Don Giovanni's serenade from Mozart's opera.

GABRIEL FAURÉ (1845–1924)

Clair de lune (Paul Verlaine)

One of the most famous Fauré settings. The voice floats, descant-like, over the accompaniment, which is really a piano solo. All voices.

Au bord de l'eau (Sully Prudhomme)

Beautiful fluid vocal line that offers practice in legato and bridging registers.

Mandoline (Paul Verlaine)

Very different from Debussy's setting which stresses poetic details. Fauré's setting emphasizes mood and atmosphere of the poetry. Extremely graceful vocal phrases with short melismas for text painting. All voices.

Automne (Armand Silvestre)

A full-textured piano accompaniment makes this *mélodie* more suited to fuller voices. Dramatic in mood.

Chanson d'amour (Armand Silvestre)

Extremely flexible vocal phrases, needs clean, clear French.

Lydia (Leconte de Lisle)

A beautiful example of a good beginning French song. Works legato, vowels, shaping phrases. Range not excessive. Male voices.

Après un rêve (Romain Bussine)

Atmospheric and Italianate in concept. Long-lined vocal phrases call for scrupulous legato. Usually taken at too slow a tempo. All voices.

Tristesse (Théophile Gautier)

Strophic setting. Comfortable vocal range and simple rhythms. Allows work with words and shaping phrases. All voices.

Sylvie (Paul de Choudens)
Early Fauré. Lyric vocal phrases. Male text.

Arpège (Albert Samain)
Wonderful example of Fauré's fluid harmonic style. Arpeggios in the L.H. of the piano accompany a graceful R.H. melody—"the soul of the flute" of the poem. The vocal line adds another layer. A neglected gem. All voices.

HENRI DUPARC (1848–1933)
Lamento (Théophile Gautier)
Offers excellent practice in sustaining legato vocal phrases, and a middle section that is dramatic and quasi-operatic in mood.

Chanson triste (Jean Lahor)
Duparc's first *mélodie*. Fairly wide range, spacious phrase lengths. Demands flexible phrasing. Better in the high key.

VINCENT D'INDY (1851–1931)
Madrigal (Robert de Bonnières)
Modified strophic setting in both voice and piano. Each stanza contains interesting "contrapuntal" interplay between the vocal line and accompaniment. Easy French.

ERNEST CHAUSSON (1855–1899)
Les Papillons (Théophile Gautier)
A stylish setting that evokes the fluttering movements of butterflies. Quick tempo, light, demands facile articulation. All voices.

Hébé (Louise Ackermann)
Describes Hébé, the cupbearer for the Greek gods, symbol of eternal youth. Austere, beautiful vocal line, transparent texture. French not difficult, musically simple. An excellent beginning song.

Le Charme (Armand Silvestre)
Expressive declaration of love. Not overly dramatic. Calls for a sense of restraint and control. Good beginning song. Low ending.

Nanny (Leconte de Lisle)

Fairly broad vocal phrases, dramatic. Interesting musical construction of vocal phrases. French not difficult.

Le Colibri (Leconte de Lisle)

A stunning song, tinged with exoticism. Its time signature, 5/4, offers practice singing in an uneven meter. Demands legato phrases, French not difficult.

CLAUDE DEBUSSY (1862–1918)

Voici que le printemps (Paul Bourget)

Early Debussy. Quick tempo, light, lyric. Requires crisply articulated consonants.

Romance (Paul Bourget)

Another early Debussy *mélodie*. Vocal phrases with nice contours and brief excursions into the upper voice. Sopranos, tenors.

Mandoline (Paul Verlaine)

Verlaine's famous poem full of images and characters—calls for textual nuance and facile French. A wonderful exercise for interpreting a dramatic text. All voices.

Beau soir (Paul Bourget)

Extremely lyric and atmospheric, perhaps the most well-known example of Debussy's very early impressionistic style. Generally tempo is taken too slowly, making one particularly long phrase even more difficult. All voices.

Noël des enfants qui n'ont plus de maisons (Claude Debussy)

Debussy's last *mélodie*, composed during the waning days of WWI, for which he wrote the text. Fast tempo demands clean articulation. Vocal line contains large intervals at points of high emotion. Despite the "regrettable words," [1] this is an effective song.

ERIK SATIE (1866–1925)

La Statue de bronze from *Trois mélodies de 1916* (Léon-Paul Fargue)

Fargue's tongue-in-cheek text about a bronze frog in a garden calls for vocal flexibility and clear diction. Last phrase is low—recitative, on one note.

Je te veux (Henry Pacory)

One of Satie's café-concert songs. Melodious waltz, fluid phrases with some arching intervals. Calls for stylish phrasing and a firm middle voice.

Ludions (Léon-Paul Fargue)

Air du rat
Spleen
La Grenouille américaine
Air du poète
Chanson du chat

Extremely short songs, like little vignettes. Some are written in popular music hall style, two are mock-serious "tongue-in-cheek" parodies. Fargue's poems are almost untranslatable.

REYNALDO HAHN (1874–1947)

A Chloris (Théophile de Viau)

An exquisite Baroque *pastiche* setting over which the vocal line floats. Wonderful rhythmic interplay between voice and piano. All voices.

Offrande (Paul Verlaine)

Beautiful legato line, recitative-like articulation. Demands that the singer carefully gauge the weight of important words and/or vowels. The poem is Verlaine's "Green," also set by Debussy and Fauré. All voices.

Tyndaris (A. de Lisle)

Hahn's quirky prosody against the rhythmic meter makes phrasing a challenge.

Le Rossignol des lilas (Léopold Dauphin)

Sweeping, lyrical vocal lines, in a style reminiscent of operetta. Sopranos, tenors.

Quand je fus pris au pavillon (Charles d'Orléans)
Nimble vocal line calls for rapid diction and good rhythmic sense. Hahn's *pastiche* of Renaissance style.

Si mes vers avaient des ailes (Victor Hugo)
Fresh, charming lyric vocal phrases. Strophic form. Composed by Hahn at age fifteen. All voices.

MAURICE RAVEL (1875–1937)

Sainte (Stéphane Mallarmé)
Atmospheric setting depicting a stained glass window of Saint Cecilia. Vocal line is undulating and chant-like and demands a legato line. High voices.

Cinq mélodies populaires grecques
(Trad. Greek, transl. M.D. Calvocoressi)
Le revéil de la mariée
Là-bas, vers l'église
Quel galant!
Chanson des cueilleuses de lentisques
Tout gai!

Good beginning Ravel set: five songs, offering varied moods, tempos, and dramatic interpretation. All voices.

GEORGE ENESCU (1881–1956)

Since Enescu is in another national section, Eastern European, and this list stops with Spanish repertoire, his beautiful cycle of *mélodies* is being filed here with the French repertoire.

Sept chansons de Clément Marot, Op. 15
Estrene à Anne
Languir me fais
Aux damoyselles paresseuses d'écrire à leurs amys
Estrene de la rose
Présent de couleur blanche
Changeons propos, c'est trop chanté amours
Du conflict en douleure

Marot was the court poet to François I. The poetry is a blend of the old and new; Enescu captures the ambience of Marot's time, portraying the poet as a troubadour. Accompaniments are suggestive of a lute or small harp. Do not let the old French stop you; use contemporary pronunciation. It is easy and perfectly fine to extract a group from this collection—in fact, it works better that way. These are beautiful songs and very effective in performance. Mezzos or baritones best.

DARIUS MILHAUD (1892–1974)

Six chansons de theater

La Bohemienne
Un petit pas
Mes amis les cygnes
Blancs son les jours d'été
Je suis dans le filet
Chacun son tour, les animaux

Six brief "theater songs" that Milhaud composed for several plays. All the songs are short; they form a little kaleidoscope of different moods and rhythms, and also present various characters: the old gypsy fortuneteller; a little dog who seems caught in a childhood rhyme; majestic swans, the passing summer days; the oppression of misspent youth, and a crazy parade of animals. Not difficult musically. All voices.

FRANCIS POULENC (1899–1963)

Priez pour paix (Charles d'Orléans)

Good beginning Poulenc song. Vocal phrases predominantly in middle voice. A prayer to the Virgin Mary, text from a seventeenth-century poet, but composed while Europe teetered on the brink of World War II. All voices.

Le Bestiaire (Guillaume Apollinaire)

Le Dromadaire
La Chèvre du Thibet
La Sauterelle
Le Dauphin
L'Écrevisse
La Carpe

Poulenc's first song cycle: five miniatures, each approximately a minute in length. Excellent for singers beginning to explore Poulenc. Middle and low male voices.

Bleuet (Guillaume Apollinaire)

Poulenc's only song specifically for tenors (sopranos have recorded it also). Fluid vocal line, intensely emotional text. Advanced singers.

Fleurs (Louise de Vilmorin) [*Fiançailles pour rire*]

The last song in Poulenc's cycle *Fiançailles pour rire*. Calls for softer dynamic work and sustained vocal phrases in the *passaggio*. The harmonic style is unmistakably Poulenc. Intermediate to advanced. Women's voices.

La Grenouillère (Guillaume Apollinaire)

Apollinaire's text describes Montreuil-sur-Mer, an island on the Seine frequented by artists and their models, and celebrated in paintings by Monet and Renoir. Vocal phrases are sustained and languid, over a slowly rocking piano accompaniment. Tessitura and overall musical texture make this more suited to low voices. Two phrases near the end climb into the *passaggio*.

Hôtel (Guillaume Apollinaire) [*Banalités*]

Bernac characterized this as "The 'laziest' song ever written." [2] Good practice for the middle voice, with one brief excursion into the passaggio.

Ce doux petit visage (Paul Eluard)

A beautiful introduction to Paul Eluard, one of Poulenc's three main poets. The simplicity of the musical setting allows the poem to shine. One of Poulenc's tiny gems.

JACQUES LEGUERNEY (1906–1997)

Je me lamente from *Poèmes de la Pléiade I* (Pierre Ronsard)

One of Leguerney's best. Broad-lined vocal phrases over a chordal accompaniment. Quasi-operatic climax. Sopranos, tenors.

Le Vallon from *Poèmes de la Pléiade VII* (Théophile de Viau)

Wonderful interplay of voice and piano, linear textures. Text describes an enchanted valley inhabited by mythological beings. Delicacy of poetic images calls for different vocal colors and firm sense of legato. All voices.

La Caverne d'Echo from *Poèmes de la Pléiade VII* (Saint-Amant)

Piano and voice combine to create the mysterious resonance of the cavern where the nymph Echo lives. Some bitonality: the vocal line is in E-flat minor, piano oscillates between E-flat and F-sharp minor. Moderate vocal demands, requires excellent pianist. Baritones, mezzo sopranos.

Come away, come away (William Shakespeare)

An attractive and evocative setting of Shakespeare's "Come away, death." One piano figure recalls and Elizabethan lute, coupled with another that images a funeral procession. This was Leguerney's last song, and his first setting of an English text. Baritones, mezzo sopranos.

ARNE DØRUMSGAARD (1921–2006), arranger

Five Early French Songs

Volume 7 of Dørumsgaard's *Canzone Scordate* is titled *Five Early French Songs*, and contains: *L'amour de moy, Cette Anne si belle, Que je plains tous ces esprits, and Le célèbre menuet d'Exaudet*. These beautifully arranged old French songs are excellent beginning materials for French song study.

BRITISH ART SONG

JOHN DOWLAND (1563–1626)

Come again, sweet love doth now invite (Anonymous)

A vibrant lover's complaint. Dowland establishes intense passion with a breathless reiteration of an ascending interval in the voice, echoed in the accompaniment—"to see, to hear, to touch, to kiss"—with a release of tension on a long climactic note "to die" (an Elizabethan metaphor for making love.) Three verses, strophic.

Fine knacks for ladies (Anonymous)

A peddler's song, probably delivered at a country fair; however, it is also a metaphor for love. Lively tempo. Good character song. Men's voices.

Away with these self-loving lads (Lord Brooke Fulke)
A knowing text, filled with archaic allusions to love. Three verses, with some harmonic changes. All voices.

Flow my tears (Anonymous)
One of Dowland's early lute songs. Slow and sustained lament. Five verses. Subtle text painting in vocal line. All voices.

HENRY PURCELL (1659–1695)

Music for a while (John Dryden)
Liberal text painting is found throughout this beautiful song: a caressing little turn on "beguile," reiteration of "all" at various pitches, a clashing half-step interval on "eternal" and the "dropping" snakes in eighth notes. One of Purcell's finest songs. All voices.

If music be the food of love (Henry Heveningham)
Purcell set this text three times (1691, 1693, and 1695). The first version is the simplest and perhaps the most tuneful. Melodic line is urged along with sequences released at the highest point of the phrase. All voices.

I'll sail upon the Dog Star from *A Fool's Preferment* (Thomas D'Urfey)
An outstanding example of English baroque song. Theatrical treatment of a rousing text. Men's voices.

Fairest Isle (John Dryden)
Tuneful song, gracefully phrased. Two verses, set strophically. High tessitura. All voices.

Sweeter than Roses (Richard Norton)
Three sections: slow and ecstatic, featuring a languid, seductive melodic line. Melismas primarily on the words "cool" and "warm." Rising sequential motives on "dear kiss" are followed by text illustration on the words "trembling" and "freeze." A short transition ushers in a faster tempo section, which dances triumphantly to the final measures. Women's voices.

RALPH VAUGHAN WILLIAMS (1872–1958)

Linden Lea- A Dorset Song (William Barnes)

A beautiful folk-like melody, fresh and appealing. Musical setting is quintessential British pastoral style- simple lyricism, natural harmonies, heartfelt sentiment. All voices.

Silent Noon (Dante Gabriel Rossetti)

Simple forms, rich lyricism, and a vocal line combine to evoke spaciousness and freedom. Luxuriant, peaceful mood of after-love. All voices.

Songs of Travel (Robert Browning)

The Vagabond
Let Beauty Awake
The Roadside Fire
Youth and Love
In Dreams
The Infinite Shining Heavens
Whither Must I Wander?
Bright is the Ring of Words
I Have Trod the Upward and the Downward Slope

This cycle has been termed an "uneven" work, some citing the failure of the piano parts to do more than fill out the harmonies in the vocal line. Melodic content is paramount in the cycle. Despite the overall theme of the vagabond's travel, songs may be excerpted from the cycle. Men's voices.

ROGER QUILTER (1877–1953)

Now sleeps the crimson petal (Alfred, Lord Tennyson)

Quilter did not set all of Tennyson's poem (see Ned Rorem's setting), but nonetheless created an attractive and romantic song that is a favorite among singers. All voices

Come away, death (William Shakespeare)

Two verses, modified strophic. Beautiful text setting. Often taken at too slow a tempo. Men's voices.

O mistress mine (William Shakespeare)

Part of *Three Shakespeare Songs*, Op. 6 (with "Come away, Death," and "Blow, blow thou winter wind"). Graceful in the Quilter style. Lively tempo. Men's voices.

Fear no more the heat o' the sun (William Shakespeare)
Gracefully written, rewarding to perform. Musically not difficult. All voices.

Love's Philosophy (Percy Bysshe Shelley)
Natural mingling of nature's elements inspires a romantic rush of metaphor from the poet. Very fast tempo from beginning to end Illustrates the ardent text. Vocal phrases broad and sweeping. Mood is fresh, youthful, intense. All voices.

Go, Lovely Rose (Edmund Waller)
This beautiful poem deals with the subject of *carpe diem* in a most delicate, elegant way. Quilter's setting is unashamedly sentimental. Fluid melody, some extended vocal phrases. Some metric variety of two-against-three. Rich song texture overall. All voices.

The Arnold Book of Old Songs
Quilter's well-done arrangements of folk songs. Contains some good beginning pieces (see especially "Drink to me only with thine eyes," "Barbara Allen," "Over the Mountains").

GEORGE BUTTERWORTH (1885–1916)

Loveliest of trees from *A Shropshire Lad* (A.E. Housman)
Duke's setting of this poem is more performed, but Butterworth's is lovely. All voices.

Is my team ploughing? from *A Shropshire Lad* (A.E. Housman)
This poem offers a dramatic story and a chance to choose different vocal colors. Dialogue between a dead soldier and his friend, still alive. Men's voices.

The lads in their hundreds from *A Shropshire Lad* (A.E. Housman)
This heart-wrenching poem is set in a quick conversational vocal line in syllabic style. Requires facile articulation. Men's voices.

REBECCA CLARKE (1886–1979)

The Cloths of Heaven (W.B. Yeats)
Rich harmonic textures including modality, duple rhythms linked with triple rhythms, and planed chords are found in this beautiful and atmospheric song. All voices.

Down by the Salley Gardens (W.B. Yeats)

Clarke sets Yeats's nostalgic words with a simple accompaniment figure, and composed a new melodic line for the singer (not using the familiar traditional Irish folk song). The texture of the song has an impressionistic sound quality that characterizes the illusory world of the lovers. All voices.

Come, o come my life's delight (Thomas Campion)

Campion's vibrant, effusive verse is given a beautiful musical setting with a harmonic treatment that gives a nod to the sixteenth century while remaining contemporary. All voices.

The Seal Man (John Masefield)

Masefield's prose text tells a chilling tale based on the Celtic myth of Selkies, shape-changing sea fairies, usually in the form of gray seals, that took on human form, often coming onto land to lure humans to their death. Dramatic, declamatory vocal writing. Piano part is spare, mainly rolled chords that give the effect of a bardic harp. Singer needs excellent diction and a flair for storytelling. All voices.

IVOR GURNEY (1890–1937)

Sleep from *Five Elizabethan Songs* (John Fletcher)

Rivals the setting by Peter Warlock. Piano figures simulate rocking motion throughout the song, creating a hypnotic mood, with subtly changing harmonic texture for the vocal lines. The vocal writing is simply beautiful. Gurney was a prolific poet, and his musical reaction to words is masterful. All voices.

The fields are full (Edward Shanks)

Lovely poem, set simply with beautiful lyric melody in the voice and simple broken-chord patterns in the piano. Two stanzas, AB. All voices. See also setting by Peter Warlock.

Under the greenwood tree (William Shakespeare)

Beautiful piano part provides rhythmic decoration and contrapuntal texture for the melodic vocal line of this fresh song. All voices.

PETER WARLOCK (1894–1930)

Pretty Ring Time (William Shakespeare)

Buoyant musical setting for text "It was a lover and his lass." Syllabic vocal line gives effect of a patter song. High note ending. All voices.

Sleep (John Fletcher)

This is one of Warlock's masterpieces. Long legato vocal lines in free speech rhythms combine with piano textures of subtle harmonic and rhythmic variations that perpetuate the poetic mood. Creative attention to detail offers the singer many changes to plumb its rich musical textures for interpretive ideas. All voices.

My Own Country (Hillaire Belloc)

A wanderer's longing for home is the theme here. Folk song quality to the setting. Vocal line set syllabically in eighth notes. In second verse, piano and voice switch ranges. Beautiful, poignant song. Men's voices.

Jillian of Berry (Beaumont & Fletcher from *The Knight of the Burning Pestle*)

Quick tempo, pounding rhythms characterize this robust drinking song. Short song, excellent ender for a group. Men's voices.

GERALD FINZI (1901–1956)

Let Us Garlands Bring, Op. 18 (William Shakespeare)

Come away, death
Who is Sylvia?
Fear no more the heat o' the sun
O mistress mine
It was a lover and his lass

These beautifully lyric adaptations of Shakespeare's verse into art songs are excellent recital repertoire, uncomplicated by sentimentality. Occasionally, surprising rhythmic patterns in the voice. May be sung separately, but together, they are very effective. Baritones.

BENJAMIN BRITTEN (1913–1976)

Folk Song Arrangements
Volumes 1, 3, and 5: British Isles
Volume 2: France
Volume 4: Moore's Irish Melodies
Volume 6: England

Britten's wonderful arrangements of folk songs offer singers many choices for recital repertoire.

On This Island (W. H. Auden)
Let the florid music praise!
Now the leaves are falling fast
Seascape
Nocturne
As it is, plenty

A wonderful early cycle of Britten's briefer settings of Auden—among the most tangible and approachable vocally. Intermediate to advanced singers. Soprano or tenor.

A Charm of Lullabies, Op. 41
A Cradle Song (William Blake)
The Highland Balou (Robert Burns)
Sephestia's Lullaby (Robert Greene)
A Charm (Thomas Randolph)
The Nurse's Song (John Philip)

This cycle is for a mezzo. There are some songs that have a low tessitura. Britten provides a wide spectrum of vocal articulation in all these lullabies, some of which do not take place in run-of-the-mill situations. The singer is given a chance for a wide range of characterizations.

MADELEINE DRING (1923–1977)

Blow, blow thou winter wind (William Shakespeare)
In Dring's hands, Shakespeare's popular text is rendered with undulating vocal phrases underpinned with interesting harmonic treatment—changing tonalities, chromaticism, and figures imaging the bitter cold of the winter wind. All voices.

Business Girls (John Betjeman)

Beguiling song tinged with a popular song "feel." Poem describes the never-changing ritual of women getting ready for work, where the work day is unvarying in its schedule. All voices.

Song of a Nightclub Proprietress (John Betjeman)

To a languid, jazzy piano part, we are introduced to the proprietress who has arrived to clean up. She is both a comic and poignant figure. The text of the song is her soliloquy recalling her "glory days" and revealing her touching and frightened insecurities. Mezzo voices best.

ITALIAN ART SONG

Every student singer needs to own a collection of early Italian songs and arias. There are numerous publications to choose from. Do your own research. Most recital repertoire for a half recital or junior recital will be chosen from one of these collections of early songs. For a senior recital, or full recital, there are some selections listed below which are not exhaustive, but will get you started exploring some more contemporary Italian repertoire for your voice.

BARBARA STROZZI (1619–1664)

The prolific and gifted composer Barbara Strozzi was a colorful figure of seventeenth century Venice. Her songs are marked by theatrical temperament and because she herself was a fine singer, a somewhat virtuosic use of the voice. These songs are fine examples of her art. All voices.

Amor, non dormir più
Spesso, per entro al petto (Cicognini)
Con male nuove, non si puo cantare
Penasci ben mio core

GIOACHINO ROSSINI (1792–1848)

La regata veneziana
Anzoleta avanti la regata
Anzoleta co passa la regata
Anzoleta dopo la regata

Rossini's *La regata veneziana (The Venetian Regatta)* is a favorite of mezzos and audiences. A singer with good dramatic sensibilities can perform this cycle with panache. The simple story is like a tiny opera: Anzoleta watches and waves from her window as her lover Momolo goes to the starting line with his gondola; her emotions are uncontrollable as she watches his progress anxiously during the regatta; and finally, she presents the winner's trophy to him, along with several kisses.

GAETANO DONIZETTI (1797–1848)

For the most part, Donizetti's songs are not among his memorable vocal works. Although he composed more than 250 examples in the genre, many remain unpublished. A number of these works are in the Neapolitan dialect. They tend toward bland accompaniments and simple melodies. Without the aid of really fine poetry, they lack the dramatic interest of his operas. That being said, judicious choices in the hands of a fine interpreter can produce effective results. Below are some choices. Intermediate. All voices.

Ah! Rammenta, o bella Irene (Pietro Metastasio)
Il barcaiolo (L. Tarantini)
Me voglio fà na casa (Canzone napoletana)

VINCENZO BELLINI (1801–1835)

Most nineteenth-century "art songs," were composed for gifted amateurs to perform in gatherings in private homes. They were akin to little arias. Bellini, Donizetti, Rossini, and Verdi composed in this opera-centered style. Bellini's *Sei ariette* are lovely examples, smaller in scale than those found in his operas, but no less demanding. Several are not as well known as are the Bellini songs we hear frequently. All of these take vocal control and are recommended for intermediate to advanced singers. This is not a cycle, so pick and choose. All voices.

Sei ariette
Malinconia, ninfa gentile (Ippolito Pindemonte)
Vanne, o rosa fortunata (Anonymous)
Bella Nice, che d'amore (Anonymous)
Almen, se non poss'io (Anonymous)

Per pietà, bell' idol mio (Pietro Metastasio)

Ma rendi pur contento (Pietro Metastasio)

GIUSEPPE VERDI (1813–1901)

Perduta ho la pace (Luigi Balestri, translated from the German of Johann Wolfgang von Goethe)

Here is the Italian Gretchen at the spinning wheel, and it has all the hallmarks of a little Verdi aria. Verdi composed only about twenty-five songs but some material from them appears much later in Verdi operas. This is a fine example. Women's voices.

Deh, pietoso, oh addolorata (Luigi Balestri, translated from the German of Johann Wolfgang von Goethe)

The companion song to the one above. Now Margarete prays to the Virgin to have pity on her and her overwhelming sense of guilt. Consistently simple piano part, vocal line a short dotted-note anacrusis into a long high note (a favorite figure of Verdi's). Intermediate to advanced. Women's voices.

Lo spazzacamino (S.M. Maggioni)

This is the song of a little chimney sweep touting his services. The charm and mood of this song—one of Verdi's most popular—brings to mind the character of Oscar in *Un ballo in maschera*, full of mischief and fun, and thoroughly ingratiating. Soprano, mezzo, tenor.

FRANCESCO PAOLO TOSTI (1846–1916)

Tosti was a popular song composer of the late Victorian and Edwardian period. His songs number in the hundreds. Great singers of the day, Caruso and Melba among them, sang his songs. Tenors love these songs, and sopranos can sing them also; in fact, they are suitable to all voices. Just do a bit of exploring.

Malìa (Emanuele Pagliara)

Two stanzas, set strophically. Delicate, tuneful melody in an ardent mood, set in waltz rhythm. Each stanza has two mini-sections, dominated by sequential phrases. Intermediate to advanced. Tenors, sopranos.

Ideale (Carmelo Errico)

Another much-performed Tosti song. A dream of the ideal one is recalled. Tosti excelled at composing songs of operatic scope on texts about love. This song fits neatly into that category. Intermediate to advanced. Tenors, sopranos.

Also see:
Mattinata
Aprile
L'ultima canzone
Lamento d'amore

STEFANO DONAUDY (1879–1925)

Donaudy's reputation as a song composer rests solely on thirty-six songs, titled *Arie di stile antico*, published in two volumes. These are charming songs emulating the *bel canto* style. Beautiful *cantabile* melodies as well as more spirited songs. Best for tenors or sopranos. Intermediate to advanced.

Amorosi miei giorni
O del mio amato ben
Freschi luoghi, prati aulenti
Vaghissima sembianza

FRANCESCO SANTOLIQUIDO (1883–1971)

Tre poesie persiane is beautifully evocative of Middle Eastern atmosphere: mysterious, exotic, languid. Vocal writing a mix of quasi-declamatory and sung phrases. Piano textures are transparent, fluid. Intermediate and advanced. All voices.

Tre poesie persiane
Quando le domandai (Negi de Kamare)
Io mi levai dal centro della terra (Omar Khayyam)
Lo domandai (Abu-Said)

MARIO CASTELNUOVO-TEDESCO (1895–1968)
Recuerdo (Edna St. Vincent Millay)

Demands an excellent pianist. Rocking rhythms image the ferry in the poem. Languid. Accompaniment, tempos, and mood change with the sections of the poem. Melodic and appealing. Compare with John Musto and Ricky Ian Gordon's settings. Intermediate to advanced. All voices.

SPANISH and SOUTH AMERICAN ART SONG

ENRIQUE GRANADOS (1867–1916)

Selections from *Tonadillas* (Fernando Periquet)

Amor y odio

El tra la la y el punteado

Callejeo

El majo discreto

El majo timido

These texts illustrate the "majos" and "majas" (men and women) of the eighteenth century Madrid made popular in Goya's paintings. A *tonadilla* is a song of theatrical character, first used as intermezzos, then developing into miniature operas. There are twelve songs total (only one is suitable for a male singer). Brilliant set of songs that captures the color and flavor of Spain in the guitar-like figures in the piano, and vocal writing rooted in Spanish traditions. Intermediate to advanced. Women's voices.

MANUEL DE FALLA (1876–1946)

Siete canciones populares españolas

El paño moruno

Séguidilla murciana

Asturiana

Jota

Nana

Canción

Polo

De Falla's stylized settings of Spanish folk songs have become staples in the Spanish art song repertoire. This cycle features brilliant piano parts with harmonies that evoke the guitar, in themes and figures derived from the songs themselves. The seven songs make the strongest effect when performed as a group. Their order, balance, and contrast in mood and tonality is meticulously planned. Advanced. All voices.

JOAQUÍN NIN (1879–1949)

Minué cantado (José Bassa)

Graceful melody in a transparent texture. Delicately drawn, simple vocal line coupled with straightforward piano figures reminiscent of the Spanish *vihuela*. Beautifully lyric, unpretentious and charming. All voices.

Paño murciano (arr. Spanish popular song)

Nin's setting of a characteristic folk song. Needs facile articulation from the singer, and requires a competent pianist. Lively rhythms in the song are that of the *guajira*, a Spanish dance. Mezzos or baritones.

Montañesa (arr. Spanish popular song)

Open fifths in the piano introduction create a reflective mood. Languid melismas embellish the vocal phrases throughout and are repeated at various points in the piano. Melodic material is the dominant element, underscored with a chordal accompaniment of wide range and open texture—an elegant *sarabande*. All voices.

JOAQUÍN TURINA (1882–1949)

Poema en forma de canciones, Op. 19 (Ramon de Campoamor)
Dedicatoria (piano solo)
Nunca olvida . . .
Cantares
Los dos miedos
Las locas por amor

Texture and harmony of these songs are more complex than Granados's *Tonadillas*, though they are immediately appealing for their romantic lyricism, color, and dramatic interpretation of the text. Requires a fine pianist. Advanced. High voices.

Tu pupila es azul (Gustavo Adolfo Bécquer)

Romantic, lyrical vocal phrases. After the opening phrase, each stanza is given a different melodic treatment. Accompaniment figures vary, ranging from a small staccato motives, to romantic arpeggiated figures, to guitar-like gestures at the end of the piece.

JESÚS GURIDI (1886–1961)

Seis canciones castellanas
Allá arriba in aquella montaña
Non quiero tus avellanas
¡Sereno!
Llámale con el pañuelo
¡Como quieres que adivine!
Mañanita de San Juan

These are six Castilian melodies harmonized by Guridi in highly original settings that add colorful, modern harmonies to the folk-like melodic vocal lines. All voices, but probably best suited to mezzos or baritones. Songs can certainly be excerpted from the group—tenors and sopranos might want to take a look also. Intermediate to advanced.

HEITOR VILLA-LOBOS (1887–1959)

Canção do poeta do século XVIII (Alfredo Ferreira)
Villa-Lobos has blended an archaic-styled vocal melody with harmonies in the piano that are decidedly contemporary. Mood is dreamy and reflective. Poem tells of a poet, dreaming of walking with his beloved in the moonlight. Not difficult, a charming song. All voices.

FEDERICO MOMPOU (1893–1987)

Combat del somni (Josep Janés)
Damunt de tu nomes les flors (1949)
Aquesta nit un mateix vent (1946)
Jo es pressentia com la mar (1948)

Mompou was half French and half Catalán by birth. He studied and worked in Paris in the last years of the nineteenth century. The cycle is perhaps closest to the characteristic style of Mompou's music—elegant and streamlined settings of atmospheric poetry. Each of the texts are melancholy, dreamlike, and abstract. The flowing melodies, simple and folk-like, have accompaniments that are quite French in style. Advanced. All voices.

FERNANDO OBRADORS (1897–1945)

Del cabello más sutil

Stunningly beautiful, long-lined melody. Vocal phrases are graceful and flowing. The piano part, consisting of arpeggios, is challenging. Despite its passionate avowal of love, Obradors's setting remains romantic and lyric. Text is gender-specific (male), however, this song could be sung by all voices. Intermediate difficulty.

El Vito (Spanish popular song)

"El Vito" was all the rage around Madrid around 1800. The *vito* is a Spanish dance, designed to be danced atop a table. Highly rhythmic setting. Variations in rhythmic stresses in voice and piano are reminiscent of castanets. All voices except very light.

JOAQUÍN RODRIGO (1901–1999)

Cuatro madrigales amatorios: Inspirados en música española del siglo XVI

¿Con que la lavaré?
Vos me matásteis
¿De dónde venis, amore?
De los alamos vengo, madre

Amatory madrigals (expressions of love) provide the texts and melodies for this cycle, probably the best-known of Rodrigo's vocal works. Skillful and attractive arrangements of well-known Spanish songs of the 16th century. Advanced. Sopranos.

CARLOS GUASTAVINO (1912–2000)

La rosa y el sauce (Francesco Silva)

A beautiful, spacious melody with opulent lyricism. Intermediate. All voices.

Se equivocó la paloma (Rafael Alberti)

The flustered dove, who has lost her way, is evoked in voice and piano using a five-note melodic cell that links both vocal and piano textures throughout. The cell repeats over and over again, as the dove realizes she cannot find her destination. All voices.

Bonita rama de sauce (Arturo Vasquez)
A lilting melody that employs syncopation and some alternation of major-minor materials. Intermediate. All voices.

XAVIER MONTSALVATGE (1912–2002)
Cinco canciones negras
Cuba dentro de un piano (Rafael Alberti)
Punto de Habanera (Siglo XVIII) (Néstor Luján)
Chévere (Nicolás Guillén)
Canción de cuna para dormir a un negrito
(Ildefonso Pereda Valdés)
Canto negro (Yoruba words)

Montsalvatge deftly integrates lush harmonic textures with sensual melodies, and a diverse array of moods. West Indies rhythms and musical style permeate the music, set to a seemingly eclectic set of poems by modern poets, but the texts are bound together by underlying themes: the disintegration of a native culture, colonialism, and racism.

ALBERTO GINASTERA (1916–1983)
Canción al árbol del olvido (Fernán Silva Valdés)
Haunting melody in a *tango* rhythm. Three stanzas, unified by an *ostinato* rhythm in the piano. Some of the accompanying figures are guitar-like. The poem refers to the tree where souls near death go to find release. All voices.

Cinco canciones populares argentinas
Chacerera
Triste
Zamba
Arrorró
Gato

These five songs cofrrespond to de Falla's *Seven Popular Spanish Songs* in that they are stylized settings of folk songs. Using anonymous traditional texts, Ginastera set five types of Argentine folk song/dance forms: *chacarera, triste, zamba, arrorró*, and *gato*. Challenging rhythmically. Vibrant settings. Advanced. Lower voices best.

ARNE DØRUMSGAARD (1921–2006), arranger

Volume 1 of Dørumsgaard's *Canzone Scordate* is titled *Ten Early Spanish Songs* (1450–1523) and contains a selection of beautifully realized sixteenth-century songs. These make interesting recital pieces, and the four songs listed below could well comprise a complete group. These are very suitable for early study of Spanish songs. Medium voices.

Con amores, la mi madre (Juan de Anchieta)

Serene melody decorated with some delicate vocal fioritura. Dørumsgaard also embroiders the introductory measures in the piano.

Pámpano verde (Francisco de la Torre)

Tender lyrical melody, accompanied by *pizzicato* figures that evoke the *vihuela*. Concludes with the voice humming the first two vocal phrases. Delicate setting perfectly captures atmosphere of fifteenth-century Spain.

De Antequera sale el Moro (Cristóbal de Morales)

A mysterious, dramatic narrative: a Moor leaves his home, Antequera, carrying letters of sorrow, written with his own blood—the blood of 120 years of suffering. Fluctuating meter follows the text stresses.

A la caza, sus, a caza (Gabriel Mena)

Delightful evocation of the hunt for love, in which everyone who joins finds sweetness as well as sadness. Highly rhythmic and energetic.

Crossover Repertoire

The list of American song above does not take into consideration the vocal contributions to the musical theater of Leonard Bernstein, George Gershwin, Richard Rodgers and Lorenz Hart, Richard Rodgers and Oscar Hammerstein II, Marc Blitzstein, Stephen Sondheim, Jerome Kern, Harold Arlen, and Cole Porter. Songs from stage works by these composers have become a viable fixture on recital programs within the last decade. Many of these songs contain texts, musical settings, and dramatic/emotional content that warrant performance in a concert setting. Musical sensitivity as well as response to textual nuance is needed for effective and communicative performances of these songs. This literature deserves to be programmed and heard more frequently on recitals.

In addition to these "pop" standards, there are selections from "Broadway Operas"—scenes or arias from theatre works that are sometimes termed operas but whose real genre is arguable. They do not easily fit into a neat category.

Some of these include: *Porgy and Bess, West Side Story, Kismet, Regina, Street Scene, The Most Happy Fella, Candide,* and *Sweeney Todd.*

Choosing Literature

Connection with the text should be the starting place for the choice of any recital repertoire, and crossovers are no exception. Interpretive expression should be a primary goal. Pick songs which suit you as a singer, and which have a variety of mood and characterization—in short, the rules of good programming hold true. You want interesting groups, good key relations, mood, tempo, and dramatic variations.

What Not to Sing:

- Songs you are uncomfortable with. Exploration of this repertoire will yield enough to keep your recitals filled for years, but a song that requires a performance over and above what you can deliver is wrong for you. If you are uncomfortable singing the lyrics or uncomfortable with the musical demands, choose something else.

- Do not sing songs so popularly identified with certain artists that the face of that person appears before your listeners when you begin to sing.

- Do not sing overexposed standards—songs that are so popular your audience practically begins to hum along when the verse is over and you launch into the chorus of the song (they may not know the verse!). Numerous musical theater songs have stood the test of time, just as countless classical art songs have. Be sure your choices have musical integrity and lasting power.

Note: Annotations are given for repertoire that may not be as well known as most selections on the list.

ERIK SATIE (1866–1925)
La diva de l'Empire
Je te veux
Allons-y Chochotte
Tendrement
Four "café concert" selections. Satie composed these with some regularity from 1900–1904. Several are cakewalks flavored with ragtime; two are romantic waltzes.

JEROME KERN (1885–1945)
Ol' Man River from *Show Boat*
Bass, baritone

Bill from *Show Boat*
Lonely Feet from *Sweet Adeline*
Not a Kern "standard" but it might be. A charming soliloquy from a wallflower at a dance.

All the Things You Are from *Very Warm for May*
The Song Is You from *Music in the Air*

COLE PORTER (1891–1964)
The Tale of the Oyster from *Fifty Million Frenchmen*
All voices

Where Is the Life That Late I Led? from *Kiss Me, Kate*
The Physician
Miss Otis Regrets

GEORGE GERSHWIN (1898–1937)
In the Mandarin's Orchid Garden from *Ming Toy*
A little known Gershwin song from an unproduced musical, composed after his journey to Paris and work with Ravel. It is Gershwin's "take" on a French *mélodie*, and has the delicacy of a Japanese print.

Someone to Watch Over Me from *Oh, Kay!*
Just Another Rhumba from *A Damsel in Distress*
Cut from the show.

Isn't It A Pity from *Pardon My English*
By Strauss
Performed by the Gershwins at private parties.

Summertime from *Porgy and Bess*

It Ain't Necessarily So from *Porgy and Bess*

FRANCIS POULENC (1899–1963)

Les Chemins de l'amour

C'est ainsi que tu es from *Métamorphoses*

Carte postale from *Quatre poèmes d'Apollinaire*

Le Tragique histoire de Petit René

A sa guitare

KURT WEILL (1900–1950)

Berlin im Licht-Song (Kurt Weill)

Nanna's Lied (Bertolt Brecht)
Soprano, mezzo soprano

My Ship from *Lady in the Dark* (Ira Gershwin)

Lonely House from *Street Scene* (Langston Hughes)

Youkali: Tango Habanera (Roger Fernay)

Le Roi d'Acquitaine from *Marie Galante*

Les Filles de Bordeaux from *Marie Galante*

That's Him from *One Touch of Venus* (Ogden Nash)

I'm a Stranger Here Myself from *One Touch of Venus* (Ogden Nash)

Speak Low from *One Touch of Venus* (Ogden Nash)

Mrs. Maurrant's Soliloquy: Somehow I Never Could Believe from *Street Scene*
Soprano

What Good Would the Moon Be? from *Street Scene*
Soprano

It Never Was You from *Knickerbocker Holiday*

September Song from *Knickerbocker Holiday*

Lost in the Stars from *Lost in the Stars*

The Saga of Jenny from *Lady in the Dark*

Pirate Jenny from *Threepenny Opera*

Solomon Song from *Threepenny Opera*

Barbara Song from *Threepenny Opera*

RICHARD RODGERS (1902–1979) and
LORENZ HART (1895–1943)

> He Was Too Good to Me from *Simple Simon*
> Falling in Love with Love from *The Boys from Syracuse*
> My Romance from *Jumbo*
> With a Song in My Heart from *Spring Is Here*
> Spring Is Here from *I Married an Angel*
> Manhattan from *Makers of Melody*
> To Keep My Love Alive from *A Connecticut Yankee*
> It Never Entered My Mind from *Higher and Higher*
> My Heart Stood Still from *A Connecticut Yankee*
> I Could Write a Book from *Pal Joey*

RICHARD RODGERS (1902–1979) and
OSCAR HAMMERSTEIN II (1895–1960)

> Lonely Room from *Oklahoma!*
> Out of My Dreams from *Oklahoma!*
> Mister Snow from *Carousel*
> Something Wonderful from *The King and I*
> I Have Dreamed from *The King and I*
> You'll Never Walk Alone from *Carousel*
> Soliloquy from *Carousel*

HAROLD ARLEN (1905–1986)

> Over the Rainbow from *The Wizard of* Oz
> Women's voices

MARC BLITZSTEIN (1905–1964)

> The Nickel Under the Foot from *The Cradle Will Rock*
> Mezzo soprano

> The Cradle Will Rock from *The Cradle Will Rock*
> Away! / The Best Thing of All from *Regina*
> A musical theater cavatina-cabaletta. Mezzo soprano.

> What Will It Be for Me? from *Regina*
> Soprano

> Blues from *Regina*

FRANK LOESSER (1910–1969)
Somebody, Somewhere from *The Most Happy Fella*
Soprano

Joey, Joey, Joey from *The Most Happy Fella*
Baritone

LEONARD BERNSTEIN (1918–1990)
Some Other Time from *On the Town*
Lonely Town from *On the Town*
I Can Cook Too from *On the Town*
Lonely Town from *On the Town*
Who Am I? from *Peter Pan*
Will You Build Me a House? from *Peter Pan*
Never-Land from *Peter Pan*
I Am Easily Assimilated from *Candide*
It Must Be Me from *Candide*
Glitter and Be Gay from *Candide*
Coloratura soprano

There's a Place for Us from *West Side Story*
Maria from *West Side Story*
Somewhere from *West Side Story*
One Hundred Ways (to Lose a Man) from *Wonderful Town*

MADELEINE DRING (1923–1977)
Song of a Nightclub Proprietress
Mezzo soprano

HARVEY SCHMIDT (b. 1929)
Much More from *The Fantasticks*
Soprano, mezzo soprano

Try to Remember from *The Fantasticks*
Baritone

Old Maid from *110 in the Shade*
Mezzo soprano

STEPHEN SONDHEIM (b. 1930)

Losing My Mind from *Follies*
Could I Leave You? from *Follies*
I Remember from *Evening Primrose*
Send in the Clowns from *A Little Night Music*
Johanna from *Sweeney Todd*
Pretty Women from *Sweeney Todd*
Children Will Listen from *Into the Woods*
Ladies Who Lunch from *Company*
Green Finch and Linnet Bird from *Sweeney Todd*
The Miller's Son from *A Little Night Music*
Anyone Can Whistle *from Anyone Can Whistle*

ANDREW LLOYD WEBBER (b. 1948)

Tell Me on a Sunday from *Song and Dance*
Mezzo soprano, soprano

NOTES

1   Pierre Bernac, *The Interpretation of French Song* (New York: W.W. Norton, Inc., 1976), 215.

2   Ibid., 281.

Afterword

Though we travel the world over to find the beautiful,
we must carry it with us, or we find it not.
—Ralph Waldo Emerson

A performer is a perpetual work in progress. Always be a student. Shun the *status quo*. Singers have been given the gift of communication—of capturing the vision of both the composer and the poet—and we need to cherish, nurture, and ultimately share that gift. Constantly seek out new repertoire that suits your voice and performing persona, and for new formats in which to perform it. New ideas are not necessarily unwelcome ideas; however, we do not have to constantly reinvent ourselves as performers. But we *do* need to keep developing and stretching our imaginations. In the final analysis, it boils down to this: you have to know who you are, and you have to be honest with the music you sing.

I attended high school in a small rural town. As was the case in most small country towns, all of the young people belonged to 4-H Clubs. The 4-H Club oath pledged "Head, Heart, Hands, and Health to serving community, country, and world."

I propose that singers keep the following "H's" in mind—they might be referred to and easily remembered as "the 3 H's."

- **HONESTY** Creating beauty is a *precious* opportunity. Respect the poetry, respect its musical setting, and be honest as a communicator.

- **HUMILITY** Creating beauty is a *unique* opportunity. Re-creating a song in performance is not about the self, but about the material.

- **HAPPINESS** Creating beauty is an *astonishing* opportunity. If the performer has completely prepared himself for the task, he will experience the greatest joy in sharing this with his listeners.

The singer's journey comes to an end onstage, performing art songs which are the products of linking the arts of poetry and music. Our investment of time, talent, and energy results in sharing beauty with others.

Distinguished French singer Jane Bathori wrote: "Tell yourself well that we are never finished learning and that in the art of singing as in every other art, one continually evolves and progresses until his last days." [1] We need to continually *challenge ourselves*. It is a never-ending process, this amazing journey from the page to the stage. For the committed artist/performer, it is simply a part of being a singer.

—Carol Kimball
May, 2012

NOTES

1   Jane Bathori, *Conseils du chant* (Paris: Schola Contorum, 1931), 19.

Appendix 1

The Poetry Poll

I thought it would be interesting to survey a number of colleagues who work with art song on a regular basis (singers, voice teachers, collaborative pianists and composers) to name a favorite poem and state why they chose it. For anyone who deals with art song daily, this proved to be a very frustrating task. The totality of repertoire that we study and perform during a lifetime in music is immense; therefore, the number of poems we have sung and played is formidable. Everyone taking part in this exercise found it to be almost impossible to pick "just one," writing comments such as: *"OK, this is so difficult…"; "I've thought and thought about this and it's so hard to come up with a favorite . . . each time I think of one I love, another one pops up and I can't pick my favorite"; "Initially, I found this somewhat like the 'pack-your-bags-and-choose-ten composers-only' for the trip to some remote desert isle! I quickly shed that frustration because, clearly, none of us could earmark one favorite poem that has been set to music!"; "Picking a favorite poem is like picking a favorite child . . . some are easier to love than others, but sometimes they snuggle up with you, touch your heart, and they become your new favorite . . .,"* and so on.

Interestingly, three people chose the same poem, but that was the only instance of duplication. One could see that people chose poems not only with the words of the poems in mind, but the musical setting of the poems as well. Most everyone mentioned the poem's setting by a particular composer. It bears pointing out the statement by composer Jacques Leguerney that in the best art songs the words and music are "…inseparable. The best poems are the ones in which you cannot read the poetry alone without thinking at once about the music."[1]

Here are some results of my "poem poll." The next time you find a poem you really connect with, try to put into words why you feel a bond with those particular words.

DEBORAH RAYMOND, SOPRANO
Associate Professor of Voice, Northern Arizona University

Die Nacht   by Hermann von Gilm zu Rosenegg

"I am touched by the mysterious quality of this poem, as it describes everything the night gently steals—from light to colors to gold. It paints such a unique picture of the power of night, which I have felt often while walking my pug Canio very late at night. It's not frightening, but it is in a subtle way, overpowering. Then at the end comes the thought-provoking sentence "O die Nacht, mir bangt, sie stehle / Dich mir auch."

Die Nacht

Aus dem Walde tritt die Nacht,
Aus den Bäumen schleicht sie leise,
Schaut sich um im weitem Kreise,
Nun gib acht.

Alle Lichter dieser Welt,
Alle Blumen, alle Farben
Löscht sie aus und stiehlt die Garben
Weg vom Feld.

Alles nimmt sie, was nur hold,
Nimmt das Silber weg des Stromes,
Nimmt vom Kupferdach des Domes
Weg das Gold.

Ausgeplündert steht der Strauch,
Rücke näher, Seel an Seele;
O die Nacht, mir bangt, sie stehle
Dich mir auch.

Night

Night steps from the wood,
she steals softly from the trees,
gazes around her in a wide arc,
now beware.

All this world's lights,
all the flowers, all the colors
she extinguishes, and steals the sheaves
from the field.

She takes all that is beautiful,
takes the silver from the stream,
and from the cathedral's copper roof
she takes the gold.

The bushes stand plundered,
come closer, soul to soul;
oh, I fear, the night will steal
you also, from me.

—Hermann von Gilm zu Rosenenegg,

THOMAS GRUBB
French Vocal Repertoire and Diction, The Juilliard School
Author, Singing in French
Coach, New York City Opera

C'est l'extase   by Paul Verlaine

"Who would not like the Fêtes galantes of Verlaine, set by either Fauré or Debussy? It's the apogee of French poetry and mélodie, in that order and in my opinion, especially the second set by Debussy. Also, 'En sourdine' by Fauré will always remain one of my favorite mélodies. It is almost perfect . . ."

C'est l'extase	It is languorous ecstasy
C'est l'extase langoureuse,	It is languorous ecstasy.
C'est la fatigue amoureuse,	It is amorous fatigue,
C'est tous les frissons des bois	It is all the trembling of the woods
Parmi l'étreinte des brises,	In the breezes' embrace,
C'est vers les ramures grises	It is, in the gray branches,
Le chœur des petites voix.	The choir of tiny voices.
O le frêle et frais murmure!	O the frail, fresh murmuring!
Cela gazouille et susurre,	The twittering and whispering,
Cela ressemble au cri doux	Is like the soft cry
Que l'herbe agitée expire...	The ruffled grass gives out…
Tu dirais, sous l'eau qui vire,	You might say, like the muted rolling
Le roulis sourd des cailloux.	Of pebbles in the swirling stream.
Cette âme qui se lamente	This soul which mourns
En cette plainte dormante	In this sleepy complaint,
C'est la nôtre, n'est-ce pas?	Is ours, is it not?
La mienne, dis, et la tienne,	Mine, and yours,
Dont s'exhale l'humble antienne	Breathing our humble hymn
Par ce tiède soir, tout bas?	On this warm evening, very softly?

—Paul Verlaine

LORI LAITMAN, COMPOSER

If I can stop one Heart from breaking   by Emily Dickinson

"'If I . . .' was composed as a gift for my father's eightieth birthday. I have often turned to Emily Dickinson when composing songs as gifts."

If I can stop one Heart from breaking

If I can stop one Heart from breaking,
I shall not live in vain;
If I can ease one Life the Aching
Or cool one Pain,
Or help one fainting Robin
Unto his Nest again,
I shall not live in Vain.

—Emily Dickinson

JENNIFER BRYANT, D.M.A., SOPRANO
Adjunct voice faculty, Mississippi State University
Birmingham Southern College

"My favorite poem is Emily Dickinson's 'If I can stop one Heart from breaking.' This poem is a life motto for me. The joy that you feel from helping someone in need is far greater than any joy that you can give yourself. I believe that meaningful relationships are the purpose in life."

JULINE GILMORE, D.M.A., MEZZO SOPRANO
Adjunct voice faculty, University of Nevada, Las Vegas

If I can stop one Heart from breaking   by Emily Dickinson

"My reason for loving this poem is centered around the importance of service, of caring for others, of helping the less fortunate or those hurting. I don't know whether Dickinson was speaking from experience here, but probably so. I assume, based on her other poems, that she lived through the pain and then wrote this as a reflection of regret, or as a warning to the reader to avoid such pain. Or it simply means to live a life of service. Regardless, this poem speaks to me and my desire to live life with purpose."

BURR COCHRAN PHILLIPS
Associate Professor of Voice, Conservatory of Music,
University of the Pacific, Stockton California

Beau soir   by Paul Bourget
"I chose this poem because of its atmosphere, simplicity, and utter direct
description of the cycle of life and the journey we all navigate."

Beau soir

Lorsque au soleil couchant
   les rivières sont roses,

Et qu'un tiède frisson court
   sur les champs de blé,

Un conseil d'être heureux semble sortir
   des choses

Et monter vers le cœur troublé;

Un conseil de goûter le
   charme d'être au monde,

Cependant qu'on est jeune et que
   le soir est beau,

Car nous nous en allons comme
   s'en va cette onde:

Elle à la mer, nous au tombeau!

Beautiful Evening

When the rivers are rosy in
   the setting sun

And a warm breeze shivers
   across the wheat fields,

A suggestion to be happy seems to
   emanate from all things—

And rises towards the restless heart;

A suggestion to savor the pleasure
   of being alive,

While one is young and the evening
   is beautiful,

For we shall go, as this wave goes:

   It to the sea, we to the tomb!

—Paul Bourget

ALAN SMITH, D.M.A.
Director of Keyboard Collaborative Arts, Thornton School of Music,
University of Southern California
Chair of Keyboard Studies, Thornton School
Voice Faculty, Tanglewood Music Center

*"A poem that keeps surfacing again and again in my life is **[i carry your heart**
with me (I carry it in] by E. E. Cummings. I first came to know the poem*
through John Duke's beautiful setting. Since coming to know that poem as
an undergraduate student I have had the joy of being loved just as the poem
describes and have tried to live up to loving just as gloriously in return."

[i carry your heart with me (i carry it in]

i carry your heart with me (i carry it in

my heart) i am never without it (anywhere

i go you go, my dear; and whatever is done

by only me is your doing, my darling)

      i fear

no fate (for you are my fate, my sweet) i want

no world (for beautiful you are my world, my true)

and it's you are whatever a moon has always meant

and whatever a sun will always sing is you

here is the deepest secret nobody knows

(here is the root of the root and the bud of the bud

and the sky of the sky of a tree called life; which grows

higher than soul can hope or mind can hide)

and this is the wonder that's keeping the stars apart

i carry your heart (i carry it in my heart)

—E. E. Cummings

276

WANDA BRISTER, D.M.A., MEZZO SOPRANO
Associate Professor of Voice, Florida State University

Le ciel est par-dessous le toit   by Paul Verlaine
"I love this Verlaine poem, set so beautifully by Gabriel Fauré as 'Prison.' The fact that some beauty came from such a hurtful experience is part of 'our miracle of song.'"

Le ciel est par-dessous le toit

Le ciel est par dessous le toit
  Si bleu, si calme!
Un arbre, par-dessus le toit,
  Berce sa palme.

La cloche, dans le ciel qu'on voit,
  Doucement tinte.
Un oiseau sur l'arbre qu'un voit
  Chante sa plainte.

Mon Dieu, mon Dieu, la vie est là
  Simple et tranquille.
Cette paisible rumeur- là
  Vient de la ville.

Qu'as-tu fait, ô toi que voilà
  Pleurant sans cesse,
Dis, qu'as-tu fait, toi que voilà,

  De ta jeunesse?

The sky is above the roof

The sky is above the roof—
  So blue, so calm!
A tree, above the roof,
  Waves its crown.

In the sky that one sees, a bell
  Gently rings.
On the tree that one sees, a bird
  Plaintively sings.

My God, my God, life is there,
  Simple and tranquil.
That peaceful sound out there
  Comes from the town.

What have you done, o you there
  Weeping unceasingly,
Say, what have you done,
    you who are there,
  With your youth?

—Paul Verlaine

DAVID SANNERUD, D.M.A., BARITONE
Coordinator of Vocal Arts, California State University, Northridge

"Chausson's sensitive setting of Armand Silvestre's Quand ton sourire me surprit ('Le Charme') has always lifted me to a lovely place. Having sung and taught this mélodie, I have always felt so moved by the poet's sweet and simple exploration of how one's heart was conquered by the display of humanity from the tear of another. This is a delicate poem that I feel Chausson set perfectly."

Quand ton sourire me surprit (from Chansons des heures)

Quand ton sourire me surprit,
Je sentis frémir tout mon être,
Mais ce qui domptait mon esprit,
Je ne pus d'abord le connaître.

Quand ton regard tomba sur moi,
Je sentis mon âme se fondre,
Mais ce que serait cet émoi,
Je ne pus d'abord en répondre.

Ce qui me vainquit à jamais,
Ce fut un plus douloureux charme;
Et je n'ai su que je t'aimais,
Qu'en voyant ta première larme.

When your smile surprised me

When your smile surprised me,
I felt all my being tremble
But what had subdued my spirit,
At first I could not know.

When your glance fell on me,
I felt my soul melt,
But what this emotion was,
At first I could not understand.

What vanquished me forever,
Was a much sadder charm,
And I did not know that I loved you,
Until I saw your first tear.

—Armand Silvestre

JUDITH CLOUD, D.M.A., COMPOSER, MEZZO SOPRANO
Coordinator of Voice, Northern Arizona University

The Lamb   by William Blake

"I loved singing various settings of this poem as a child in church and later on as a music student. I've always been attracted to the spiritual in words and music. Blake's poetry, written from a child's point of view, appeals to the child in me. I also love the fact that Blake illustrated his poems."

The Lamb

Little Lamb, who made thee?
Dost thou know who made thee?
Gave thee life, and bid thee feed
By the stream and o'er the mead;
Gave thee clothing of delight,
Softest clothing, woolly, bright;
Gave thee such a tender voice,
Making all the vales rejoice?
Little Lamb, who made thee?
Dost thou know who made thee?

Little Lamb, I'll tell thee,
Little Lamb, I'll tell thee:
He is called by thy name,
For he calls himself a Lamb.
He is meek, and he is mild;
He became a little child.
I a child, and thou a lamb.
We are called by his name.
Little Lamb, God bless thee!
Little Lamb, God bless thee!

—William Blake

ROZA TULYAGANOVA, D.M.A., SOPRANO
Artist in Residence at Dicapo Opera Theater, New York City

Nastojashchuju nezhnost'   by Anna Akhmatova

"My choice is a poem by Anna Akhmatova, set by Prokofiev (Five Poems of Anna Akhmatova, Op. 27, No. 2). It's just so true and real. It's like singing with the soul. You either have it or you don't."

Nastojashchuju nezhnost'	True tenderness is silent
Nastojashchuju nezhnost' ne sputajesh'	True tenderness is silent
Ni s chem, i ona tikha.	and can't be mistaken for anything else.
Ty naprasno berezhno kutajesh'	In vain with earnest desire
Mne plechi i grud' v mekha	you cover my shoulders
	with fur;
I naprasno slova pokornyje	In vain you try to persuade me
Govorish' o pervoj ljubvi.	of the merits of first love.
Kak ja znaju `eti upornyje,	But I know too well the meaning
Nesytyje vzgljady tvoji!	of your persistent burning glances.
— Anna Akhmatova	—Anonymous translation

SERDAR ILBAN, D.M.A., BARITONE
Assistant Professor of Voice and Opera, Lamar University

Clair de lune by Paul Verlaine

"I think it is the subtlest and the most polite way of declaring love or admiration to someone—referring to their soul or being as a chosen landscape. The first line sells the poem for me. It's one of those lines that I wish I were talented enough to have written. Also, there is so much music in this poem already. I think it begged to be a song from the first moment it was imagined."

Clair de lune	Moonlight
Votre âme est un paysage choisi	Your soul is a chosen landscape
Que vont charmant masques et bergamasques,	Charmed by masks and bergamasks
Jouant du luth et dansant, et quasi	Playing the lute and dancing, and almost
Tristes sous leurs déguisements fantasques.	Sad beneath their fantastic disguises.
Tout en chantant sur le mode mineur	While singing in the minor key
L'amour vainqueur et la vie opportune.	Of victorious love and the good life,
Ils n'ont pas l'air de croire à leur bonheur,	They do not seem to believe in their happiness,
Et leur chanson se mêle au clair de lune,	And their song blends with the moonlight.
Au calme clair de lune triste et beau,	With the calm moonlight, sad and beautiful,
Qui fait rêver, les oiseaux dans les arbres,	That makes the birds dream in the trees,
Et sangloter d'extase les jets d'eau,	And the fountains sob with rapture,
Les grands jets d'eau sveltes parmi les marbres.	The tall slender fountains among the marble statues.

—Paul Verlaine

JEANETTE FONTAINE, D.M.A., MEZZO-SOPRANO
Instructor of Voice, Mississippi State University

The Tyger   by William Blake
*"I really love William Blake's poem 'The Tyger,' which has been set by Rebecca
Clarke ('The Tiger'). I prefer Blake's spelling, which symbolizes an ancient time. Like
much of Blake's poetry, there is an element of good vs. evil, God vs. the devil. I love
the comparison between 'the Tyger' and 'the Lamb' (Lamb of God perhaps?) and
the reference to the war in heaven and Lucifer's fall from grace ('When the stars
threw down their spears and water'd heaven with their tears'). Another favorite
moment is the alteration of one word between the first and last stanza. ('What
immortal hand or eye **could** frame thy fearful symmetry?' becomes 'What immortal
hand or eye **dare** frame thy fearful symmetry?') Blake was a genius!"*

The Tyger

Tyger! Tyger! burning bright,
In the forests of the night,
What immortal hand or eye,
Could frame thy fearful symmetry?

In what distant deeps or skies
Burnt the fire of thine eyes?
On what wings dare he aspire?
What the hand dare seize the fire?

And what shoulder & what art,
Could twist the sinews of thy heart?
And when thy heart began to beat,
What dread hand? & what dread feet?

What the hammer? what the chain,
In what furnace was thy brain?
What the anvil? what dread grasp,
Dare its deadly terrors clasp?

When the stars threw down their spears
And water'd heaven with their tears:
Did he smile his work to see?
Did he who made the Lamb make thee?

Tyger! Tyger! burning bright
In the forests of the night,
What immortal hand or eye,
Dare frame thy fearful symmetry?

—William Blake

DEBRA GRESCHNER, SOPRANO
Voice Faculty, Lamar University
Book Reviewer, Journal of Singing

The Taxi   by Amy Lowell

*"The choice of adjectives and verbs in this poem paint such strong pictures.
I know it has been set to music by Celius Dougherty, but I am hoping Nick*
will write one for me to sing."*

The Taxi

When I go away from you
The world beats dead
Like a slackened drum.
I call out for you against the jutted stars
And shout into the ridges of the wind.
Streets coming fast,
One after the other,
Wedge you away from me,
And the lamps of the city prick my eyes
So that I can no longer see your face.
Why should I leave you,
To wound myself upon the sharp edges of the night?

—Amy Lowell

*composer Nick Rissmann is Greschner's husband.

VEERA KHARE ASHER, D.M.A., SOPRANO
Producer and Creator of Pilates2Voice

Sure on this shining night   by James Agee

"This is a solemn poem. The text consists of simple and accessible words that when combined, create a deeper symbolic meaning. My interpretation evolved as I grew from a young artist to a mature artist. It is introspective and insightful but not religious. There is a feeling of a deep emotional appreciation for life, while at the same time addressing the journey to a higher place, beyond life and this earth."

Sure on this shining night

Sure on this shining night
Of star-made shadows round,
Kindness must watch for me
This side the ground.

The late year lies down the north,
All is healed, all is health.
High summer holds the earth.
Hearts all whole.

Sure on this shining night
I weep for wonder
wand'ring far alone
Of shadows on the stars.

—James Agee

TOD FITZPATRICK, D.M.A., BARITONE
Associate Professor of Voice, University of Nevada, Las Vegas

My Life's Delight   **by Thomas Campion**
"I love the unencumbered and energetic outpouring of love in this poem!"

My Life's Delight

Come, O come, my life's delight,
 Let me not in languor pine!
Love loves no delay; thy sight,
 The more enjoyed, the more divine:
O come, and take from me
The pain of being deprived of thee!

Thou all sweetness dost enclose,
 Like a little world of bliss.
Beauty guards thy looks: the rose
 In them pure and eternal is.
Come, then, and make thy flight
As swift to me, as heavenly light.

—Thomas Campion

KATHLEEN ROLAND-SILVERSTEIN, D.M.A., SOPRANO
Assistant Professor of Voice, Syracuse University,
Setnor School of Music
Author, Northern Lights: Swedish Song for Studio and Concert Stage

Flickan under nymånen   by Bo Bergman
*"This poem (and the 'romans' setting by Ture Rangström) is well beloved by
the Swedes, and is a perfect picture of that particularly Swedish mixture of
paganism, pantheism, and the connection between nature and human feeling."*

Flickan under nymånen
Jag har nigit för nymånens skära
Tre ting har jag önska mig tyst.
Det första är du, och det andra är du,
och det tredje är du, min kära.
Men ingen får veta ett knyst.

Jag har nigit för nymånens skära tre gånger till jorden nu.
Och om månen kan ge vad vi önska,
så önskar jag tre gånger till,
och krona jag här, när marken sig klär,
och björkarna gunga af grönska och lärkorna spela sin drill.

Det är långsamt att önska och önska.
O, vore min kära här!
Lyft nu upp honom, stormolnen,
på vingen och tag honom, våg,
på din rygg.

Han är ung som jag, han är varm som jag,
han är härlig och stark som ingen,
och säll skall jag sofva och trygg
in hans armar engång under vingen af natten,
tills natt blir dag.

—Bo Bergman

Girl under the New Moon

I have curtseyed to the crescent of the new moon
Three things have I silently wished for.
The first is you, the second is you, and the third is you, my love.
But none may know at all.
I have curtseyed to the new moon, three times now to the earth.
And if the moon can give me what I wish,
   so shall I wish three times more!
A crown I wear, when the earth is ready,
   and the birches swing green and the larks trill.
It is tiresome to wish and wish. Oh, were my love here!
Lift him up now, storm clouds, and take him, waves, on your back.
He is young, like I, he is warm like I, he is wonderful and strong,
   like no other!
And I shall sleep and be safe in his arms once again
   under the wings of the night,
until night becomes day.

—Translation by Kathleen Roland-Silverstein

REBECCA FOLSOM, D.M.A., MEZZO-SOPRANO
Voice Faculty, The Boston Conservatory

Morgen!   **by John Henry Mackay**

"The first time I heard the Richard Strauss setting, I was a first year graduate student attending a recital sung by Frederica von Stade (she has always been one of my favorite singers and was such a role model for me as a young lyric mezzo). Her performance of that piece brought me to tears and that had never happened to me before while listening to someone sing. Something in the way she delivered the text and expressed it through the musical phrasing touched the core of me."

Morgen!	Morning
Und morgen wird die Sonne wieder scheinen,	And tomorrow the sun will shine again,
und auf dem Wege, den ich gehen werde,	and the way that I take
wird uns, die Glücklichen*, sie wieder einen	will bring us together again, we happy ones,
in mitten dieser sonnenatmenden Erde…	in the midst of this sun-breathing earth…

Und zu dem Strand, dem weiten, wogenblauen,	And to the beach, the wide shore with blue waves,
werden wir still und langsam niedersteigen,	we will go quietly and slowly
stumm werden wir uns in die Augen schauen,	we will look silently into each other's eyes
und auf uns sinkt des Glückes stummes** Schweigen…	and the quiet of happiness will descendupon us.

*Mackay *[Seligen], **[grosses]

—John Henry Mackay

All translations by Carol Kimball, except where indicated

NOTES

1   Jacques Leguerney, in an interview with Mary DIbbern, Paris, France. Quotation used by permission. In Carol Kimball, *Song: A Guide to Art Song Style and Literature* (Milwaukee, WI: Hal Leonard Corp., 2005), 238.

Appendix 2

The Printed Program: Guidelines

"The time has come," the Walrus said,
"To talk of many things:
Of shoes and ships—and sealing wax
Of cabbages and kings."

—Lewis Carroll (from *Through the Looking-Glass*)

The recital program given to each member of the audience is an extension of you. It showcases your work in a different way than your musical performance does, but is nevertheless representative of you—in planning, format, program notes, texts and/or translations. In a sense it is a formal document, a souvenir of—it is hoped—a wonderful musical evening. I still have many recital programs that I can look at today and remember exactly how artistic and communicative the singer was—or was not. The good programs are remembrances of satisfying musical experiences. The not-so-good programs are generally full of mistakes of one sort or another—the repertoire and its formatting was not stellar. Therefore, you want your program to be as perfect as possible in format and content, with everything that those two terms encompass.

General Format: The Look of the Program

Your school may have a template for recitals that is mandatory for the front page and the program page (inside page). They may dictate the size of the paper and the number of pages. If you are working with a fairly simple program, one 8 ½ X 11 page folded in half, you will need to make decisions as to *how much print* you can easily fit on two pages, since the front page and inside front page will be taken up with the program. Many schools only print a leaflet, front and back. If this is the case, and you want to print program notes, you will need to do that *apart* from the program that will be printed by the music office.

In most instances, the singer turns his program into the music office where someone else who does not necessarily know vocal literature or the niceties of song titles in various languages sets it. Make sure that what you hand in is *absolutely accurate* and that you *keep a copy* for easy proofreading. *Insist* upon proofing the program *before* it goes to the printer. The music office will make sure that the format meets the department standards.

Between this step and the actual printing of the program, the singer has one more crucial task: **proofread**. There will always be typos, uppercase/lowercase mistakes, misspellings, and so on. If your teacher has time to proof the program, ask them to do so as well. This is after all, an example of your work and also an example of work coming from their studio.

1. Cover Page
School logo if there is an official format
Type of recital (Junior Recital, Senior Recital, Masters Recital,
   Doctoral Recital, or if not at a school, In Recital)
Singer's name and voice type
Pianist's name
Any other assisting artists' names
Date / venue / time

2. Program Page
Program (centered at top or flush left)
Program groups with composers' names and dates (set the groups
   apart from one another so they are clearly delineated as groups.
   See Appendix 3: Sample Programs for varying formats)
Poets (if space is a problem, the poets can be listed in the text/
   translation part of the program)
Note: Watch font size on the program page (12 pt. is a good rule of
   thumb), and program notes should be somewhat smaller (11 pt. is
   good, but no smaller than 10 pt.)

3. Program Notes, Texts and Translations

Depending on how large your program is, this section will vary in length. You may be able to print only program notes, only translations, or use paraphrases. If space is an issue, you might want to have a separate handout with program notes, texts and translations to accompany the program.

If foreign language texts and translations are printed, these should be in two columns and may be preceded by a short paragraph that speaks to the songs or the song cycle to be performed. Make sure that each line of the poem lines up with the correct line of translation. If you are printing full texts for foreign languages with translations, full texts for songs in English should be printed also if space permits.

Finally, *do not* print your program on colored paper. When going through old program files, I found a number of recitals printed on red, blue, or green paper in too-small or hard-to-read fonts. If a font is difficult to read on white, off-white, or ecru paper **it is going to be unreadable on colored paper**. Stick to white, or shades of white. A red or blue recital program doesn't guarantee a successful recital.

A Word About Fonts

The more decorative and ornate a font appears, the more difficult it will be to read. *Keep it simple*. There are hundreds of fonts available. Choose one that combines ease of reading and an elegance of presentation that fits the formal character of a recital. Thicker, heavier bold fonts appear too cumbersome and give the program a less streamlined look. Additionally, parts of the program will use boldface type that will render many fonts almost unreadable.

Often students think that the more flowery a font is, the more its curlicues will enhance the printed program. Not so! See the examples below. Use easy-to-read fonts and your program will look sleek, clean, and reader-friendly. All fonts are printed here in 14 pt. font size, and the font names are identified in parentheses.

This is difficult to read (Snell Roundhand)

This is also difficult to read (Lucida Blackletter)

Help! Too much! Amazingly, we see this one often! (Curlz MT)

This looks like a term paper (American Typewriter)

𝕿𝖍𝖎𝖘 𝖔𝖓𝖊 𝖎𝖘 𝖏𝖚𝖘𝖙 𝖘𝖈𝖆𝖗𝖞 (Blackmoor LET)

Try reading an entire program with this one (Bernard MT Condensed)

Be careful with this one! (Mona Lisa Solid IT ITT)

This font is just irritating (Bauhaus 93)

How informal can you get? (Handwriting Dakota)

Papyrus is often a favorite, but it gets old (Papyrus Condensed)

This is also a bit much (Zapfino)

Some suggestions for readable fonts: Arial, Geneva, Times, Times New Roman, Helvetica Neue, Verdana, Palatino. If you want a wee bit of more formal decoration: Cochin, Calabria, Didot. You need to experiment with font size. Some fonts are smaller than others, and you need to make sure your content is readable.

There are myriad numbers of fonts; the ones listed above are only suggestions. Search until you find the one that suits your visual specifications.

Example 1: A song group, written in Snell Roundhand, 16 pt., bold.

Fêtes galantes 1   *Claude Debussy*
> *En sourdine*
> *Fantoches*
> *Clair de lune*

Comments:

This group is a perfect example of a font that is too decorative for a program. It might work for a wedding invitation, but not for your recital. Try Palatino instead (see below).

Fêtes galantes 1   Claude Debussy
> En sourdine
> Fantoches
> Clair de lune

Example 2: An excerpt from program notes, written in Zapfino, 10 pt., bold.

Sweet Suffolk Owl   *(Richard Hundley)*

Hundley balances the witty mood of this Elizabethan verse with a slightly pompous accompaniment of heavy chords that retains a buoyant feeling throughout this brief song. The vocal lines feature dotted rhythms and gentle syncopation.

Comments:

If you must have a bit of decoration in your font, try using Didot.

Sweet Suffolk Owl   **(Richard Hundley)**

Hundley balances the witty mood of this Elizabethan verse with a slightly pompous accompaniment of thick chords that retains a buoyant feeling throughout this brief song. The vocal lines feature dotted rhythms and gentle syncopation.

Example 3: Choosing a too-small font

I would not use any font size smaller than 10 pt. on a program. This is not a vision exam, and you do not want your audience squinting to find out what you are going to sing.

This happened some years ago when I attended the recital of a distinguished professional artist. Most often, the program is sent to the hosting venue by the artist's management, and that office takes care of the typing and printing the program. In this case, the program was a one-fold 8 ½ X 11 page. This left three 3 pages for the program, any program notes, and the artists' bios. The secretary in charge typed everything in 8 pt. font, rendering the program page and bios of the artists frustratingly microscopic. If you forgot to bring your reading glasses, you were out of luck. See the lines below to compare Arial 10 pt. font with Arial 8 pt. font.

10 pt. font:

_____ Tonight's program features the premiere performance of a piece by American composer _____. The work was commissioned by the National Endowment for the Arts.

8 pt. font:

Example 4: Another example of fonts trumping format

In order to get all the information on one line, even using a smaller font size does not work. Another distinguished recitalist whose professional representative sent a program ahead to have it typed by the secretary in the office of the performing venue, had this happen to the program:

I

Selections from *Colección de tonadillas escritas en estilo antigua* (1912)
Enrique Granados
  La maja de Goya
  El mirar de la maja
  El majo timido
  La maja dolorosa (No. 2)
  El majo discreto

II

Rheinlegendchen, from *Des Knaben Wunderhorn*
Gustav Mahler
Liebst du um Schönheit (1902)
Blicke mir nicht in die Lieder (1901)
Lob des hohen Verstandes, from *Des Knaben Wunderhorn*

Comments:

The composers' names reverted to the left side of the page, under the title of the first song in the group. Some audience members might have been confused by this—possibly not—but this audience member was incredulous that no one in the office caught this little gaffe. In this situation, using the format that places the composers' names in caps on the left hand side of the program and the musical titles on the right would have provided enough wiggle room to place everything where it could be read easily.

What to Leave Out...

1. Effusive thanks at the end of the program expressing gratitude to your voice teacher, the voice faculty, your friends, family, and even the Almighty really have no place on a printed recital program. This is a formal document. As far as possible, the program should document you as a serious, committed performer. You probably will want to use the program later—perhaps to apply for graduate school or a young artist program, and there will be all those fussy "thank-you's" on the last page. Keep it professional! Deliver your thanks in person at the reception after the recital. There will be those readers who will insist this is a sacrosanct part of the printed program, but I respectfully beg to differ.

2. Spelling or punctuation errors. There should be none. This is a given.

3. Song titles written without proper lower case/upper case characters. These differ from language to language. Check the rules and stay consistent!

4. Decorative fonts that hinder ease of reading.

5. Font sizes that are too small to read comfortably in low light.

6. Materials or translations without the proper citations.

7. Program printed in light ink (example light white) on colored paper.

Perhaps this is the place to mention another practice which is proliferating in recitals—that of speaking to the audience about the pieces you are about to sing. If you have provided program notes, there is no need to break that fourth wall and be chatty with your audience. This little exercise usually trails off in some mood of embarrassment, either on your part, or that of the audience, and it is difficult to regain the professional atmosphere of the performance.

Sundry Slip-Ups

Example 1: Mixing Upper Case/Lower Case

VERGIN, TUTTO AMOR	Durante
DANZA, DANZA FANCIULLA GENTILE	Durante
SE TU M'AMI, SE SOSPIRI	Pergolesi

Comments:

This upper case/ lower case example is awkward, pairing all capital letters for the song titles and the composers' names in lower case,
without their first names *or* any dates.

Example 2: Excerpting Songs from a Cycle

If you are singing only *part* of a song cycle, it is not necessary to
put the numbers of the songs you have excerpted to sing. Instead, use
"Selections from" or even ". . . from _____"

Die Winterreise (Müller)   Franz Schubert

I.	Gute Nacht
II.	Die Wetterfahne
VII.	Auf dem Flusse
XIII.	Die Post
XXIV.	Der Leiermann

Comments:

The numbers of the songs excerpted from a cycle need not be
noted. If you cannot do without imparting this information to your
audience, do it in the program notes. It's neater. This recital had
three additional groups, formatted similarly, and it made the program
page look messy. The title of the cycle should always be italicized.
Schubert's dates should be noted. Compare the neatness of the format
below with the one above:

Selections from *Die Winterreise*, Op. 89 (Müller)   Franz Schubert
   Gute Nacht   (1797–1828)
   Die Wetterfahne
   Auf dem Flusse
   Die Post
   Der Leiermann

Example 3: Using numbers to delineate songs in a complete cycle

Le Bestiaire (Apollinaire)   Poulenc

        I.   Le Dromadaire

        II.   Le Chevre du Thibet

        III.   La Sauterelle

        VI.   Le Dauphin

        V.   L'Ecrevisse

        VI.   La Carpe

Comments:

Since all of this little cycle is being performed, there is really no need for numbering the songs, nor for the right justification of the Roman numerals, which have a typo besides. Listing the poet's full name would be nice. (Guillaume Apollinaire) and the first name of the composer (Francis Poulenc).

Example 4: Arabic numbers

Octaves and Sweet Sounds   R. Hundley
                                                              (b. 1931)

1. Strings in the Earth and Air   James Joyce
2. Seashore Girls   e. e. Cummings
3. Moonlight's Watermelon   Jose Garcia Villa
4. Straightway Beauty on Me Waits   James Purdy
5. Well Welcome   Gertrude Stein

Comments:

- Using Arabic numbers is just as messy as using Roman numerals. Leave them out. Audiences are intelligent enough to know that the second title is the second song in the group or cycle, and so forth. There were three cycles programmed on this recital, and in each case, Arabic numerals were used for each song in the cycle. It was superfluous, to say the least.

- In the example above, the composer's first name is not given, but all the poets for each song are listed with their full names. Again, please be consistent.

- The poet, e.e. cummings, can be written in lower case (as he wrote all his poems) or E.E. Cummings, but don't mix them up, as this listing did.

- Finally, the composer's name (Richard Hundley) should be moved farther right to make it easier to read the composer's name *and* the poets' names for each poem. A right justification of the poets' names makes reading the entire entry more difficult.

- This would have been easier to see if the following had been done: lose the numbers; put the poets' names in parentheses immediately following the song titles. For instance:

Octaves and Sweet Sounds   **Richard Hundley**
    Strings in the Earth and Air (James Joyce)   (b. 1931)
    Seashore Girls (e.e. cummings)

    and so on…

Example 5: More on excerpting from sets or volumes
Old American Songs, vol.I, II   Aaron Copland
    Zion's Walls
    At the River
    The Dodger
    Long Time Ago
    I Bought Me a Cat

Comments:

- Here is another case where "Selections from _____" would have worked.

- Copland's work is designated in "sets" and not "volumes." As they are given here, the Roman numerals do not specify *which* songs are in *which* set of the *Old American Songs*.

- *Old American Songs* should be italicized.

- Copland's dates should appear under his name

- Since the program notes for this group began with a sentence that states that there are two sets (not volumes) of songs, this might be left out altogether, or put in the program notes. *If* you specify set numbers, put them in parentheses *after the song title*, with Set capitalized. For instance:

Selections from *Old American Songs*   Aaron Copland
   Zion's Walls (Set 2)   (1900–1990)
   At the River (Set 2)
   The Dodger (Set 1)

     and so on…

Example 6: Do not forget your collaborators!

Here is the printed program line for Schubert's "The Shepherd on the Rock" with obbligato clarinet. It is missing the name of the clarinetist.

Der Hirt auf dem Felsen   **Franz Schubert**

Please place the name of the instrumentalist assisting you on a particular piece, centered *below* the musical title (see below) on the program page. Omitting the clarinetist's name on this particular work is *not* a good idea. The clarinetist is also a soloist, and is not there just to make you look good. This should read:

Der Hirt auf dem Felsen   **Franz Schubert**
                                           (1797–1828)

John Reed, clarinet

Also, do not forget to list any assisting artists' names on the front page of the program.

Setting the Tone: Program Notes

"When I use a word," Humpty Dumpty said in a rather scornful tone, "it means just what I choose it to mean— neither more nor less."

—Lewis Carroll (from *Through the Looking Glass*)

Program notes can run the gamut from *excellent*, through *boring*, to *terrible*, ending with *embarrassing*. Keep program notes short if the texts are printed; however, in most cases it is good to have a sentence or two to help guide the listener.

Admittedly, it's often difficult to strike the right tone in program notes. Don't talk down to your audience; this is not a scholarly paper.

Conversely, don't be too elementary; this is not a *Recitals for Dummies* book. The purpose of program notes is to provide your readers factual information about the work(s) you are singing—notes that will help them connect with the repertoire. Keep your notes fairly brief, but interesting. You do not want to overwhelm your audience with program notes that resemble a term paper.

Program notes should speak to the music and should not be simply biographical information about the composer. Printed comments should help clarify the musical and/or textual content of the pieces to be heard. Program notes should be short and to the point.

Paraphrasing

Paraphrasing song texts is tricky, and takes practice. Paraphrases are generally used when space is at a premium, to prevent having to print the entire poem. When foreign languages are being sung, instead of printing the poem in the original language and a translation, paraphrases in English are often used. Another option is to print the entire poem in English and not the original foreign language text.

If paraphrases are used, they are usually put below the song title. Often if the entire poem is printed in English, it goes in the same place. It really depends on how many pages the program contains and how much space you have.

Example 1: Paraphrases of poems

Here is an opening group of Mozart songs. Under each song's title is a well-done, brief paraphrase. The audience was directed to reserve applause for those points in the program indicated by asterisks. This broke the group for audience, singer, and pianist, and also effectively set up the final song in the group. Notice the formatting of composer's name and dates, centered.

Wolfgang Amadeus Mozart
(1756–1791)

Ridente la calma
> Contentment reposes in my soul
> For my beloved is bound to my heart with sweetest chains.

Der Zauberer
> Girls, watch out for Damoetas!
> Believe me, he's a magician.
> He caught me in his spell, but fortunately
> Mother came along just in time.

Das Veilchen
> A violet growing in the meadow
> Longed to be carried off by the shepherdess.
> Alas, the shepherdess came by
> And merely trampled the lovely flower underfoot.

Als Luise die Briefe ihres ungetreuen Liebhabers verbrannte
> Go into the flames, you ill-begotten love letters,
> For I know that your author wrote such lines to others, too.
> (But, alas, the memory of that man
> Will continue to burn in my heart.)

Un moto di gioia
> My heart beats with joy,
> For in love all sorrow will vanish. [1]

Example 2: Succinct and Informative Program Notes

Here is an example of a succinct program note that precedes full text translations in English. No foreign texts were given. The information in these notes describes the songs as a group.

Trois mélodies   **Manuel de Falla**

The young Spanish composer Manuel de Falla composed *Trois mélodies* in 1909 during an extended stay in Paris. Falla's exposure to French impressionsim is evident in his setting of these poems by Théophile Gautier. [2]

Les colombes
Chinoiserie
Séguidille

Comments:

In two sentences, we have the following information:

- Falla is a Spanish composer.

- Falla composed these songs in Paris in 1909 where he lived for a time.

- These *mélodies* contain musical influences of French impressionism

- Théophile Gautier is the poet.

The program note was followed by *each song title*, and a full English translation of that specific poem under the title. The original French was not printed, and if space is an issue, this is a perfectly good way to do this.

Example 3: Good program notes that reference each song in the group

In a program that opened with three art songs by Giuseppe Verdi (Perduta ho la pace; Deh, pietoso, oh Addolorata; and Lo spazzacamino), the singer wrote brief but informative program notes.

The first two songs of this group, *Perduta ho la pace* and *Deh, pietoso, oh Addolorata*, are Italian settings of German texts by Goethe. In both songs the character is Margarete, the unfortunate woman who falls in love with Faust, a man who has sold his soul to the Devil. The operatic quality of these works is apparent and lays the groundwork for Verdi's future heroines. The little chimney sweep in *Lo spazzacamino* ends the Italian group of a lighter note. His character is one of mischief and fun, and the effect is intoxicating. [3]

Comments:

The information in these notes described each song in the group rather than treating them as a group; however, they still told us that these works were all operatic in style and the characters in the texts could have been derivatives of Verdi's later operatic heroines. Below the notes were full texts and translations.

Example 4: Program notes in lieu of texts

> Songs occupy a special place in the music of Charles Ives. Throughout his creative life, he repeatedly turned to that medium, perhaps because he was not only profoundly musical, but also highly verbal. Viewed as a whole, Ives's song texts reflect a richness of outlook and experience consistent with his philosophy of taking in life to the fullest. The hymn tunes, village bands, personalities, color and history of his native New England inspired his songs. The four songs heard today are included in the collection *114 Songs* that Ives had privately printed in 1921. [4]

Comments:

The Ives song group to which the program notes refer consisted of:

The Things Our Fathers Loved

Tom Sails Away

Memories (Very Pleasant, Rather Sad)

The Greatest Man

Because the performing venue provided only a leaflet for a program, it was necessary to print program notes separately. Since space was an issue, and the songs were in English, the notes were deliberately concise.

Translations

There will be audience members who want to follow or have the original language text line by line in front of them. Translations may be poetic line-by-line translations, or paraphrase translations. Using paraphrase translations saves a lot of space, and if this is done, you will probably *not* print the original texts. If paraphrases are used, coupling them with brief program notes might be nice. Another option: print the paraphrase in the body of the program under the song title.

Program notes by themselves give the audience very little to reference. Texts, translations, *and* program notes are usually expected at a graduate recital or on any university recital where the student receives a grade for the recital.

Credit Where Credit is Due

You must also give proper citations for using translations from books, CD liner notes, etc. In almost every case, these are copyrighted materials. At the end of the translation, give the name of the translator, for example: Translation by John Doe, perhaps in a smaller font. If you have done your own translations, then cite it as: Translations by (your name), and put it at the end of all the texts and translations. If you have program notes with quotations from other sources, cite these also. This may be done with an asterisk *in the note at the point of the cited material*, and an asterisk *with the citation* at the end of the notes. This may also be in a smaller size font.

Are Any of These Yours?

Below are some authentic program note bloopers. They are genuine mistakes, taken from real programs, most of them long since sung. Obviously, they escaped the proofreader's eagle eye, or they didn't get to a proofreader, which really is inexcusable.

Example 1: Distressing Program Notes

Below are some rather clumsy program notes, made worse by typos. They are printed exactly as they appeared on the program. Bolded type indicates the "bloopers."

Mignon Lieder (Goethe)   Hugo Wolf (1860–1903)
    Hiess mich nicht **reder**
    Mignon asks that she be allowed to remain silent because she is sworn to secrecy.

Nur wer die Sehnsucht kennt
    Only those who have known love's **yearnaing** can know **wghat** Mignon is feeling.

So lasst mich scheinen
> **The young Mignon is wearing a white dress for a play and asks that she be allowed to keep it on.**

Example 2: Program Notes for an Aria

This particular senior recital featured the aria "Adieu, notre petite table" from Jules Massenet's opera *Manon*. Instead of several brief sentences about the aria, the singer chose to print as program notes "The Story of Manon" (all five acts)—an entire synopsis of the opera! All the audience needed to know was this: the opera and composer, the character singing the aria, where the aria takes place, and something about Manon's state of mind as she leaves Des Grieux. The five-act synopsis was haltingly and poorly written. It is not reproduced here.

Example 3: More Distressing Program Notes

The program notes below are embarrassing. They feature incomplete sentences, poor syntax in some of the sentences which *are* complete, incorrect use of "there" for "their" *and* misspellings. The examples are presented *exactly* as they appeared in the printed program. Ellipses (. . .) indicate an omission in the quotation.

Leonard Bernstein's *I Hate Music!*
"Leonard Bernstein (1918–1990) His talents are formidable to say the least. As composer, pianist, and conductor he has moved in the diverse worlds of Broadway and the concert hall, and has left a distinct mark on both . . . This song cycle is based on children and there outlooks on life."

The program notes below suffer the same biographical disease as the Bernstein above.
"Schubert wrote more than 600 Lieder. Some of these are among the best-loved pieces of music in the world. One of which is the ever popular Ave Maria."
(and finally)
"He only lived a tragically short life of 31 years."

Proofread Your Program!

Putting all the print together is *not* the final step. There are *always* "print gremlins" lurking in every program. Proofread your work, *including the cover presentation page*. For foreign texts, check all words, all diacritical markings, upper case and lower case on all repertoire titles and throughout any program notes, texts and/or translations, italicizations, and margins. Errors in spelling, punctuation, and just general typographical slips need to be found and corrected. The time it takes to do this painstaking task will be rewarded with a recital program that is as error-free as you can make it.

What do all these upper-lower-case, readable fonts, intelligent program notes exercises mean? It is training in organization, and it compels one to focus on details, which is not a bad thing. We have to do this if we're preparing a song for performance, and we should follow through with the program also.

A Proofreader's Quiz

Finally, to review the material just discussed, here is a little quiz for you. Look at this list of songs, which has a number of mistakes. *These are real mistakes and typos* from student programs that thought they had everything "right." The answers may be found following the "Notes" section at the end of this chapter.

Claire de Lune	Après un Reve
Steal me Sweet Theif!	Allersellen
Ouvre to cœur	Das Veichlen
Il Pleure Dans Mo Cœur	Ramance de Mignon
Caro Nome (Rioletto)	Ah had I Jubol's Lyre
Rastlost Liebe	Nui d'Etoiles
Faites-lui mes aveaux	Phydile
Perla Gloria d'aroravi	Nachtwandrer
Les Rosignol des Lilas	

Guidelines for Song Titles
Titles

Titles of individual songs should appear within quotation marks, but titles of larger works should be italicized. For example, one writes about "Morgengruss" from Schubert's *Die schöne Müllerin*, and "The Vagabond" from Vaughan Williams's *Songs of Travel*.

Capitalizations

English

For aria/song/cycle/poem titles, leave capitalization as is for titles that originated in English. For translations into English, use headline capitalization.

French

If the title does not begin with an article, capitalize the first word only,
> Examples:
>> "Au cimetière"
>> "Clair de lune"
>> "Dans le ruines d'une abbaye"

If the title begins with an article, capitalize through the first noun; use lower case after that.
> Examples:
>> *Les Nuits d'été*
>> "Le Papillon et la fleur"
>> "La Fleur qui va sur l'eau"
>> *L'Horizon chimérique*

German

Capitalize the first word and any nouns thereafter.
> Examples:
>> *Sieben frühe Lieder*
>> "Auf ein altes Bild"
>> "Alte Laute"
>> "Auf dem Wasser zu singen"
>> "Der Tod und das Mädchen"

Italian and Spanish

Capitalize the first word only.
> Examples:
>> "Che fa il mio bene"
>> "La mar"
>> "Danza, danza fanciulla gentile"
>> "Le violette"
>> "Amarilli, mia bella"

Guidelines for Printed Materials: Suggested Reading

Below are some articles dealing with style and format as regards the printed recital program. They are helpful sources to reference, but with the *caveat* that guidelines used for articles and other manuscripts vary in a number of details for the style guidelines used for producing recital programs. Whatever style rules you use, *be consistent*.

Chicago Manual Of Style, 14th rev. edition (Chicago: The University of Chicago Press, 1993).

Dana C. Gorzelany-Mostak, **"Writing Program Notes: A Guide for Teachers of Undergraduate Voice Students,"** *Journal of Singing* 65, no. 4 (March/April 2009): 431–440. Students should write program notes as a part of their preparation for lessons.

D. Kern Holoman, *Writing about Music* (Berkeley, CA: University of California Press, 1988). This diminutive paperback book is a style sheet from the editors of the journal *19th-Century Music.* It is a most useful resource for producing accurate program copy for the printed recital program.

Patricia Robertson, **"Producing Accurate Recital Program Copy: An Annotated Style Sheet,"** *Journal of Singing* 62, no. 1 (September/October 2005): 19–25. A helpful reference, providing a brief, annotated style sheet for recital programs with proper style and format accuracy. A valuable resource for producing programs with proper style and format accuracy.

NOTES

1   Notes by unknown author. A Lieder Recital, Benita Valente, soprano, Thomas Grubb, piano, with William Wrzesien, clarinet. New York City, Jewett Arts Center, February 14, 1971.

2   Amy Hunsaker, soprano. Masters Recital. University of Nevada, Las Vegas Rando Recital Hall, November 7, 2002

3   Jeanette Fontaine, mezzo soprano. Senior Recital, April 27, 2004, Rando Recital Hall, University of Nevada, Las Vegas, Las Vegas, NV.

4   Song Translations and Program Notes, an additional handout printed separately Carol Kimball, mezzo soprano; Thomas Grubb, pianist. In Recital, Library and Museum of the Performing Arts at Lincoln Center, New York City, June 18, 1976.

ANSWERS TO THE PROOFREADER'S QUIZ:

Clair de lune

Steal me, sweet thief

Ouvre ton cœur

Il pleure dans mon cœur

Caro nome (Rigoletto)

Rastlose Liebe

Faites-lui mes aveux

Per la gloria d'adorarvi

Le Rossignol des lilas

Après un rêve

Allerseelen

Das Veilchen

Romance de Mignon

O had I Jubal's lyre

Nuits d'étoiles

Phidylé

Nachtwanderer

Appendix 3

A Selection of Various Recital Programs

Here are some examples of different types of song recitals. Looking through them may give you ideas for designing a different type of recital for yourself.

Note: Composers' dates and spellings are presented as they were on the original programs. Some composers have since died and many spellings have become standardized. The names of the performers have been purposefully omitted.

Some Junior Voice Recitals
JUNIOR RECITAL 1: SOPRANO

~ Program ~

I

Das Veilchen	Wolfgang Amadeus Mozart
Ridente la calma	(1756–1791)
Un moto di gioia	
Oiseaux, si tous les ans	

II

Trois chants de Noël	Frank Martin
Les Cadeaux	(1890–1974)
Image de Noël	
Les Bergers	

_____, flute

III

Music, when soft voices die	Ernest Gold (b. 1921)
Why do they shut me out of Heaven?	Aaron Copland (b. 1900)
Sure on this shining night	Samuel Barber (1910–1981)
Sigh no more, ladies	Virgil Thomson (1896–1989)

Commentary: A very nicely programmed Junior recital, which includes a brief cycle with flute and piano. Eleven selections, four languages (three in the Mozart group).

JUNIOR RECITAL 2: SOPRANO
~ Program ~

I.

Lascia ch'io pianga (*Rinaldo*)	George Frideric Handel
Tornami a vagheggiar (*Alcina*)	(1685–1759)

II.

Green (*Ariettes oubliées*)	Claude Debussy
C'est l'extase (*Ariettes oubliées*)	(1862–1918)
Fantoches (*Fêtes galantes I*)	

III.

The Lament of Ian the Proud	Charles T. Griffes (1884–1920)
Hymn (*Six Elizabethan Songs*)	Dominick Argento
Winter (*Six Elizabethan Songs*)	(b. 1927)

IV.

Plenivshis' rozny, solovey (The Nightingale and the Rose)	Nikolay Rimsky-Korsakov (1844–1908)
Zdes' khorosho (It is Beautiful Here)	Sergey Rakhmaninov (1873–1943)
Vessenniya vody (Spring Waters)	

Commentary: This Junior Recital features some challenging repertoire, but the student was a bit older and advanced vocally. Very colorful repertoire, four languages, eleven selections. A slow tempo Handel aria to open the program seems just right.

JUNIOR RECITAL 3: BARITONE
~ Program ~

Recitative and aria (from *Scipione*) Null temer da un generosa core: Generoso chi sol brama	George Frideric Handel (1685–1759)
Selections from *Die Winterreise* Gute Nacht Gefrorne Tränen Die Krähe	Franz Schubert (1797–1828)
Deux épigrammes de Clément Marot D'Anne qui me jecta de la neige D'Anne jouant de l'espinette	Maurice Ravel (1875–1937)
Soliloquy (from Carousel)	Richard Rodgers (1902–1979)

Commentary: Repertoire-wise, this recital is on the slim side, but given the length of the "Soliloquy" from *Carousel* (really a musical theater "aria"), and the level of difficulty of the French and German, one could argue the case. It might have been better perhaps, to have a three-song group in Italian to follow the Handel. Seven selections, four languages.

JUNIOR RECITAL 4: SOPRANO
~ Program ~

I.

Se voi bramate
   from *Il re Teodoro in Venezia*

Giovanni Paisiello
(1740–1816)

II.

Nachtigall, op. 97, no. 1

Johannes Brahms
(1833–1897)

An die Nachtigall, op. 98, no. 1

Franz Schubert
(1797–1828)

An die Nachtigall, op. 46, no. 4

Johannes Brahms

III.

Mandoline
Les berceaux
Ouvre ton cœur

Gabriel Fauré
(1845–1924)
Georges Bizet
(1838–1875)

IV.

The Blue Madonna

John Jacob Niles
(1892–1980)

Come ready and see me

Richard Hundley
(b. 1931)

Where the music comes from

Lee Hoiby
(b. 1926)

Commentary: There are 10 selections in this Junior Recital. The second group offers a nice comparison in setting poetry based on the nightingale, the French group is colorful in content, and the last group is lighter fare but ends the program nicely. Instead of opting for the flashier Bizet at the end of the French group, singing one more or even two more Fauré would have made a more compact and balanced group. If a fast song was needed to supplant the Bizet, Fauré's quick-tempo "Nell" or "Notre amour" would work just fine.

The singer obviously wanted to end with the "high note" Bizet. In this case, for balance, you could precede "Ouvre ton cœur" with another Bizet. Two Fauré plus two Bizet, or three Fauré would work nicely.

JUNIOR RECITAL 5: SOPRANO
~ Program ~
I.

De pena, de susto	Antonio Rodriguez de Hita
from *Las Labradoras de Murcia*	(ca. 1725–1787)
Amor y olvido	Fermín Maria Álvarez
	(1833–1898)
Lo que está de Dios	Francisco Asenjo Barbieri
	(1823–1894)

II.

Liebst du um Schönheit	Clara Wieck Schumann
	(1819–1896)
Liebst du um Schönheit	Gustav Mahler
	(1860–1911)

III.

Si mes vers avaient des ailes	Reynaldo Hahn
	(1875–1947)
Le Colibri	Ernest Chausson
	(1855–1899)
Green	Gabriel Fauré
	(1845–1924)

IV.

Take, o take those lips away	Amy Marcy Cheney Beach
The year's at the Spring (*Three Browning Songs*)	(1867–1944)

Commentary: Nicely programmed, 10 selections. A different opening group features 18th and 19th century Spanish selections. A comparison setting of the same poem makes up the second group, which could have had a third song to flesh it out a bit. The French group has nice contrast in tempos and poetic content, but the Chausson stylistically is a heavyweight in between two lighter bookends. Another two-song group ends the program. Note: Having two groups of two songs each is questionable. A three-song group is generally better. In the case of the Beach songs, the last is very short, and an obvious "high note/fast tempo ender."

Some Senior Voice Recitals
SENIOR RECITAL 1: MEZZO SOPRANO
~ Program ~

Nobles seigneurs, salut! from *Les Huguenots*	Giacomo Meyerbeer (1791–1864)

La regata veneziana
    Anzoleta avanti la regata
    Anzoleta co passa la regata
    Anzoleta dopo la regata
	Gioachino Rossini
	 (1792–1868)

Assisa a piè d'un salice from *Otello*	Gioachino Rossini

~ Intermission ~

Banalités
    Chanson d'Orkenise
    Hôtel
    Fagnes de Wallonie
    Voyage à Paris
    Sanglots
	Francis Poulenc
	 (1899–1963)

Cinco canciones populares argentinas
    Chacarera
    Triste
    Zamba
    Arrorró
    Gato
	Alberto Ginastera
	 (b. 1916)

Commentary: This recital features some colorful and vibrant repertoire, but omits a group in English, which ought to have been a part of a senior recital. The program opens with a dramatic salutation by Meyerbeer, and moves to Rossini's vivacious Venetian regatta. Desdemona's aria from Rossini's *Otello* pulls the momentum backward and closes the first half with an aria from a composer the audience had just heard. Two arias on the program is a bit much for an undergraduate recital, but the Rossini is not sung as often. However, since the Rossini cycle had already been offered, another short group (in English) could have been programmed. The Poulenc cycle could have been put in the first half instead of the Rossini, but problems of length and the chronological unity kept it in the second half. Ginastera's animated Argentinean folk songs ends the program on a lively note. A challenging program.

SENIOR RECITAL 2: TENOR

~ Program ~

Leonardo Vinci (ca. 1690–1730)	From: *La caduta del Decemviri* Teco, sì
Carlo Caproli (ca. 1617–1692)	Tu mancavi a tormentarmi
Franz Schubert (1797–1828)	From *Schwanengesang* Liebesbotschaft Ständchen Das Fischermädchen Ihr Bild Frühlingssehnsucht

~ Intermission ~

Francis Poulenc (1899–1963)	*Calligrammes* L'Espionne Mutation Vers le sud Il pleut La Grâce exilée Aussi bien que les cigales Voyage

Arthur Farwell	I'll Tell You How the Sun Rose
(1872–1952)	Safe in Their Alabaster Chambers
	I'm Nobody! Who Are You?
	Wild Nights! Wild Nights!
	Tie the Strings to My Life

Commentary: Good length, although first half is a not completely balanced with the second half in length. Interesting Poulenc cycle, not often heard, and a dramatic stretch for some undergraduates. Arthur Farwell's group of five songs on poems by Emily Dickinson provides a solid group to end the program. The second half of the program should normally be on the lighter side, not the other way around.

SENIOR RECITAL 3: MEZZO SOPRANO
~ Program ~

Zigeunermelodien (1880)	Antonín Dvořák
Mein lied ertönt	(1841–1904)
Ei!: Wie mein Triangel…	
Rings ist der Wald	
Als die alte Mutter	
Reingestimmt die Saiten	
In den weiten, breiten luft'gen	
Darf des Falken Schwinge…	

Fêtes galantes II (1904)	Claude Debussy
Les Ingénus	(1862–1918)
Le Faune	
Colloque sentimental	

~ Intermission ~

Four Sonnets by Pablo Neruda, Set 2 (2008)	Judith Cloud
If your eyes were not the color of the moon	(b. 1954)
Your hand flew from my eyes into the day	
Maybe—though I do not bleed—I am wounded	

With poetry readings by _____

Cinco canciones populares argentinas (1943)   Alberto Ginastera
  Chacarera   (1916–1983)
  Triste
  Zamba
  Arroró
  Gato

Commentary: Here is another lively program that blends gypsy songs by Dvořák with the concentrated musical style of Debussy's second set of *Fêtes galantes*. A contemporary group by composer Judith Cloud follows the intermission, punctuated by readings of the poetry. The recital ends with another colorful group, the Ginastera Argentinean folk songs, a nice balance to the opening group of gypsy songs. This is colorful repertoire, and a musically sophisticated program.

SENIOR RECITAL 4: SOPRANO
~ Program ~

Blute nur, du liebes Herz !   Johann Sebastian Bach
  from *St. Matthew Passion*   (1685–1750)

La conocchia   Gaetano Donizetti
A mezzanotto   (1797–1848)

…from *Sonnets from the Portuguese*   Libby Larsen
  My letters!   (b. 1950)
  If I leave all for thee
  How do I love thee?

~ Intermission ~

Chanson   Francis Poulenc
Ce doux petit visage   (1899–1963)
Parisiana
  Jouer du bugle
  Vous n'écrivez plus?

Nichts   Richard Strauss
Befreit   (1864–1949)

Lamento della Ninfa Claudio Monteverdi
   Non havea ancora Febo (1567–1643)
   Amor
   Si tra sdegnosi

      _____, baritone

      _____, tenor

      _____, tenor

      _____, cello

      _____, harpsichord

Commentary: This program opens with a soprano solo from Bach's *St. Matthew Passion*, followed by a rather slim "group" of two Donizetti songs. This could have been a longer group, fleshed out by some Bellini to begin, and then the Donizetti.

Three songs of Libby Larsen (from her *Sonnets from the Portuguese*) end the first half. This is a quite wide range of disparate composers and musical styles. This distinct contrast appears again in the second half, which mixes Poulenc, Strauss, and Monteverdi (with assisting voices). It would have been better to switch the Monteverdi with the Larsen for a better mix of composers, poetry, and styles.

SENIOR RECITAL 5: SOPRANO
~ Program ~

Meine Seele hört im Sehen (HWV 207) George Frideric Handel
  from *Neun Deutsche Arien* (Brockes) (1685–1759)

      _____, violin

      _____, cello

Airs chantés Francis Poulenc
   Air romantique (1899–1963)
   Air champêtre
   Air grave
   Air vif

*I Spill My Soul** (E.E.Cummings)	Judith Cloud
thy fingers make early flowers of all things	(b. 1954)
this is the garden: colours come and go	
(sitting in a tree-)	
o thou to whom the musical white spring	

~ Intermission ~

In dem Schatten meiner Locken (Heyse)	Hugo Wolf
Die Spröde (Goethe)	(1860–1903)
Die Bekehrte (Goethe)	
Ich hab' in Penna einen Liebsten wohnen (Heyse)	

Sul fil d'un soffio etesio	Giuseppe Verdi
from *Falstaff* (Boito)	(1813–1901)

Commentary: This is an interesting mixture of repertoire, with some appealing choices for soprano voice. The Handel German arias are a good source for opening pieces and offer a chance to involve instruments right away. It is a strong presentational opening. The Poulenc offers a 20th century romp into poetry he disliked vehemently. The first half closes with a North American premiere of poems by e.e. cummings, set by composer Judith Cloud. The second half features songs by Wolf and closes with the lovely aria from Verdi's *Falstaff*. Despite its beauty, closing with an aria on a student recital, and especially this ethereal one, leaves one open to some risk at the end of the program. Unfortunately, the singer chose to sing an encore that had nothing whatsoever to do with the program just heard, and was a rather self-indulgent exercise. This practice is as annoying as printing profuse thank yous on the printed program.

SENIOR RECITAL 6: SOPRANO
~ Program ~

Ach! Dieser süsser Trost – Ich wünsche mit den Tod	J. S. Bach
from *Selig ist der Mann*	(1685–1750)

L'abbandono	Vincenzo Bellini
Almen se non poss'io	(1801–1835)
Per pieta, bell idol mio	

Ich wollt ein Sträusslein binden	Richard Strauss
Morgen!	(1864–1949)
Breit' über mein Haupt	
Nichts	

~ Intermission ~

Folksong Arrangements	Benjamin Britten
I will give my love an apple	(1913–1976)
Sailor-boy	
Master Kilby	
The Soldier and the Sailor	
Bonny at Morn	
The Shooting of his Dear	

featuring _____, guitar

Chansons pour les oiseaux	Louis Beydts
La colombe poignardée	(1896–1953)
Le petit pigeon bleu	
L'oiseau bleu	
Le petit serein en cage	

Commentary: This is a nicely balanced program with attractive repertoire, some of it not heard often. Bach, followed by Bellini and Strauss comprise the first half. After intermission, Britten's lovely folksong arrangements for voice and guitar offer a different tone color. The program ends with the little-heard French composer Louis Beydts's birdsongs.

Some Masters Voice Recitals

MASTERS RECITAL 1: SOPRANO
~ Program ~

Ch'io mi scordi di te?	Wolfgang Amadeus Mozart
Concert Aria, K.505	(1756–1791)

La regata veneziana	Gioacchino Rossini
Anzoleta avanti la regata	(1792–1868)
Anzoleta co passa la regata	
Anzoleta dopo la regata	

Selections from the *Italienisches Liederbuch*	Hugo Wolf
Auch kleine Dinge	(1860–1903)
Mein Liebster singt	
Wohl kenn ich Euren Stand	
Du denkst mit einem Fädchen mich zu fangen	
Heut' Nacht erhob ich mich um Mitternacht	
Ich hab' in Penna einem Liebsten wohnen	

~ Intermission ~

Trois mélodies	Manuel de Falla
Les colombes	(1876–1946)
Chinoiserie	
Séguidille	

The Astronomers	Richard Hundley
Bartholomew Green	(b. 1931)
Moonlight's Watermelon	
Ballad on Queen Anne's Death (1619)	
Sweet Suffolk Owl	
Seashore Girls	

Commentary: Graduate recitals call for more sophistication in repertoire choices, and a good balance between groups. Repertoire should be chosen with exploration and challenge in mind. This program begins with a Mozart concert aria, followed by Rossini's Venetian regatta songs. A selection of six songs from the distilled and emotional miniatures of Wolf's *Italienisches Liederbuch* closes the first half. Falla's three songs feature brilliant piano textures and a Spanish flavor to finish. Six songs by American Richard Hundley close the program. This recital has good balance and variety of musical styles.

MASTERS RECITAL 2: SOPRANO
~ Program ~

La Promessa L'invito La pastorella delle Alpi	Gioacchino Rossini (1792–1868)
Bachianas Brasilieras No. 5: Aria	Heitor Villa-Lobos (1887–1959)

_____, guitar

Der Hirt auf dem Felsen	Franz Schubert (1797–1828)

_____, clarinet

~ Intermission ~

Fiançailles pour rire	Francis Poulenc (1899–1963)

La dame d'André
Dans l'herbe
Il vole
Mon cadavre est doux comme un gant
Violon
Fleurs

Songs from Letters: Calamity Jane *to her daughter, Janey* (1880-1902)	Libby Larsen (b. 1950)

So Like Your Father
He Never Misses
A Man Can Love Two Women
A Working Woman
All I Have

Commentary: A varied and colorful choice of repertoire, with two pieces utilizing assisting artists. The Villa-Lobos piece with its familiar and haunting melody takes on a newer sound with the guitar instead of cellos, and provides a good introduction to the heftier sound of the clarinet in Schubert's venerable *Der Hirt auf dem Felsen*. These works are beautiful and expressive in their own right, but juxtaposing them gives a bit of "sameness" of style to the first half, saved only by the last allegro section of the Schubert. The second half, featuring two cycles on poems/texts by women (Louise de Vilmorin and Calamity Jane), offers a striking contrast of material to say the least.

MASTERS RECITAL 3: BARITONE
~ Program ~

Endlich, endlich wird mein Joch
    third aria from BWV 56
    Ich will den Kreuzstab gerne tragen
	Johann Sebastian Bach
	(1685–1750)

_____, organ

_____, oboe

_____, bassoon

Lieder eines fahrenden Gesellen
    Wenn mein Schatz, Hochzeit macht
    Ging heut morgen übers Feld
    Ich hab ein glühend Messer
    Die zwei blauen Augen
	Gustav Mahler
	(1860–1911)

~ Intermission ~

Chansons Villageoises
    Chanson du clair tamis
    Les gars qui vont à la fête
    C'est le joli printemps
    Le mendiant
    Chanson de la fille frivole
    Le retour du sergent
	Francis Poulenc
	(1899–1963)

Eight Folksong Arrangements	Benjamin Britten
Lord! I Married me a Wife	(1913–1976)
She's like the Swallow	
Lemady	
Bonny at Morn	
I was Lonely and Forlorn	
David of the White Rock	
The False Knight Upon the Road	
Bird Scarer's Song	

Commentary: A Bach cantata aria pairs with Mahler's *Songs of a Wayfarer* in the first half of this graduate recital. This is demanding literature, and its somber atmosphere is balanced in the second half by Poulenc's delightful *Chansons villageoises*. Almost twelve minutes in length, it presents a review of bucolic "snapshots" for a strong yet supple baritone voice in the musical style of Maurice Chevalier. The Britten *Folksong Arrangements* close the recital on a different sort of light note, creating two recital halves with good balance.

MASTERS RECITAL 4: SOPRANO
~ Program ~

Poems by e. e. cummings	John Duke
in Just-spring	(1899–1984)
[i carry your heart with me (i carry it in]	
hist … whist	

* *

Three songs by e. e. cummings	Vincent Persichetti
lady will you come with me into	(1918–1987)
now (more near ourselves than we)	
Spring is like a perhaps hand	

* *

Though Love be a Day	Gwyneth Walker
thy fingers make early flowers	(b. 1947)
lily has a rose	
after all white horses are in bed	
meggie and milly and molly and may	

~ Intermission ~

Estlin
    let's live suddenly
    move deeply, rain
    in time of

Mark Scearce
(b. 1960)

* *

Songs about Spring
    who knows if the moon's a balloon
    Spring is like a perhaps hand
    in Just-spring
    in Spring comes
    when faces called flowers float out of the ground

Dominick Argento
(b. 1927)

Commentary: Here is a one-poet recital in English, using the poems of e. e. cummings (Edward Estlin Cummings), one of America's most prolific and well-known poets. Cummings was known for his unusual way of handling language and his radical experimentation with spelling, punctuation, and syntax. At the time of his death, he was the second most widely read American poet after Robert Frost. Cummings's poetry has been set by numerous composers. This recital featured an assortment of settings by American composers.

MASTERS RECITAL 5: SOPRANO
~ Program ~

Arie Barocche
    Spesso per entro al petto (Barbara Strozzi)
    Sperar io non dovrei (Giacomo Perti)

arr. Arne Dørumsgaard
(1921–2006)

Das zitternde Glänzen
    from *Neun Deutsche Arien*

George Frideric Handel
(1685–1759)

_____, oboe

_____, cello

_____, harpsichord

Aus dem *Italienisches Liederbuch*   Hugo Wolf
 Ihr jungen Leute…   (1860–1903)
 Wie viele Zeit verlor ich…
 Mein Liebster singt…
 Heut' Nacht erhob ich mich um Mitternacht
 Ich hab' in Penna…

~ Intermission ~

Fêtes galantes I   Claude Debussy
 En sourdine   (1862–1918)
 Fantoches
 Clair de lune

Six Elizabethan Songs   Dominick Argento
 Spring   (b. 1927)
 Sleep
 Winter
 Dirge
 Diaphenia
 Hymn

Commentary: This recital opens with three attractive and effective pieces featuring assisting artists. Five selections from Wolf's *Italienisches Liederbuch* follow. Debussy's *Fêtes galantes I* opens the second half, and the program closes with Argento's *Six Elizabethan Songs*. Here is an example of a program in which the number of pieces may seem a bit light, but the vocal demands and sophistication of the repertoire, and length of the first group balances this beautifully.

MASTERS RECITAL 6: MEZZO SOPRANO

A TITLED THEME RECITAL: Spectres, Spirits, and Spooks
~ Program ~

I.

Mad Bess   Henry Purcell
                                                        (1659–1695)

with _____, cello

II.

Voyez dans la nuit brune (from *Fantasio*)   Jacques Offenbach
                                                        (1819-1880)

Colloque sentimental (from *Fêtes galantes II*)   Claude Debussy
                                                        (1862-1918)

Danse macabre   Camille Saint-Saëns
                                                        (1835-1921)

III.

Pesni i plaski smerti   Modest Musorgsky
(Songs and Dances of Death)   (1839–1881)
  Kolybel'naya (Lullaby)
  Serenada (Serenade)
  Trepak (Trepak)
  Polkavodets (The Field-Marshal)

~ Intermission ~

IV.

Fünf Ophelia-Lieder   Johannes Brahms
  Wie erkenn' ich dein Treulieb   (1833–1897)
  Sein Leichenhemd, weiss wie Schnee
  Auf morgen ist Sankt Valentins Tag
  Sie trugen ihn auf der Bahre bloß
  Und kommt er nicht mehr zurück?

V.

Eight Epitaphs   Theodore Chanler
  Alice Rodd   (1902–1961)
  Susannah Fry
  Three Sisters
  Thomas Logge
  A Midget
  "No Voice to Scold"
  Ann Poverty
  "Be Very Quiet Now"

VI.

Evening Prayer from *Hansel and Gretel*   Engelbert Humperdinck
(1854–1921)

with _____, soprano

Commentary: This recital has a theme that runs throughout the
repertoire selections, creating unity, while interesting repertoire
choices create musical and dramatic variety. Additionally, the
repertoire provides plenty of vocal challenges and offers the audience
a sumptuous smorgasbord of styles. Purcell's dramatic *scena*, "Mad
Bess," sets the stage, followed by three French selections, including
the well known tune "Danse macabre." Musorgsky's *Songs and
Dances of Death* ends the first half. Brahms's *Ophelia-Lieder* are
folk-like and attractive; Chanler's settings of epitaphs by Walter de
la Mare are somber yet appealing; and Humperdinck's poignant duet
from *Hansel and Gretel* ends the recital effectively on an inspirational
note.

Some Doctoral Voice Recitals

DOCTORAL RECITAL 1: MEZZO SOPRANO

~ Program ~

Where shall I fly? (from *Hercules*)	George Frideric Händel (1685–1750)

Mignon Lieder Heiss mich nicht reden Nur wer die Sehnsucht kennt So lasst mich scheinen Kennst du das Land	Hugo Wolf (1860–1933)

Au pays où se fait la guerre Extase La vie antérieure	Henri Duparc (1848–1933)

~ Interval ~

Despite and Still, op. 41 A Last Song My Lizard In the Wilderness Solitary Hotel Despite and Still	Samuel Barber (1910–1981)

Hermano Abismo de sed La rosa y el sauce	Carlos Guastavino (1922–1999)

Commentary: Handel's aria from *Hercules* opens this doctoral recital, revealing the character Dejanira in what is, in effect, her mad scene from that musical drama. She is the first of a varied group of characters. *Mignon Lieder* by Hugo Wolf reveals the child-waif Mignon, and Duparc's group reveals the noble lady who watches and waits for her knight to return from the war. The second half is filled with a kaleidoscope of moods in Samuel Barber's cycle *Despite and Still*. Three colorful songs by Argentine composer Carlos Guastavino end the program. The first two songs, shot through with dance rhythms, are followed by the lyric and ethereal "La rosa y el sauce." A demanding group of repertoire interestingly programmed.

DOCTORAL RECITAL 2: BARITONE
~ Program ~

Dolente imagine di Fille mia	Vincenzo Bellini
Il fervido desiderio	(1801–1835)
Per pietà, bell' idol mio	
Ma rendi pur contento	

Flight for Heaven (Robert Herrick)   Ned Rorem
   To Music, To becalm his Fever   (b. 1923)
   Cherry-ripe
   Upon Julia's Clothes
   To Daisies, not to shut so Soon
   Epitaph upon a Child that died
   Another Epitaph
   To the Willow-tree
   Comfort to a Youth that had lost his love
   Piano interlude
   To Anthea, who may command him Any thing

~ Interval ~

Net, tól 'ka tót, kto znál	Pyotr Il'ich Tchaikovsky
Rastvaril ja aknó	(1840–1893)
Snóva, kak prézhde, adin	
Serenáda Don-Zhuana	

Chansons gaillardes   Francis Poulenc
   La maîtresse volage   (1899–1963)
   Chanson à boire
   Madrigal
   Invocation aux Parques
   Couplets bachiques
   L'Offrande
   La belle jeunesse
   Sérénade

Commentary: A colorful choice of repertoire, musical styles, and languages. It includes Rorem's first published cycle, *Flight for Heaven*, in the first half place of honor. Tchaikovsky's vibrant *romans* includes two familiar Tchaikovsky melodies—the first and last songs in the group. Poulenc's often neglected, vivacious but naughty *Chansons gaillardes* closes the recital. An effective, sophisticated program.

DOCTORAL RECITAL 3: SOPRANO

A Doctoral Recital of Contemporary Song
~ Program ~

Selections from *Poèmes de la Pléiade,*   Jacques Leguerney
1er Recueil   (1906–1997)
    Je vous envoie
    Je me lamente
    Bel aubépin

Selections from *The Emily Dickinson Songbooks,*   Virko Baley
Bks. 1 and 2   (b. 1938)
    He was weak, and I was strong—then **
    'Hope' is the thing with feathers **
    There is a Languor of the Life **
    I held a Jewel in my fingers *
    There is a solitude of space *

        ** from Songbook 2
        * from Songbook 1

~ Intermission ~

Mr. Tambourine Man: Seven Poems of Bob Dylan   John Corigliano
    Prelude: Mr. Tambourine Man   (b. 1938)
    Clothes Line
    Blowin' in the Wind
    Masters of War
    All Along the Watchtower
    Chimes of Freedom
    Postlude: Forever Young

Commentary: This doctoral recital features art songs from twentieth-century composers. The repertoire is musically advanced, calling for a singer with excellent musicianship and dramatic sensibilities. The Dylan poems, commissioned from John Corigliano by soprano Sylvia McNair, is interesting in that the Dylan poems are re-created in a totally different soundscape from the familiar "tunes" we are accustomed to hearing. About his choice of Emily Dickinson's poems, composer Virko Baley said: "I am particularly struck by their tonal intricacies and complex juxtaposition of opposed or perhaps even irreconcilable feelings . . . The songs are each composed around a musical metaphor, usually stated in the piano. The vocal line is both part of it and separate." [1]

DOCTORAL RECITAL 4: MEZZO SOPRANO
~ Program ~

***

Illalle	Jean Sibelius
Svarta Rosor	(1865–1957)
Säv, säv, susa	
Marssnön	

***

Vingar i natten	Ture Rangström
	(1884–1947)
Skogen Sover	Hugo Alfvén
	(1872–1960)
Vandraren	Wilhelm Stenhammar
Det far ett skepp	(1871–1927)

***

Flickan kom ifrån sin älsklings möte	Wilhelm Stenhammar
Flickan kom ifrån sin älsklings möte	Jean Sibelius

334

~ Interval ~

Selections from *Einfache Lieder op. 9*   Erich Wolfgang Korngold
    Nachwanderer   (1897–1957)
    Liebesbriefchen
    Das Heldengrab am Pruth
    Sommer

***

American composers on texts for children
    The Children's Hour   Charles Ives
    To Edith   (1874–1954)
    Two Little Flowers

    Frustration   Ernest Charles
                                             (1894–1984)

    The Serpent   Lee Hoiby
                                              (b. 1926)

Commentary: Doctoral recitals are required to program some unusual repertoire choices with sophisticated musical challenges. The first half of this recital is in Finnish (Sibelius) and Swedish, and presents a vibrant selection of repertoire, including one extended art song set by two composers, Stenhammar and Sibelius. Four songs by Erich Korngold, composed in his teens, open the second half, followed by five American art songs on texts for children. The recital ends with the always humorous and engaging "The Serpent" by Lee Hoiby.

DOCTORAL RECITAL 5: MEZZO SOPRANO

A Doctoral Chamber Music Recital
~ Program ~

I.

Three Cantata Arias for Alto   Johann Sebastian Bach
with Instruments   (1685–1750)

BWV 79: *Gott der Herr ist Sonn' und Schild! (Reformation Day,
     Leipzig, 1725)*
Aria: *Gott is unsre Sonn' und Schild!*
BWV 102: *Herr, deine Augen sehen nach dem Glauben*
        (10th Sunday after Trinity, Leipzig, 1726)
Aria: *Weh! der Seele*

Alto, Oboe and Continuo

BWV 39: *Brich dem Hungrigen dein Brot*
        (1st Sunday after Trinity, Leipzig, 1726)
Aria: *Seinem Schöpfer noch auf Erden*

Alto, Oboe, Violin and Continuo

II.

Works for Voice and Flute
    Une flûte invisible   Camille Saint-Saëns
        (1835–1921)

    Viens! Une flûte invisible   André Caplet
        (1878–1925)

Voice, Flute, and Piano

Écoute, mon cœur

Deux stèles orientées   Jacques Ibert
    Mon amante a les vertus de l'eau   (1890–1962)
    On me dit…Vous ne devez pas l'épouser

Voice and Flute

~ Interval ~

III.

Seven Romances on Poems of   Dmitri Shostakovich
Alexander Blok, Opus 127   (1906–1975)
   Ophelia's Song
   Gamayun, the Prophet Bird
   We were together
   The city sleeps
   The Storm
   Secret signs
   Music

Soprano, Violin, Cello and Piano

Commentary: This doctoral recital listed the assisting artists' names on the program cover, but on the program page, lists the instrumentation. Since the program is fairly dense as far as repertoire titles are concerned, this is a professional way to format information. The Shostakovich cycle is a powerful choice to end the program. Each movement involves the singer in duos, trios, and in the final movement, all the musicians are united.

DOCTORAL RECITAL 6: SOPRANO

~ Program ~

The Blessed Virgin's Expostulation   Henry Purcell
                                                     (1659–1695)

_____, continuo

Misera, dove son! Ah! Non son io che parlo   W. A. Mozart
Concert aria, K. 369   (1756–1791)

Selections from *Brentano Lieder*   Richard Strauss
   An die Nacht   (1864–1949)
   Ich wollt' ein Sträusslein binden
   Säusle, liebe Myrthe
   Amor

~ Intermission ~

Quatre chansons de jeunesse Claude Debussy
  Pantomime (1862–1918)
  Clair de lune
  Pierrot
  Apparition

Songs About Spring Dominick Argento
  who knows if the moon's a balloon (b. 1927)
  Spring is like a perhaps hand
  in Just – spring
  in Spring comes
  when faces called flowers float out of the ground

Selections from *Canciones clásicas españolas* Fernando Obradors
  La mi sola, Laureola (1897–1945)
  Al amor
  Del cabello más sutil
  Coplas de curro dulce

Commentary: Five languages and a variety of musical styles are programmed in this Doctoral recital. The Obradors and Argento could have been switched one with another, but putting the English between the French and Spanish introduced English into the program in the second half and offered a new language sound. The Purcell, which opened the first half, was a nice touch before the Mozart concert aria.

DOCTORAL RECITAL 7: MEZZO SOPRANO
~ Program ~

I.

Selections from *Le Bestiaire* Louis Durey
  La Chèvre du Thibet (1888–1979)
  Le Serpent
  Le Dromadaire
  L'Eléphant
  Le Dauphin
  La Méduse

II.

Histoires naturelles	Maurice Ravel
Le Paon	(1875–1937)
Le Grillon	
Le Cygne	
Le Martin-Pêcheur	
La Pintade	

~ Intermission ~

III.

Gadkiy Utyonok	Sergei Prokofiev
(The Ugly Duckling)	(1891–1953)

IV.

The Monk and His Cat	Samuel Barber
(from *Hermit Songs*)	(1910–1981)
Tiger, Tiger	Rebecca Clarke
	(1886–1979)
Sweet Suffolk Owl	Richard Hundley
	(b. 1931)
The Seal Man	Rebecca Clarke
In the Beginning	Jake Heggie
(from *Of Gods and Cats*)	(b. 1961)

Commentary: Though not titled as a theme recital, the repertoire in this recital is linked by art songs about animals, birds, and insects. It is good to hear Louis Durey's *Le Bestiaire*, an interesting and effective contrast to Poulenc's cycle of the same title. The Prokofiev piece is an extended story. The final group in English presents a mix of American and British composers. It contains unity in titles but wide diversity in musical styles, including two stunning selections by Rebecca Clarke.

More Recitals of Different Types

EXAMPLE 1: A Theme Recital

Commentary: Here is a faculty recital that chronicles groups of songs having to do with a variety of different kinds of journeys. In addition to introductory program notes, there were brief notes that prefaced each "journey." Each song group was a microcosm of the larger theme (journeys), yet was complete as a group within itself. The "theme" allowed the juxtaposition of songs in different languages and styles (see German and English mixed in Groups 3 and 4) that might not normally be put in a group together.

Below are some excerpts from the opening program notes:

> We are all on journeys throughout our lives. There are vacation trips and business trips on the physical plane, not to mention that we are passengers on the earth as it moves through space. Our emotions travel between highs and lows, and our world views are in constant flux. We all partake in the journey from birth to death.

> . . .With the ties between music and poetry in song, there is an obvious connection to journeys and travel in this genre. Some works, like *Die Winterreise* of Schubert, specifically outline journeys. Others can be easily grouped and/or interpreted so as to form a journey. This has been the aim here. Some of these journeys are physical, but all include an emotional, psychological or spiritual component. [2]

DAVID BRADLEY, BARITONE; CAROL URBAN, PIANIST
A Faculty Recital
Five Journeys
March 24, 1987
Alta Ham Fine Arts Little Theatre
University of Nevada, Las Vegas

FIVE JOURNEYS

~ Journey to the Sea ~

L'Horizon chimérique	Gabriel Fauré
La mer est infinie...	(1845–1924)
Je me suis embarqué...	
Diane, Séléné...	
Vaisseaux, nous vous aurons aimés …	

~ Journey to Madness ~

From *Die Winterreise* (Müller)	Franz Schubert
Gute Nacht	(1797–1828)
Der Lindenbaum	
Die Post	
Das Wirtshaus	
Der Leiermann	

~ Journey on Land ~

Wanderlied (Kerner)	Robert Schumann
	(1810–1856)
The Vagabond (Stevenson)	Ralph Vaughan Williams
	(1872–1958)
Der Musikant (Eichendorff)	Hugo Wolf
	(1860–1903)
Whither Must I Wander (Stevenson)	Ralph Vaughan Williams
Wanderers Nachtlied (Goethe)	Franz Schubert

~ INTERMISSION ~

~ Journey to God ~

In a Churchyard (Hardy)	Gerald Finzi (1901–1956)
Die Allmacht (Pryker)	Franz Schubert
Herr, was trägt der Boden hier	Hugo Wolf
The Desire for Hermitage	Samuel Barber
Litanei (Jacobi)	Franz Schubert

~ Journey to Love ~

Heimliche Aufforderung (Mackay)	Richard Strauss (1864–1949)
Der Nachtgang (Bierbaum)	
Ach Lieb, ich muss nun scheiden (Dahn)	
Heimkehr (Schack)	
Zueignung (von Gilm)	

EXAMPLE 2: A Storyline Recital

Commentary: Here is an Artists Program from the summer program SongFest, featuring artists-in-residence Graham Johnson and baritone Brandon Verlarde. It has a simple storyline running through it, with each group linking to the next until the recital's conclusion. This was a program in one language, but the variety of composers created both balance and contrast. Any of the groups could stand alone on other programs, but using a simple "love stories" theme links the songs together by a slender thread that allows each part of the story to have vitality and contrast: boy meets girl, they fall in love, they marry, they separate, but live to love another day.

BRANDON VELARDE, BARITONE
GRAHAM JOHNSON, PIANO
Artists Recital: A Journey of French Song
July 8, 2001
SongFest, Chapman University
Orange, California

HISTOIRES D'UNE LIAISON
A Journey of French Song

Love stories. . .

I. RENCONTRES
Meetings. . .

Ou voulez-vous aller (Gautier)	Gounod
Le charme (Silvestre)	Chausson
Quand je fus pris au pavillon (d'Orleans)	Hahn
Le manoir de Rosemonde (Bonnieres)	Duparc
Le roi s'en va-t-en chasse (Anon.)	arr. Britten

II. ENAMOURÉS
In love. . .

Chanson d'amour (Silvestre)	Fauré
Offrande (Verlaine)	Hahn
Si tu le veux (Marsan)	Koechlin
Je tremble en voyant ton visage (Tristan l'Hermite)	Debussy
La maîtresse volage (Anon.)	Poulenc
Cœur en péril (Chalupt)	Roussel
Epipalinodie (Ronsard)	Leguerney

~ Interval ~

III. MARIAGES ET LUNES DE MIELS
Marriages and honeymoons. . .

Le reveil de la mariée (Calvocoressi)	Ravel
Extase (Lahor)	Duparc
Le paon (Renard)	Ravel
L'îsle heureuse (Mikhael)	Chabrier
Phidylé (Leconte de Lisle)	Duparc

IV. LA CROISÉE DES CHEMINS…ET RÉCUPERATION
Parting of the ways…and recovery

Infidelité (Gautier)	Hahn
L'impossible pardon (Debussy)	Debussy
Soupir (Prudhomme)	Duparc
Chansons pour Jeanne (Mendes)	Chabrier
Adieu from *Poème d'un jour* (Grandmougin)	Fauré
Colloque sentimental (Verlaine)	Debussy
La belle jeunesse (Anon.)	Poulenc

EXAMPLE 3:
A Doctoral Recital That Contrasts Two Song Cycles

Commentary: Here is a doctoral recital that juxtaposes two cycles from diverse musical and historical periods: Robert Schumann's *Frauenliebe und -leben* and Dominick Argento's *From the Diary of Virginia Woolf*.

A Doctoral Recital

Frauenliebe und –leben	Robert Schumann
Seit ich ihn gesehen	(1810–1856)
Er, der Herrlichste von Allen	
Ich kann's nicht fassen, nicht glauben	
Du Ring an meinem Finger	
Helft mir, ihr Schwestern	
Süsser Freund	
An meinen Herzen, an meiner Brust	
Nun hast du mir den ersten Schmerz getan	

~ Intermission ~

From the Diary of Virginia Woolf	Dominick Argento
The Diary	(b. 1927)
Anxiety	
Fancy	
Hardy's Funeral	
Rome	
War	
Parents	
Last Entry	

The singer used this program as the topic for her doctoral (DMA) document and for this recital, which was performed prior to its writing. Dominick Argento described his cycle and its relation to the Schumann work like this: "I decided on a sort of twentieth-century *Frauenliebe und -leben* and even my last song's return to the musical material of the first is Schumannesque," [3]

The singer described her rationale for pairing the two cycles this way:

> Both cycles depict chronological glimpses of a woman's thoughts and feelings. While the two characters are quite different in personality, their disclosure of highly intimate emotions and experiences unites them. Form is another important bonding quality between the two works. Similarities in the overall form—eight songs unified by recurring material throughout, in particular a return in the last song to material from the opening song—and smaller formal structures offer a sense of unity between the cycles. Musically, both composers use techniques such as word painting, recurring leitmotivs, and piano figures that provide pictorial settings. Additionally, both cycles were inspired by a particular woman: *Frauenliebe und -leben* was a wedding gift to Schumann's fiancée Clara Wieck, while *From the Diary of Virginia Woolf* was conceived for and premiered by mezzo soprano Janet Baker.
>
> Contrasting elements between Schumann and Argento's works are many, and are an absolute necessity for variety and interest in recital programming. Schumann's writing is notably conservative and simple, while Argento's is highly cerebral, incorporating elements such as twelve-tone technique. In both cases, the composers' musical choices are always at the service of the character and text. Schumann's Frau is a traditional wife and mother, while Virginia Woolf is a troubled genius. The overall mood or atmosphere of each cycle is also quite distinct: *Frauenliebe und -leben* is largely cheerful, only featuring tragedy in the last song of the cycle, while *From the Diary of Virginia Woolf* is generally depressive, punctuated by fleeting moments of happiness. [4]

EXAMPLE 4:
A Musical Theatre Program in "Recital" Format

Commentary: This program was presented at the Cal-Western Regional conference of the National Association of Teachers of Singing at the University of Nevada, Las Vegas, August 10, 1979. It was titled "An Afternoon of Musical Theatre." The recital developed as a collaboration between the singer and Jack Lee, who has had a distinguished international career as a musical conductor in the musical theatre, and also as a teacher/coach/director in the musical theatre division of New York University's Steinhardt School in Vocal Performance. The object of the program was to plan a group of songs/arias from musical theatre productions, assigning musical genre headings to each of them. Within each group, the songs were loosely related by mood: relationships; several aspects of love; a short song cycle; and happiness and triumph in liaisons. Due to time limits for the conference, the program was shorter than the usual art song recital. The program was effective and very well received.

> *Note: due to a last minute professional engagement, Jack Lee could not accompany this recital that had given him so much pleasure to plan.*

CAROL KIMBALL, MEZZO SOPRANO
REX WOODS, PIANO
An Afternoon of Musical Theatre
NATS Cal-Western Regional Conference
August 20, 1979
Judy Bayley Theatre
University of Nevada, Las Vegas

An Afternoon of Musical Theatre

I.

LAMENT

Can't Help Lovin' That Man   Oscar Hammerstein II-Jerome Kern
(*Showboat*, 1927)

FRENCH ART SONG

In the Mandarin's Orchid Garden   Ira Gershwin-
(*George White's Scandals*, 1930)   George Gershwin

RONDO

The Tale of the Oyster   Cole Porter
(*Fifty Million Frenchmen*, 1931)

BALLADE

The Ballad of Sexual Dependency   Bertolt Brecht-Kurt Weill
(*The Threepenny Opera*, 1933)

II.

REVERIE

He Was Too Good to Me   Lorenz Hart-Richard Rodgers
(*Simple Simon*, 1930)

AIR

Lonely Feet   Oscar Hammerstein II-Jerome Kern
(*Sweet Adeline*, 1934)

LA VALSE

Falling in Love with Love   Lorenz Hart-Richard Rodgers
(*The Boys from Syracuse*, 1938)

SOLILOQUY

Ev'ry Time   Ralph Blane-Hugh Martin
(*Best Foot Forward*, 1941)

CHANSONETTE

Now!   Robert Wright-George Forrest
(*The Song of Norway*, 1951)   (with special thanks to Edvard Grieg)

. . .and after a brief intermission

III.

SONG CYCLE

Four Songs from *Peter Pan* (1950)   Leonard Bernstein
  Never-Land
  My House
  Peter, Peter
  Who Am I?

IV.

ROMANCE

A Sleepin' Bee   Truman Capote-Harold Arlen
(*House of Flowers*, 1954)

PASTORALE

The Miller's Son
(*A Little Night Music*, 1974)   Stephen Sondheim

SCENE and ARIA

Away!
The Best Thing of All   Lillian Hellman-Marc Blitzstein
(*Regina*, 1954)

EXAMPLE 5: An Artist Recital
DAME JANET BAKER, MEZZO SOPRANO
WITH GEOFFREY PARSONS, PIANIST
Les Lundis Musicaux de L'Athenée
Théâtre de L'Athenée-Louis Jouvet
4, square de l'Opéra-Louis Jouvet
75009 PARIS

LES LUNDIS MUSICAUX DE L'ATHENEE
SAISON 1 9 8 3 – 1 9 8 4

LUNDI 16   JANVIER à 20 H 30   DAME JANET BAKER
                                                   Geoffrey Parsons, piano

~ PROGRAMME ~

WOLFGANG AMADEUS MOZART	Vado, ma dove?
(1756–1791)	Al desio di chi t'adora

FRANZ SCHUBERT	Auf dem See (Goethe)
(1797–1828)	Abendstern (Mayrhofer)
	Der Tod und das Mädchen (Claudius)
	Der Jüngling und der Tod (von Spaun)
	Auflösung (Mayrhofer)

JOSEPH HAYDN	Scena di Berenice
(1732–1809)	

~ ENTRACTE ~

CLAUDE DEBUSSY	Sur des poèmes de Verlaine:
(1862–1918)	Il pleure dans mon cœur
	Green
	En sourdine
	Mandoline

GABRIEL FAURÉ	Spleen (Verlaine)
(1845–1924)	Mandoline (Verlaine)
	Aurore (Silvestre)
	Clair de lune (Verlaine)
	Notre amour (Silvestre)

Commentary: This program, presented in Paris by mezzo soprano Dame Janet Baker and pianist Geoffrey Parsons, shows beautiful symmetry. The first half begins with two works by Mozart: a concert aria, K. 583. and Susanna's rondo, K. 577 from *Le nozze di Figaro*, one of two additions to the opera in 1789. This is followed by a generous group of Schubert *Lieder*, and the first half finishes with a dramatic scene by Haydn. The length of the Haydn (approx. 11:52 min.) balances the two Mozart pieces (11:56) that began the recital, and the five Schubert *Lieder* provide a striking contrast.

The second half of the program is all French repertoire, featuring two of France's greatest 19th century *mélodie* composers, Gabriel Fauré and Claude Debussy. The two groups are settings of poet Paul Verlaine, whose interest in word sounds as resonances and fascination with poetry as pure sensation inspired superb settings from both these composers. Two settings of poet Armand Silvestre, a favorite poet of Fauré, are also programmed. Dame Janet offered two encores: Martini's "Plaisir d'amour" and Mendelssohn's "Auf flügeln des Gesänges"— both beautifully simple and familiar melodies.

Note: The program format with the composers' names on the left makes the program easy-to-read, vis-à-vis putting the titles on the left. It is easier and more comfortable for any audience members who are unfamiliar with the musical works being performed, to immediately see the composer, and then the musical titles, rather than vice versa. Of course, both formats are fine, but the first choice seems elegantly simple.

EXAMPLE 6: An Artist Recital
An Evening of German *Lieder* to Poems by Goethe

DIETRICH FISCHER-DIESKAU, BARITONE, WITH NORMAN SHETLER, PIANO

Commentary: This program was presented in Tempe, Arizona at the Grady Gammage Memorial Auditorium, December 10, 1969 by baritone Dietrich Fischer-Dieskau with Norman Shetler, pianist. The program of twenty-three songs to poems by Germany's great Romantic poet, Johann Wolfgang von Goethe, featured some rarely heard *Lieder*. Since it was an all-Goethe evening, it was possible to creatively program these lesser known songs with more familiar

German repertoire, creating groups of four and five *Lieder*. It was a seamlessly designed evening, magically performed.

Poems by Johann Wolfgang von Goethe
set to music by

Herzogin Anna Amalia 1739–1807	Auf dem Land und in der Stadt
Johann Friedrich Reichardt 1752–1814	Feiger Gedanken bängliches Schwanken
Carl Friedrich Zelter 1758–1832	Gleich und gleich
Ludwig van Beethoven 1770–1828	Mailied Neue Liebe, neues Leben

---

Franz Schubert 1797–1828	An den Mond An Schwager Kronos Meeres Stille Erlkönig

Intermission

Robert Schumann 1810–1856	Freisinn Sitz ich allein Setze mir nicht
Johannes Brahms 1833–1897	Serenade Unüberwindlich

Richard Strauss 1864–1949	Gefunden
Othmar Schoeck 1886–1957	Dämmerung senkt sich von oben
Max Reger 1873–1916	Einsamkeit

| Ferruccio Busoni | Zigeunerlied |
| 1866–1924 | |

Hugo Wolf	Wanderers Nachtlied
1860–1903	Frühling übers Jahr
	Anakreons Grab
	Cophtisches Lied
	Der Rattenfänger

EXAMPLE 7: Joy in Singing Award Recital

Commentary: *Joy in Singing* began as a series of master classes given by its founder, Winifred Cecil. In 1958, it also became a publicly supported award program. Winners of the annual awards received a prize recital, first given in Town Hall (NYC) and later moved to Alice Tully Hall in Lincoln Center. After Cecil's death in 1984, countless singers appealed to the organization to keep the unique idea of *Joy in Singing* alive, and it has continued to flourish since that time.

Below is an awards recital given by mezzo soprano Eunice Hall in 1975. The program featured a colorful selection of repertoire. Paraphrase translations were printed under the musical titles. The program is reproduced as printed, in columns to fit a 9 x 6 program booklet. A continuous line marks the bottom of the page. Blank space was left on the RH column of the last program page for a biography of the singer.

EUNICE HALL, MEZZO SOPRANO
THOMAS GRUBB, PIANO
WITH DAVID MILLER, VIOLIST
Joy in Singing Award Recital
October 20, 1975
Alice Tully Hall
Lincoln Center for the Performing Arts
New York City

I.

CLAUDIO MONTEVERDI

Pròlogo: La Musica (*L'Orfeo*)
I greet you, great heroes. I am
Music. As I sing, let no wave
sound, let no wind stir.

Illustratevi, o cieli
(*Il ritorno d'Ulisse in patria*)
Shine brightly, Heavens. Rejoice
and be merry again, for from
Trojan ashes, my phoenix is risen.

BERNARDO PASQUINI

Si misera Regina
So wretched a queen. I cannot
mourn. Merciful grasses, tender
dew, limpid brooklets, you weep
for me.

Giran' pure in ciel le sfere
The spheres whirl in the heavens,
the sun and moon spin. Time
whirls like the sea, as does all
creation.

II.

JOHANNES BRAHMS

Zwei Gesänge, Opus 91,
with viola
Gestillte Sehnsucht
(Longing at Rest)
O wishes forever raging in
my heart, when will you
sleep? When no more my soul
dreams, then whisper with all
my longing my life away.

Geistliches Wiegenlied
(Cradle Song of the Virgin)
Holy angels, my child is
sleeping. This heavenly boy
has borne pain and anguish.
Still the rocking palms of
Bethlehem.

Intermission

III.

GIOACCHINO ROSSINI

La Regata Veneziana
(The Venetian Regatta)
in Venetian dialect

**Anzoleta Avanti la regata
(Before the Regatta)**
The pennant is waving. Drive
your gondola forward, Momolo.
for Anzoleta is anxiously
watching.

**Anzoleta co passa la regata
(During the Regatta)**
Look at the poor fellows bent
over their oars. There is Momolo.
He overtakes them all.

**Anzoleta dopo la regata
(After the Regatta)**
Take a kiss, dear Momolo. All
Venice hails you. You have no
equal at the oars.

IV.

NED ROREM
  The Rain in Spring
  The Lordly Hudson
JOHN CORIGLIANO
  Fort Tryon Park: September
  Christmas at the Cloisters

V.

ERIK SATIE
Ludions (Bottle Imps)

Air du Rat (Air of the Rat)

Abi, Abirounère, who were you after all? A white rat with an eye like an old geezer; a pretty little glutton.

Spleen (Melancholy)

In an old square, on a sad bench with rainy eyes; it's for an ornery, well-endowed blonde that you remain depressed.

La Grenouille américaine

The American frog looks at me. I think of Casadesus who has performed no music on this love scene; nostalgic fragrance comes out of a can of Armour.

Air du poète (Air of the Poet)

I caressed Pouasia. The blessing that I yearn for is not to be Papouet.

**Chanson du chat
(Song of the Cat)**

He is a silly little girl, a little white one; a little potasson. He's my little urchin, my little pig, Tirelo the little unnecessary one.

Je te veux (I Desire You)

Understanding your distress, beloved, as your mistress, I give in to your will. I have but one desire: to live all my life with you.

VI.

JOAQUÍN TURINA
Tres Arias (Three Arias)

Romance (Story)

A brave warrior enters Cordoba in triumph. He has lost his love while away at war and now has no one to share his triumphs.

El Pescador (The Fisherman)

My little fishermaiden, listen to the song of the fisherman. Your beautiful face would calm even the sea.

Rima (Rhyme)

I see your eyes, only your eyes, even when I sleep. They are luring me—but where or to what danger I know not.

MEET THE ARTIST
(biography of Ms. Hall)

EXAMPLE 8: A One-Language Recital (Spanish)
VICTORIA DE LOS ANGELES, SOPRANO, WITH ALICIA DE LARROCHA, PIANO.

Commentary: This is a recital given by the renowned soprano Victoria de los Angeles, partnering with her friend, concert pianist Alicia de Larrocha. Both artists were from Barcelona, and had been friends for over 30 years, but this was the first time they had appeared together in recital. It is amazing to note that Larrocha played the entire recital from memory.

Victoria de los Angeles, soprano
Alicia de Larrocha, pianist
At Hunter. Saturday Evening Series
November 13, 1971 and November 22, 1971
Hunter College Assembly Hall
Hunter College of the City University of New York.

~ Program ~

CUATRO CANCIONES ANTIGUAS ESPAÑOLAS:

Confiado jilguerillo	Antonio Literes
Seguidillas religiosas	Manuel Pla
Canción de cuna	Anónimo
El tripili	Blas de la Serna

DOCE TONADILLAS: Enrique Granados

La Maja de Goya
Amor y odio
El Majo tímido
El mirar de la Maja
Callejeo
La Maja dolorosa, Nums. 1, 2 y 3
El tra-la-la y el punteado
Las Currutacas modestas
El Majo olvidado
El Majo discreto

~ Intermission ~

SEIS CANCIONES AMATORIAS   Enrique Granados
  Llorad corazón
  Ilban al pinar
  No lloreis ojeulos
  Mananica era
  Mira que soy niño
  Gracia mía

SIETE CANCIONES   Manuel de Falla
POPULARES ESPAÑOLAS
  El Paño moruno
  Seguidilla murciana
  Asturiana
  Jota
  Nana
  Canción
  Polo

EXAMPLE 9: A Multi-Media Recital

As referenced in Chapter 4, Francis Poulenc's *Le Travail du peintre* is a cycle of *mélodies* that links images in poetry with images in the paintings of the seven artists whose names are the titles of the songs in the cycle: Pablo Picasso, Marc Chagall, Georges Braque, Juan Gris, Paul Klee, Joan Miró, and Jacques Villon.

Le Travail du peintre is an inventive experiment of artistic synthesis that will communicate more strongly to an audience if the singer has done some research on the artists in the poems, their paintings, and the cultural milieu in which they worked. This is a work that easily lends itself to programming as a multi-media presentation, presenting paintings by the artists in the cycle as a slide show, before each song is performed. If done in this manner, a few words about the artists' style could appear on the program as notes, followed by an English translation of the poem.

If slides are too distracting from the music, or for the singer to feel comfortable, visual representations of the artists' work could be displayed for reference in the lobby. If the recital is in a university situation, collaboration with the Art Department's art historian would certainly be in order.

Perhaps the best option would be for the singer (or another person) to read the English translation of each poem while the slides of that specific artist's work are being shown, and then perform the piece. Since the cyclical link between the songs is the work of the artists themselves, breaking the cycle's performance in this manner would not be distracting. The images in the paintings complement the poetry so well, that choosing the paintings to show becomes happy research for the singer and pianist who perform this cycle.

Because our contemporary culture is strongly oriented towards the visual, this type recital format seems perfect for this piece, or for any other song cycles whose content lends itself to such a presentation. Below is a list of paintings that I used when I presented a multimedia recital of this Poulenc work.

A List of Paintings Used as Illustrations in One Recital

Pablo Picasso:	Cover of *Le Travail du peintre* (1957)
	Three Masked Musicians (1921)
	Seated Woman (1927)
	Woman with Pigeons (1930)
	Drawing of Paul Eluard
	Guernica (1937)
Marc Chagall:	Frontispiece for *Le Désir du Durer* (1946)
	Me and My Village (1911)
	The Lovers in the Lilacs (1931)
	Bride and Groom of the Eiffel Tower (1938)
	Self-Portrait with a Wineglass (1917)
George Braque:	The Birds (1960)
	L'Oiseau et son nid (1957-58)
	Les Arbres à L'Estaque (1908)
	Guitare, pichet, et fruits (1927)

Juan Gris:	Guitar, Glasses and Bottle (1914)
	Guitar with Clarinet (1920)
	Fruit-Bowl, Book and Newspaper (1916)
	Fruit-Bowl with Bottle (1914)
Paul Klee:	Conqueror (1930)
	Stricken Place (1922)
	Perspective of a Room with Occupants (1921)
	Florentine Villa District (1926)
	Fish Magic (1925)
Joan Miró:	Red Disk (1960)
	The Gold of the Azure (1967)
	Blue II (1961)
	The Flight of the Dragonfly Before the Sun (1968)
	Poem III (1968)
Jacques Villon:	Soldiers Marching (1913)
	Little Girl at the Piano (1912)
	Man Reading a Paper (n.d.)
	Farm Yard with Pigeon-House (1953)

NOTES

1 Virko Baley, Program Notes. NEXTET concert, premiere of his Emily Dickinson Songbooks, Books 1 and 2, Lucy Shelton, soprano, with Virko Baley and Sallie Pollack pianists. January 24, 2006, Dr. Arturo-Grillot Rando Recital Hall, University of Nevada, *Note: The concert above is not the recital listed as an example doctoral recital.*

2 David Bradley, program notes "Five Journeys," a faculty recital presented by David Bradley, baritone, with Carol Urban, pianist. March 24, 1987. Grant Hall Little Theatre, University of Nevada, Las Vegas.

3 Dominick Argento, quoted in Leslie Kandell, liner notes to *Permit Me Voyage, Songs by American Composers.* Albany Records CD TROY 118, 1994.

4 Material in this section taken from Jeanette Fontaine, DMA Document Proposal, University of Alabama, August 2011. Used by permission.

Poetry Permissions

James Agee, "Sure on this shining night," from *Samuel Barber: 65 Songs*, edited by Richard Walters, by permission of G. Schirmer, distributed by Hal Leonard Corporation. Text, stanzas 6-8 from *Permit Me Voyage*, published 1934. Used by permission of Yale University Press, Publishers.

Anna Akhmatova, "Nastojashchuju nezhnost'," from The Lied, Art Song, and Choral Texts Archive website (www.recmusic.org). Russian text and English translation (anonymous translation) given. Set by Sergey Prokofiev in his *Five Poems of Anna Akhmatova, Op.27*, in 1917. Poem is in Public Domain.

Anonymous, "Amarilli," from *28 Italian Songs and Arias of the Seventeenth and Eighteenth Centuries*, based on the Editions of Alessandro Parisotti, edited by Richard Walters, by permission of G. Schirmer Inc., distributed by Hal Leonard Corporation. Poem in the Public Domain.

Anonymous, "Del cabello más sutil," from *Standard Vocal Literature (Tenor)*, edited by Richard Walters, by permission of Hal Leonard Corporation. Poem in the Public Domain.

Anonymous, "El vito," from *The Spanish Song Companion* by Jacqueline Cockburn and Richard Stokes, by Permission of Victor Gollancz LTD. Poem in the Public Domain.

Anonymous, "Have you seen but a bright lilie grow?" from *Standard Vocal Literature (Tenor)*, edited by Richard Walters, by permission of Hal Leonard Corporation. Poem in the Public Domain.

Anonymous, "Intorno all'idol mio," from *28 Italian Songs and Arias of the Seventeenth and Eighteenth Centuries*, based on the Editions of Alessandro Parisotti, edited by Richard Walters, by permission of

G. Schirmer Inc., distributed by Hal Leonard Corporation. Poem in the Public Domain.

Anonymous, "Paño murciano," from *The Spanish Song Companion* by Jacqueline Cockburn and Richard Stokes, by Permission of Victor Gollancz LTD. Poem in the Public Domain.

Guillaume Apollinaire, "Il pleut," from *How to Read a Poem: And Fall in Love with Poetry* by Edward Hirsch, by permission of Harcourt, Inc. Calligramme only. In the Public Domain. Poem in The Complete Songs of Poulenc, Vol. 3, Signum Classics CD booklet, SIGCD272. Poem in the Public Domain.

Matthew Arnold, "Dover Beach," from *The Poet's Corner*, compiled by John Lithgow, by permission of Grand Central Publishing, New York. Poem in the Public Domain.

Bo Bergman, "Flickan under nymånen," from *Black Roses*, Virgin Classics CD booklet, edited by Paula Kennedy, Virgin Classics CDC7243-5-45273-2-6, by permission of Virgin Classics Limited. Poem in the Public Domain.

Elizabeth Bishop, "Sonnet 1928 (I am in need of music)," from *Elizabeth Bishop: Complete Poems 1927–1979* by Elizabeth Bishop, by Permission of Farrar, Straus & Giroux, LLC copyright © 1983, by Elizabeth Bishop

William Blake, "The Lamb," from *The Complete Poetry and Prose of William Blake (1757-1827)*, by permission of the University of California Press, Berkeley. Poem is in Public Domain

William Blake, "The Tyger," from *The Poet's Corner*, compiled by John Lithgow, by permission of Grand Central Publishing, New York. Poem in the Public Domain.

Paul Bourget, "Beau soir," from *The French Song Anthology*, edited by Carol Kimball and Richard Walters, by permission of Hal Leonard Corporation. Poem in the Public Domain.

Lewis Carroll, "Jabberwocky," from *The Poet's Corner*, compiled by John Lithgow, by Permission of Grand Central Publishing, New York. Poem in the Public Domain.

Thomas Campion, "My life's delight," from *Rebecca Clarke: Songs and Chamber Works*, Guild Music Ltd. CD booklet GMCD 7208, by permission of Guild Music Ltd. Poem in the Public Domain.

Giacento Andrea Cicognini, "Delizie contente," from *28 Italian Songs and Arias of the Seventeenth and Eighteenth Centuries*, based on the Editions of Alessandro Parisotti, edited by Richard Walters, by permission of G. Schirmer Inc., distributed by Hal Leonard Corporation. Poem in the Public Domain.

e.e. cummings, "i carry your heart with me (i carry it in)," from *Complete Poems 1904–1962* by e.e. cummings, edited by George J. Firmage, by permission of W.W. Norton & Company copyright © 1991, by the trustees for the e.e. cummings Trust and James J. Firmage.

Emily Dickinson, "Heart, we will forget him," from *The Collected Poems of Emily Dickinson*, with an introduction and notes by Rachel Wetzsteon, consulting editorial director George Stade, by permission of Barnes & Noble Classics, New York. Poem in the Public Domain.

Emily Dickinson, "If I can stop one Heart from Breaking," from *The Collected Poems of Emily Dickinson*, with an introduction and notes by Rachel Wetzsteon, consulting editorial director George Stade, by permission of Barnes & Noble Classics, New York. Poem in the Public Domain.

Emily Dickinson, excerpt from "Safe in their Alabaster Chambers—," from *The Collected Poems of Emily Dickinson*, with an introduction and notes by Rachel Wetzsteon, consulting editorial director George Stade, by permission of Barnes & Noble Classics, New York. Poem in the Public Domain.

Robert Frost, "Stopping by Woods on a Snowy Evening," from *Poetry: A Longman Pocket Anthology* by R.S. Gwynn, by permission of Longman, an imprint of Addison Wesley Longman, Inc. Poem in the Public Domain.

Théophile Gautier, "Lamento," from *The French Song Anthology*, edited by Carol Kimball and Richard Walters, by permission of Hal Leonard Corporation. Poem in the Public Domain.

Charles Ives, "The Circus Band," from *114 Songs by Charles E. Ives*, by permission of Theodore Presser Co., distributed by Hal Leonard Corporation. Poem is in the Public Domain.

Charles-Marie-René Leconte de Lisle, "Lydia," from *The French Song Anthology*, edited by Carol Kimball and Richard Walters, by permission of Hal Leonard Corporation. Poem in the Public Domain.

Amy Lowell, "The Taxi," from Sword Blades and Poppy Seed, published 1914 in *Complete Poetical Works*, by Amy Lowell, with an introduction by Louis Untermeyer, by permission of Houghton Mifflin Co. Poem in the Public Domain.

John Henry Mckay, "Morgen!," from *The Fischer-Dieskau Book of Lieder*, by Dietrich Fischer-Dieskau, trans. George Bird and Richard Strokes, by permission of Limelight Editions, New York. Poem in the Public Domain.

Edna St. Vincent Millay, "Recuerdo," from *Poem A Day, Volume 2*, edited by Laurie Sheck, by permission of Steerforth Press, Hanover, NH. Poem in the Public Domain.

Eduard Möricke, "Das verlassene Mägdlein," from *The Fischer-Dieskau Book of Lieder*, by Dietrich Fischer-Dieskau, trans. George Bird and Richard Strokes, by permission of Limelight Editions, New York. Poem in the Public Domain.

Fernando Periquet, "El tra la la y el punteado," from *The Spanish Song Companion* by Jacqueline Cockburn and Richard Stokes, by Permission of Victor Gollancz LTD. Poem in the Public Domain.

Ippolito Pindemonte, "Malinconia, ninfa gentile," from *15 composizione da camera per canto e pianoforte*, by Vincenzo Bellini, by permission of G. Ricordi, Milan, distributed by Hal Leonard Corporation. Poem is in Public Domain

Edward Arlington Robinson, "Richard Cory," from *Poetry: A Longman Pocket Anthology* by R.S. Gwynn, by permission of Longman, an imprint of Addison Wesley Longman, Inc. Poem is in the Public Domain.

Paolo Antonio Rolli, "Se tu m'ami, se sospiri," from *28 Italian Songs and Arias of the Seventeenth and Eighteenth Centuries*, based on the Editions of Alessandro Parisotti, edited by Richard Walters, by permission of G. Schirmer Inc., distributed by Hal Leonard Corporation. In the Public Domain.

Hermann von Gilm zum Rosenwegg, "Die Nacht," from *Richard Strauss: 40 Songs*, edited by Laura Ward and Richard Walters, by permission of Hal Leonard Corporation. Poem in the Public Domain.

Dante Gabriel Rosetti, "Silent Noon," from *Standard Vocal Literature (Mezzo-Soprano)*, edited by Richard Walters, by permission of Hal Leonard Corporation. Poem in the Public Domain.

Friedrich Rückert, "Liebst du um Schönheit," from *The Fischer-Dieskau Book of Lieder*, by Dietrich Fischer-Dieskau, trans. George Bird and Richard Strokes, by permission of Limelight Editions, New York. Poem in the Public Domain.

Friedrich Rückert, "Widmung," from *The Fischer-Dieskau Book of Lieder*, by Dietrich Fischer-Dieskau, trans. George Bird and Richard Strokes, by permission of Limelight Editions, New York. Poem in the Public Domain.

William Shakespeare, "O Mistress mine, where are you roaming?," from *Poem A Day, Vol. 1*, edited by Karen McCosker and Nicholas Albery, by permission of Zoland Books, an imprint of Steerforth Press. Poem in the Public Domain.

William Shakespeare, "When Icicles Hang by the Wall," from *Poem A Day, Vol. 1*, edited by Karen McCosker and Nicholas Albery, by permission of Zoland Books, an imprint of Steerforth Press. Poem in the Public Domain.

Armand Silvestre, "Quand ton sourire me surprit," from *The Interpretation of French Song* by Pierre Bernac, by permission of W. W. Norton & Co., Inc., New York. In the Public Domain.

Robert Louis Stevenson, "Bright Is the Ring of Words," from *Art Song in English: 50 Songs by 21 American and British Composers*, edited by Carol Kimball, by permission of Boosey & Hawkes, distributed by Hal Leonard Corporation. Poem in the Public Domain.

Sara Teasdale, "Barter," from Love Songs (1917) in *The Collected Poems of Sara Teasdale* (1884-1933), by permission of The Macmillan Company. Poem is in Public Domain.

Francisco de la Torre, "Pampano verde," from *Canzone Scordate: Book 1, Ten Early Spanish Songs*, fifteenth century texts, arr. Arne Dorumsgaard, by permission of Recital Publications, Huntsville, Texas. Poem in the Public Domain.

Paul Verlaine, "C'est l'extase," from *The Interpretation of French Song by Pierre Bernac*, by permission of W. W. Norton & Co., Inc., New York. In the Public Domain.

Paul Verlaine, "Clair de lune," from *The Interpretation of French Song* by Pierre Bernac, by permission of W. W. Norton & Co., Inc., New York. In the Public Domain.

Paul Verlaine, "Le ciel est par-dessous le toit," from *The Interpretation of French Song* by Pierre Bernac, by permission of W. W. Norton & Co., Inc., New York. In the Public Domain.

Paul Verlaine, "Mandoline," from *The French Song Anthology*, edited by Carol Kimball and Richard Walters, by permission of Hal Leonard Corporation. In the Public Domain.

Richard Wilbur, "Museum Piece," from *Richard Wilbur: Collected Poems 1943–2004* by Richard Wilbur, by permission of Harcourt, Inc. Copyright © 2004.

W. B. Yeats, "He wishes for the cloths of heaven," from *Poem A Day, Vol. 1*, edited by Karen McCosker and Nicholas Albery, by permission of Zoland Books, an imprint of Steerforth Press. Poem in the Public Domain.

A Selected Bibliography

This bibliography is intended as a guide to vocal literature and is by no means exhaustive. General references are provided as well as entries by national area. Books on the songs of specific composers are listed under that composer's national area, and these have been limited for space considerations. Books that have substantial discussions of the composer's songs have been included. Since the study of vocal literature encompasses diction concerns, selected diction books treating specific song literature also appear. Although there are many excellent periodical and journal articles dealing with vocal literature, both general and specific, this listing is confined to books.

Since new vocal literature is being added to the repertoire yearly, readers should note that surveys of literature are only as current as their publication date. It is hoped that this list will supply information that will initiate further exploration and discovery in the study of vocal literature.

General Studies of Song Repertoire and History

Elaine Brody, *Paris: The Musical Kaleidoscope, 1870–1925* (New York: George Braziller, 1987). Presents a panorama of the artistic movements, people and works existing in Paris during the decades of the Great Expositions and *La Belle Époque*.

Berton Coffin, ed. *Singer's Repertoire*, 2nd edition (New York: Scarecrow Press, 1960–1962). In five volumes: 1 - Coloratura, Lyric, Dramatic Sopranos; 2 - Mezzo-soprano and Contralto; 3 - Lyric and Dramatic Tenor; 4 - Baritone and Bass. Song lists for each voice. 5 - Program notes for the Singer's Repertoire, with Werner Singer. Sketchy paraphrases of selected song literature. Repertoire listed by voice type, categorized by arbitrary categories.

Barbara Doscher, *From Studio to Stage: Repertoire for the Voice*, edited and annotated by John Nix (Lanham, MD: The Scarecrow Press, 2002). A compendium of annotated repertoire, arranged by broad category (art songs, arias, oratorios, etc.) Taken from the late Barbara Doscher's repertoire files. Helpful format of song entries for matching students' abilities with repertoire.

Martha Elliott, *Singing in Style: A Guide to Vocal Performance Practices* (New Haven, CT: Yale University Press, 2006). An overview of performance practice and style from the Baroque to the present. Includes information on each historical period—singers, and composers, vocal repertoire, and stylistic conventions of the period.

Shirlee Emmons and Stanley Sonntag, *The Art of the Song Recital* (New York: Schirmer Books, 1979, revised 2001). Excellent reference covering all facets of the song recital. including program building, musical resources and research. Extensive appendix of repertoire current to the publication date.

——— and Wilbur Watkins Lewis, *Researching the Song* (New York: Oxford University Press, 2006). A lexicon of terms and names found in art songs. There are 2,000 topical entries providing information about historical, mythological, geographical, literary, and technical references found in poetic song texts. Art songs from the German, French, Italian, Russian, Spanish, South American, Greek, Finnish, Scandinavian, and both American and British English repertoire are included. Sources, narratives, and explanations of major song cycles are also given. Organized alphabetically, the lexicon includes brief biographies of poets, lists of composers who set each poet's work, bibliographic materials, and brief synopses of major works from which song texts were taken. A most useful reference.

Noni Espina, *Repertoire for the Solo Voice* (Metuchen, NJ: Scarecrow Press, 1977). Extensive two-volume reference of works for solo voice with annotations covering material from the 13th century to the publication date.

Raymond Erickson, *Schubert's Vienna* (New Haven, CT: Yale University Press, 1997). A most interesting study. Beautiful book giving the cultural and artistic milieu in Vienna during the time of Schubert.

Thomas Goleeke, *Literature for Voice, Vol. I: An Index of Songs in Collections and Source Book for Teachers of Singing* (Lanham, MD: Scarecrow Press, 1984). Lists composer, title, key and range in musical notation of each song.

————, *Literature for Voice, Vol. II: An Index to Songs in Collections, 1985–2000* (Lanham, MD: Scarecrow Press, 2002). See above.

James Husst Hall, *The Art Song* (Norman, OK: University of Oklahoma Press, 1953). General survey of French, German, English song. Specific, selected songs discussed. Limited by publication date.

James Harding, *The Ox on the Roof: Scenes from Musical Life in Paris in the Twenties* (New York: Da Capo Press, 1986). A portrait of literary, artistic and social *milieu* of Jean Cocteau and the influential "Les Six"—Georges Auric, Louis Durey, Arthur Honegger, Darius Milhaud, Francis Poulenc, and Germaine Tailleferre—the central innovators in French classical music during the 1920s.

D. Kern Holoman, *Writing about Music* (Berkeley, CA: University of California Press, 1988). A most useful resource for producing accurate program copy for the printed recital program. The style sheet of the musicological journal *19th-Century Music.*

Donald Ivey, *Song: Anatomy, Imagery, and Styles* (New York: Free Press, 1970). A study of the component elements of song. Also covers principal style elements of representative composers in a compact but informative history of song.

Sergius Kagen, *Music for the Voice,* revised ed. (Bloomington, IN: Indiana University Press, 1968). Annotated listing of available songs, airs, operatic excerpts and folk songs from the seventeenth century to 1968. Entries are arranged by composer and list song titles, general style and form of each song, tessitura and compass, problems of execution for singer and accompanist, available editions, and recommended translations and transpositions. A dated but classic source.

Carol Kimball, **Song: A Guide to Art Song Style and Literature**, revised ed. (Milwaukee, WI: Hal Leonard Corporation, 2006). An overview of classical song. Biographies and discussions of the works of 150 composers of various nationalities with annotations of representative cycles and single songs for each. Bibliographies for each composer and introductory overview of each national repertoire area. Introductory unit on style and its musical components.

Carol MacClintock, **The Solo Song, 1580–1730** (New York: W.W. Norton & Co., 1973). Selected English, French, German, Italian songs of the Renaissance–Baroque periods. Helpful introductory chapter on performance practices.

Barbara Meister, **An Introduction to the Art Song** (New York: Taplinger Publishing Co., 1980). A general overview of the genre.

————, **Art Song: The Marriage of Music and Poetry** (Wakefield, NH: Hollowbrook Publishing, 1992). Selected song literature is examined as to the fusion of poetic and musical elements.

Roger Nichols, **The Harlequin Years: Music in Paris 1917–1929** (Berkeley, CA: University of California Press, 2002). During the inter-war years, Paris was the hub of the musical world, rich in musical personalities in music and art. Nichols also chronicles the opera houses, orchestras, conservatoires, publishers, and salons in his usual thorough style. A fine source.

Charles Osborne, **The Concert Song Companion** (New York: Da Capo Press, 1974). The art song 1650–1950 separated according to language and country. Concisely written, excellent resource.

Charles Rosen, **The Romantic Generation** (Cambridge: Harvard University Press, 1995). A thorough exploration of the musical language, styles, and spirit of the Romantic period. See especially Chapter 3: "Mountains and Song Cycles."

Douglass Seaton, **The Art Song: A Research and Information Guide** (New York: Garland Publishing Co., 1987).

Roger Shattuck, **The Banquet Years: The Origin of the Avant-garde in France 1885 to World War I** (New York: Vintage Books, 1968).

Excellent discussion of the arts in France during this period. Chapters on Rousseau, Satie, Jarry, and Apollinaire.

Jack M. Stein, *Poem and Music in the German Lied from Gluck to Hugo Wolf* (Cambridge: Harvard University Press, 1971). A study of the fusion of poetry and music in the songs of Schubert, Schumann, Brahms, and Wolf and the evolution of the German *Lied* between 1750–1900.

Denis Stevens, *A History of Song*, revised ed. (New York: W.W. Norton & Co., 1970). Comprehensive narrative of the history of song from the troubadours to the 20th century organized by country.

Poetry: References for Study

Alfred Corn, *The Poem's Heartbeat: A Manual of Prosody* (Ashland, OR: Story Line Press, 1998). A general and user-friendly guide to rhyme, rhythm, meter, and form—the patterns of rhythm and sound used in poetry.

Babette Deutsch, *Poetry Handbook: A Dictionary of Terms*, 4th ed. (New York: Harper Resource, an Imprint of Harper Collins Publishers, 1974). A handy paperback book of less than 200 pages that provides easy reference for finding the difference between a literary *ballad* and a *ballade*.

James Fenton, *An Introduction to English Poetry* (London: Penguin/ Viking, 2002). Provides a good introduction for comparing methods of versification in English and French.

Emily Fragos, ed., *Music's Spell: Poems about Music and Musicians* (New York: Alfred A. Knopf Everyman's Library, 2009). A collection of over 160 absorbing poems about music and musicians by well-known poets, divided into ten sections for easy reference.

Dana Gioia, *"Can Poetry Matter?": Essays on Poetry and American Culture* (Minneapolis, MN: Graywolf Press, 2002). A collection of essays including the provocative essay of the title.

Edward Hirsch, *How to Read a Poem: And Fall in Love with Poetry* (Orlando, FL: Harcourt, Inc., 1999). Twelve chapters explore poetry and the imagery/emotions it evokes. There are two useful appendices titled "The Glossary and the Pleasures of the Text," and "A Reading List and the Pleasure of the Catalog." Although not an anthology per se, there are many poetic examples. Good resource book.

Helen Handley Houghton and Maureen McCarthy Draper, eds., *The Music Lover's Poetry Anthology* (New York: Persea, 2007). An anthology of more contemporary poetry focusing on poets of the twentieth and twenty-first centuries. Celebrates the connection between poetry and music in 150 poems by an exceptional array of poets from Baudelaire to Kerouac.

David Hunter, *Understanding French Verse: A Guide for Singers* (New York: Oxford University Press, 2005). Explains the formal structure of French verse using examples drawn from many well-known song settings. A clear and succinct resource for singers who want to know more about the complexities of French versification.

John Lithgow, compiler. *Poet's Corner* (New York: Grand Central Publishing, 2007). Subtitled "the one and only poetry book for the entire family," this attractive volume contains fifty of Lithgow's favorite poems. Each poet is represented by a short bibliography and a poem, followed by a succinct annotation. Included with the book is an MP3 CD of poetry readings by Lithgow and some "very special guests," including Morgan Freeman, Lynn Redgrave, Sam Waterston, and Glenn Close. The bonus CD provides students with some outstanding model readers.

Frances Mayes, *The Discovery of Poetry: A Field Guide to Reading and Writing Poems* (Orlando, FL: Harcourt, Inc., 2001). Mayes's goal is to show that poetry is accessible and fun rather than intimidating. Discussions of rhyme, free verse, choice of subject, style, and interpretation—in plain language, how poetry works. Uses hundreds of examples of poetry from all time periods. A well-written, interesting resource.

Karen McCosker and Nicholas Albery, eds., *Poem a Day, Volume 1* (Hanover, NH: Steerforth Press, 1994). Contains 366 poems old and new—one for each day of the year. Most pages include brief annotations about the poet and/or the poem. There are two other books in this series, Volumes 2 and 3.

Jack Myers and Don C. Wukasch, **Dictionary of Poetic Terms** (Denton, TX: University of North Texas Press, 2003). Formerly The Longman Dictionary of Poetic Terms, newly updated. Contains over 1,600 entries on devices, techniques, history, theory, and terminology of poetry from the Classical Age to the present. A good "go-to" resource.

Mary Oliver, **Rules for the Dance: A Handbook for Writing and Reading Metrical Verse** (Boston: A Mariner Original, Houghton Mifflin Company, 1998). A wonderful book by one of America's distinguished poets. Oliver presents her concise and cogent thoughts on sound, rhyme, and metrical poetry. Includes an anthology of fifty poems in English from the Elizabethan Age to Elizabeth Bishop.

————, **A Poetry Handbook: A Prose Guide to Understanding and Writing Poetry** (New York: Harcourt Brace & Company, 1994). A compact, slender book that introduces the reader to poetry— lessons on sound, line, poetic forms, tone, and imagery. Although aimed at budding poets, there is enough information for the novice reader of poetry. Oliver's engaging writing is infused throughout with her passion for her craft.

Ron Padgett, ed., **The Teachers and Writers Handbook of Poetic Forms**, 2nd edition (New York: Teachers and Writers Collaborative, 2000). Discusses over seventy-five poetic forms—their histories, how their forms work (rhyming schemes), and gives sample poems and a bibliography for each form. Clear, direct explanations, easy-to-read. This short book is valuable as a reference guide for anyone interested in learning about poetic forms.

Robert Pensky and Maggie Dietz, eds., **An Invitation to Poetry: A New Favorite Poem Project Anthology** (New York: W.W. Norton Co., 2004). A collection of 200 poems with an accompanying DVD featuring project participants reading their favorite poems from Shakespeare to Szymborska. These are people from diverse backgrounds and professions, speaking about their connection to poetry and the pleasure they derive from it. The Favorite Poem Project was begun in 1997. The National Endowment for the Arts provided major funding for its video presentations, which were broadcast on *The News Hour with Jim Lehrer*.

Laurence Perrine, **Sound and Sense: An Introduction to Poetry** (New York: Harcourt, Brace & World, Inc., 1963). Easy to read textbook with example poems and questions for the insatiable.

Clive Scott, **French Verse-Art: A Study** (Cambridge: Cambridge University Press, 1980). Designed to help students master technicalities and techniques of French verse.

Mark Strand and Eavan Boland, **The Making of a Poem: A Norton Anthology of Poetic Forms** (New York: W.W. Norton & Co., 2000). Another good reference that discusses poetic forms such as sonnet, ballad, villanelle, elegy, pastoral, and sestina. Contains an abundance of poetic examples for each form. An excellent text and/or reference for everyone's bookshelf.

Brian Woledgy, ed., **The Penguin Book of French Verse, Volume I** (Baltimore, MD: Penguin Books, 1961). In four volumes with plain prose translations of each poem.

Susan Goldsmith Wooldridge, **poemcrazy: freeing your life with words** (New York: Three Rivers Press, 1996). A book of ideas and techniques for teachers of poetry, this little book also is "a field guide to imagination." Wooldridge's enthusiasm for her craft and for working with words in all sorts of ways is thoroughly infectious.

WEBSITE of the **Academy of American Poets** (www.poets.org) is a treasure house of poems, interviews, essays, notable books, audio archives. Look up a poet, or poem, or explore the website for discussions, videos, and "poetry near you." This is an informative, absorbing website with something for everyone.

WEBSITE of the **Poetry Foundation** (www.poetryfoundation.org) is another excellent resource for interviews, articles, audio archives. There is a wealth of information about poets and poetry: the PF supports monthly poetry lectures, talks given by notable scholars and critics on poets, poetry, and their intersections with other art forms. In addition to live events, these talks feature recordings from historic archives. The Foundation also supports a project PoetryOutLoud, a national competition for poetry recitation.

Texts and Translations

David Adams, *The Song and Duet Texts of Antonín Dvořák* (Geneseo, NY: Leyerle Publications, 2003).

Paula Boire, *Romanian Art Songs, Vol. 1: Soprano; Vol. 2: Mezzo Soprano* (Geneseo, NY: Leyerle Publications, 2002).

Natalia Challis, ed., *The Singer's Rachmaninoff* (New York: Pelion Press, 1989). Includes original Russian texts with English translations and IPA.

Margaret Cobb, *The Poetic Debussy: A Collection of His Song Texts and Selected Letters,* trans. Richard Miller (Boston: Northeastern University Press, 1982). A collection of the song texts of Debussy with translations, dates of composition, and location of original manuscripts. Also contains selected letters.

Jacqueline Cockburn, Richard Stokes, and Graham Johnson, *The Spanish Song Companion* (London: Victor Gollancz, 1992). Texts, translations, and introductory notes on early Spanish song, *tonadillas, zarzuelas*, and representative literature by major Spanish song composers. Excellent source.

Dietrich Erbelding, *Translations of 106 French Poems, Set to Music by French Composers*, edited by Martial Singher, as recorded on two cassette tapes, recitation by Martial Singher (Novato, CA: Pocket Coach Publications,1990). Recorded originally on two cassette tapes, later on one CD. Recitation of all 106 poems by the distinguished French baritone and teacher Martial Singher. A very useful source for working with French song. Contains much of what we consider the generic French repertoire, read idiomatically by Singher. May be difficult to locate, but persevere.

Dietrich Fischer-Dieskau, *The Fischer-Dieskau Book of Lieder,* trans. by George Bird and Richard Stokes (New York: Limelight Editions, 1984). Texts and translations for over 750 selected songs by every major composer of *Lieder.*

Martha Gerhart, *Italian Song Texts from the 17th to the 20th Centuries, Vol. I and II* (Geneseo, NY: Leyerle Publications, 2003). Covers all the basic Italian song texts through four centuries, with International Phonetic Alphabet transliteration, word-for-word English translations, and idiomatic translations.

Beaumont Glass, **Schubert's Complete Song Texts, Vol. I and II** (Geneseo, NY: Leyerle Publications, 1996). Schubert's more than 600 songs are split between volumes 1 and 2. Songs are presented alphabetically by title. Volume 1 begins wih "Abend" and ends with "Frühlingslied." Volume 2 begins with "Frühlingslied/Geöffnet sind des Winters Riegel" and ends with "Zur Namensfeier des Herrn Andreas Siller." Song cycles are presented alphabetically as a unit. Format for each song is four lines: IPA transliteration, German text, word-for-word translation, and idiomatic translation.

———, **Schumann's Complete Song Texts** (Geneseo, NY: Leyerle Publications, 2002). One volume.

———, **Brahms's Complete Song Texts** (Geneseo, NY: Leyerle Publications, 1999). One volume.

———, **Hugo Wolf's Complete Song Texts** (Geneseo, NY: Leyerle Publications). One volume.

———, **Strauss's Complete Song Texts** (Geneseo, NY: Leyerle Publications. 2004). One volume.

———, **Miscellaneous Song Texts (Schubert, Schumann, Brahms, Wolf and Strauss)** (Geneseo, NY: Leyerle Publications).

Note: when dates are omitted from Leyerle Publications, they were not given on the website nor on other Internet resources.

Laurence Kramer, **Music and Poetry: The Nineteenth Century and After** (Berkeley: University of California Press, 1984).

Timothy LeVan, **Masters of the French Song** (Metuchen, NJ: Scarecrow Press, 1991). Texts and translations of the complete songs of Chausson, Debussy, Duparc, Fauré, and Ravel.

Timothy LeVan, **Masters of the Italian Song** (Metuchen, NJ: Scarecrow Press, 1990). Word-by-word and poetic translations of the complete songs for voice and piano of Bellini, Donaudy, Donizetti, Puccini, Rossini, Tosti, and Verdi.

Ann L. Leyerle and William D. Leyerle, **French Diction Songs: From the 17th to the 20th Centuries** (Geneseo, NY: Leyerle Publications, 1983).

Candace A. Magner, *Phonetic Readings of Brahms Lieder* (Metuchen, NJ: Scarecrow Press, 1987). A pronunciation guide to the German in every song composed by Johannes Brahms. Each line of German is presented with its pronunciation clearly spelled in IPA. Included are 297 texts of Brahms *Lieder* and folk songs, along with four appendices and cross-referencing.

————, *Phonetic Readings of Schubert Lieder* (Metuchen, NJ: Scarecrow Press, 1994).

Philip Miller, ed. *The Ring of Words: An Anthology of Song Texts* (New York: Doubleday & Co., Inc., 1962). Anthology of selected poetry set by major song composers, arranged by poet. An excellent resource.

Marie-Thérèse Pacquin, *Ten Cycles of Lieder* (Montreal: University of Montreal Press, 1977). Translations (poetic and word-for-word) of ten selected cycles by Beethoven, Brahms, Mahler, Schubert, and Schumann.

Lois Phillips, *Lieder Line by Line* (New York: Charles Scribner's Sons, 1980). Word-for-word and poetic translations of selected *Lieder* of Beethoven, Schubert, Schumann, Wagner, Brahms, Wolf, Mahler, and Strauss.

Jean Piatek and Regina Arashov, *Russian Songs and Arias* (Dallas: Pst...Inc., 1991). Phonetic readings, word-by-word translations for 150 songs and arias, with a concise guide to Russian diction.

S. S. Prawer, ed. and trans. *The Penguin Book of Lieder* (Baltimore, MD: Penguin Books, 1964). This little paperback is a good introduction to German repertoire. Contains short biographies plus words and translations of song texts from Haydn to Hindemith. Includes complete texts of major song cycles from Beethoven's *An die ferne Geliebte* to Strauss's *Vier letzte Lieder*. Succinct, valuable general resource.

Lawrence Richter, *Prokofiev's Complete Song Texts* (Geneseo, NY: Leyerle Publications, 2009). A series of 6 volumes of Russian song texts. Phonetic transcriptions, literal and idiomatic English translations.

————, ***Tchaikovsky's Complete Song Texts*** (Geneseo, NY: Leyerle Publications, 1999). See above.

————, ***Rachmaninov's Complete Song Texts*** (Geneseo, NY: Leyerle Publications, 2000). See above.

————, ***Mussorgsky's Complete Song Texts*** (Geneseo, NY: Leyerle Publications, 2002). See above.

————, ***Selected Nineteenth Century Russian Song Texts*** (Geneseo, NY: Leyerle Publications, 2005). See above.

————, ***Shostakovich's Complete Song Texts*** (Geneseo, NY: Leyerle Publications, 2007). See above.

Claire Rohinsky, ed., ***The Singer's Debussy*** (New York: Pelion Press, 1987). Brief notes on each of Debussy's songs, with translations and IPA phonetic transcriptions.

Josep M. Sobrer and Edmon Colomer, ***The Singer's Anthology of 20th Century Spanish Songs*** (New York: Pelion Press, 1987). Concert songs of Enrique Granados, Manuel de Falla, and Frederic Mompou. Some discussion of composers and poets. Word-by-word and poetic translations, IPA transcriptions.

Richard D. Sylvester, ***Tchaikovsky's Complete Songs: A Companion with Texts and Translations*** (Bloomington, IN: Indiana University Press, 2002). Tchaikovsky's songs are presented chronologically with annotations that present musical and biographical information. Texts are presented in their original Cyrillic with a transcription of each into the Latin alphabet. English translations are also supplied as well as a list of recordings. An exceptional and very useful resource.

Richard Wigmore, ***Schubert: The Complete Song Texts*** (London: Victor Gollancz, 1988). Complete texts and translations for all of Schubert's *Lieder*.

Mei Zhong, ***Newly Arranged Chinese Folk Songs, Vol. I*** (Geneseo, NY: Leyerle Publications, 2005). An anthology of Chinese folk songs arranged by contemporary Chinese composers. Directions for pronunciation by Dr. Zhong.

———, *Traditional and Modern Chinese Art Songs, Vol. II* (Geneseo, NY: Leyerle Publications, 2009). A second volume of Chinese songs by the author above. CDs for both volumes are available for separate purchase.

Performance Preparation

Kurt Adler, *The Art of Accompanying and Coaching* (Minneapolis, MN: University of Minnesota Press, 1965). Thorough discussion of style, diction, and interpretation from the coach/pianist's viewpoint.

Lynn Eustis, *The Singer's Ego: Finding Balance Between Music and Life* (Chicago, IL: GIA Publications, Inc., 2005). The "how-to" of keeping the relationship of "the voice" and "the human being" in a healthy balance. Explores the serious issues that singers encounter during a professional career.

Harry Plunket Greene, *Interpretation in Song* (New York: Da Capo Press, 1979). Published in 1912, this diminutive volume contains some valuable observations about singing and performing music.

Thomas Hemsley, *Singing and Imagination: A Human Approach to a Great Musical Tradition* (New York: Oxford University Press, 1998). Hemsley believes that "Imagination is an essential prerequisite of singing and not an optional extra." The role that imagination, feelings, and intuition play in vocal training is explored.

Martin Katz, *The Complete Collaborator: The Pianist as Partner* (New York: Oxford University Press, 2009). Drawing from his more than forty years of experience, distinguished pianist Martin Katz discusses the collaborative process partnering singers in recital. Audio recordings of the author and two vocalists can be accessed on a companion website. Not only pianists but also singers will find this a rich and rewarding resource.

Lotte Lehmann, *More Than Singing: The Interpretation of Songs* (New York: Praeger, 1972). Lehmann's highly personalized comments on interpretation.

Sharon Mabry, ***Exploring Twentieth-Century Vocal Music: A Practical Guide to Innovations in Performance and Repertoire*** (New York: Oxford University Press, 2002). An excellent summary of vocal works by twentieth-century composers and the performance challenges they present. Explores new and unusual notation systems, suggests rehearsal techniques and vocal exercises for this repertoire.

Richard Miller, ***On the Art of Singing*** (New York: Oxford University Press, 1996). A collection of essays dealing with the art of singing. The sections on "Style and Interpretation," and "Professional Preparation" are particularly relevant.

————, ***Singing Schumann: An Interpretive Guide for Performers*** (New York: Oxford University Press, 2005). In-depth look at style and interpretation of Schumann's widely performed middle and late *Lieder*, as well as the early songs.

Gerald Moore, ***Singer and Accompanist: The Performance of Fifty Songs*** (Westport, CT: Greenwood Press, 1975). Performance notes on selected repertoire, written from a pianist's viewpoint by the noted accompanist/coach.

————, ***The Schubert Song Cycles*** (London: Hamish Hamilton, 1975). Moore's thoughts on performance and interpretation for *Die Schöne Müllerin* and *Winterreise*.

————, ***Poet's Love: The Songs and Cycles of Schumann*** (New York: Taplinger Co., 1981). Moore discusses performance of Schumann's *Dichterliebe* and selected songs.

Alain Pâris, ed., ***Dictionnaire des Interprètes*** (Paris: Robert Laffont, 1985). A dictionary of famous singers with brief biographies of each. In French.

David Ostwald, ***Acting for Singers: Creating Believable Singing Characters*** (New York: Oxford University Press, 2005). How to develop a character through studying the text.

Aksel Schiøtz, ***The Singer and His Art*** (New York: Harper & Row, 1970). The distinguished Danish tenor writes about his career. The last section of the book is a discussion of *Winterreise* and *Die Schöne Müllerin*, with Schiøtz's suggestions for interpretation.

Diction

David Adams, *A Handbook of Diction for Singers* (New York: Oxford University Press, 1999). Covers the basics of French versification using examples drawn from a wide range of well-known song settings.

Kurt Adler, *The Art of Accompanying and Coaching* (Minneapolis, MN: University of Minnesota Press, 1965). See chapters 4–8 "Phonetics and Diction in Singing."

Jeannine Alton and Brian Jeffery, *Bele Buche e Bele Parleure* (London: Tecla Editions: Preachers' Court Charterhouse, 1976). A guide to the pronunciation of Medieval and Renaissance French.

Pierre Bernac, *The Interpretation of French Song* (New York: W. W. Norton, Inc. 1970). Chapter 2: "On Singing French" is a helpful guide to the basics of French lyric diction.

Nico Castel, *A Singer's Manual of Spanish Lyric Diction* (New York: Excellent Publishing, 1994). Castel, a distinguished singer and diction coach at the Metropolitan Opera, has provided a most useful book. There is an introduction to Spanish vocal music, pronunciation, vowels and consonants, syllabification, and much more. For Castel, Castilian Spanish is correct, but he also deals with Latin American pronunciations and Ladino in separate sections.

Timothy Cheek, *Singing in Czech: A Guide to Czech Lyric Diction and Vocal Repertoire* (Lanham, MD: Scarecrow Press, 2001). A much-needed book addressing singing in Czech. Presents the language sounds (with IPA) and goes on to composers, with a section on Smetana, Dvořák, Janácek, and Martinů. Selected arias and songs, transcribed with word for word translations and IPA. A very useful reference.

Berton Coffin, *Phonetic Readings of Songs and Arias*. 2nd ed. (Lanham, MD: Scarecrow Press, 1982). This venerable resource has been serving teachers and students since 1964. There are 413 songs and arias with lyric and phonetic transcriptions representing the most performed repertoire. More German and Italian listings than French.

Evelina Colorni, **Singers' Italian** (New York: Schirmer Books, 1995). Originally published in 1970, Colorni's book on Italian lyric diction is a classic. It is also a bit daunting in its thorough discussion, but it is worth the study.

Eileen Davis, **Sing French: Diction for Singers** (Ashland, OR: Eclairé Press, 2004). Using the International Phonetic Alphabet, seven songs are presented with text analyses and vocal lines. Piano-vocal scores are in an appendix. Includes a CD with examples and songs.

Thomas Grubb, **Singing in French: A Manual of French Diction and French Vocal Repertoire**. 2nd edition (New York: Schirmer Books, 1990). The definitive guide to French diction for singers, accompanists, and coaches. An appendix contains an excellent repertoire list of *mélodies* and arias, by vocal *fach*.

Annette Johansson, ed. and author, **Thirty Songs of Wilhelm Stenhammar** (Geneseo, NY: Leyerle Publishing, 1999). Contains the most comprehensive guide to Swedish lyric diction for English speaking singers available today. IPA and English translations for all thirty songs with information about the composer and poets.

Kathryn LaBouff, **Singing and Communicating in English: A Singer's Guide to English Diction** (New York: Oxford University Press, 2007). An accessible and helpful guide to the principles of English diction by renowned diction coach Kathryn LaBouff. Covers aspects of phonetics, includes multiple practical exercises in IPA transcriptions, helpful diagrams, and pronunciation drills. All exercises chosen from English art song and operatic repertoire. In addition to standard American and British English, a variety of regional dialects and accents are covered in depth. A companion website features numerous helpful exercises and additional information.

Madeleine Marshall, **The Singer's Manual of English Diction** (New York: G. Schirmer, 1943). A classic resource, still informative and useful to students and teachers.

John Moriarty, **Diction** (Boston: E. C. Schirmer, 1975). Moriarty's classic book covers the Italian, Latin, French, and German languages—the sounds and exercises for singing them.

William Odom, **German for Singers: A Textbook of Diction and Phonetics**, 2nd ed. (New York: Schirmer Books, 1997). Since its first printing in 1981, Odom's book has been a helpful resource with clear presentation and examples for practice. The second edition is revised and updated and includes an audio CD demonstrating the sounds of the German language.

Emily Olin, **Singing in Russian: A Guide to Language and Performance** (Lanham, MD: Scarecrow Press, 2012). A comprehensive, accessible approach to understanding, mastering, and performing Russian vocal music. Covers the basics of the Cyrillic alphabet, Russian grammar and diction, English sound comparisons, linguistic and musical examples. Repertoire lists and practical recommendations. Accompanying CD with exercises.

Jean Piatek and Regina Avrashov, **Russian Songs and Arias** (Dallas: Pst...Inc., 1991). Phonetic readings and word-by-word translations for 150 songs and arias with a concise guide to Russian diction.

Dorothy Uris, **To Sing in English** (New York: Boosey & Hawkes, 1971). A very good study of good American English. Correct pronunciation of vowels and consonants, separately, and in context. Introduction to the IPA.

Repertoire Studies and Style
German *Lieder*
A. Craig Bell, **The Songs of Schubert** (London: Alston Books, 1954). A small volume that discusses Schubert's song style.

Elaine Brody and Robert Fowkes, **The German Lied and Its Poetry** (New York: New York University Press, 1971). A study of selected 19th century *Lieder*, its poetry and text setting from Mozart through Berg.

Maurice Brown, **BBC Music Guides: Schubert Songs** (Seattle: University of Washington Press, 1967). Brief monograph on Schubert's songs.

Astra Desmond, **BBC Music Guides: Schumann Song** (Seattle: University of Washington Press, 1972). Brief monograph on Schumann's songs.

Dietrich Fischer-Dieskau, **Schubert's Songs: A Biographical Study of His Songs** (New York: Alfred A. Knopf, 1977). In addition to his treasurable legacy of recordings, the distinguished baritone Fischer-Dieskau gave us many written treasures. Musical studies of Schubert, Schumann, and Brahms are among his writings. Places Schubert's songs in chronological context of his life.

————, **Robert Schumann: Words and Music, the Vocal Compositions** trans. by Reinhard Pauly (Portland: Amadeus Press, 1988). The vocal compositions of Schumann.

Lorraine Gorrell, **The Nineteenth-Century German Lied** (Portland, OR: Amadeus Press, 1993). In-depth discussion of the *Lieder* of Schubert, Schumann, Brahms, Wolf, and other composers of the period. Examines social and literary factors that impacted the development of the *Lied* as a genre.

Max Harrison, **The Lieder of Brahms** (New York: Praeger, 1972). Discusses Brahms's songs in context of historical and artistic developments of his time.

Alan Jefferson, **The Lieder of Richard Strauss** (New York: Praeger, 1971). Detailed study of selected *Lieder* with texts and translations grouped by text subject.

Arthur Komar, ed. **Schumann: Dichterliebe** (New York: W.W.Norton, 1971). Musical score, historical background, essays in analysis, views and comments. An excellent resource on this important cycle.

James Parsons, ed., **The Cambridge Companion to the Lied** (New York: Cambridge University Press, 2004). A collection of essays by distinguished scholars in the field.

Theo Reinhard, ed., **The Singer's Schumann** (New York: Pelion Press, 1988). A collection of Schumann's *Lieder* with translations, IPA transcriptions, and brief essays. Includes the complete song cycles as well as the most frequently performed songs (Peters, Vol. 1 plus others).

Eric Sams, **The Songs of Robert Schumann**, 3rd edition (London: Methuen, 1993). Excellent discussion of Schumann's songs and general style with song translations.

————, *The Songs of Hugo Wolf,* revised and enlarged edition (London: Methuen, 1993). Classic reference to Wolf's compositional style in his songs. Each song is translated and discussed.

————, *Brahms Songs* (Seattle: University of Washington Press, 1973). BBC Music Guides series No. 12. A small but informative book on Brahms's compositional style in his songs.

Lawrence D. Snyder, *German Poetry in Song* (Berkeley, CA: Fallen Leaf Press, 1995). Snyder Indexes 9,800 *Lieder* composed after 1770 and the poetry from which the composers drew their inspiration.

Susan Youens, *Hugo Wolf: The Vocal Music* (Princeton: Princeton University Press, 1992). An examination of Wolf's songs from the beginning the end of his creative lifetime. A valuable resource by a distinguished scholar.

————, *Retracing a Winter's Journey: Schubert's Winterreise* (Ithaca: Cornell University Press, 1991). Schubert's cycle with analysis of each song, overview of poetry, and biographical information about the poet, Müller.

————, *Schubert: Die Schöne Müllerin* (Cambridge: Cambridge University Press, 1992). Softcover edition. Genesis of the work from poetry to song cycle, romantic illusion of the poems, discussion of musical settings.

French *Mélodie*

Betty Bannerman, ed. and trans. *The Singer as Interpreter: Claire Croiza's Master Classes* (London: Victor Gollancz, 1989). Croiza (1882–1946), like Jane Bathori, was a singer who championed the music of her time. Notes from her master classes are commentaries on the art of singing and interpretation, particularly referencing the composers for whom she had been a chosen interpreter.

Jane Bathori, *On the Interpretation of the Mélodies of Claude Debussy*, trans. and with an introduction by Linda Laurent (New York: Pendragon Press, 1998). Jane Bathori (1877–1970) was a tireless champion of the music of her time. She sang first performances of vocal works by virtually every major twentieth century French composer of song, and had many works dedicated to her. Bathori also disseminated her firsthand knowledge of style and interpretation through teaching and writing.

Pierre Bernac, *The Interpretation of French Song* (New York: W. W. Norton & Co., 1978). Classic, indispensable reference to French song study. Texts of 200 selected songs, with translations, indicated liaisons and elisions, and suggestions for performance.

———, *Francis Poulenc: The Man and His Songs* (New York: W.W. Norton & Co., 1977). Texts and translations of Poulenc's complete song output plus definitive discussions of style and interpretation.

Sidney Buckland, ed. and trans., *Francis Poulenc: "Echo and Source," Selected Correspondence 1915–1963* (London: Victor Gollancz, 1991). Three hundred fifty letters to and from Poulenc which give insight into his creative processes and compositions, personal relationships, and important events in his career.

——— and Miriam Chimenes, *Francis Poulenc: Music, Art and Literature* (Ashgate Publishing Ltd., 1999). Fourteen articles by Poulenc scholars. Excellent source for information on interrelationship of the arts.

Keith W. Daniel, *Francis Poulenc: His Artistic Development and Musical Style* (Ann Arbor: U.M.I. Research Press, 1982). Excellent reference on Poulenc. Chapter 11 deals with the *mélodies*. Contains an extensive bibliography current to the time of publication.

Laurence Davies, *The Gallic Muse* (New York: A. S. Barnes, 1967). Biographical sketches and discussion of the songs of Fauré, Duparc, Debussy, Satie, Ravel, and Poulenc.

Mary Dibbern, Carol Kimball, and Patrick Choukroun. *Interpreting the Songs of Jacques Leguerney: A Guide for Study and Performance* (New York: Pendragon Press, 2001). Leguerney (1906–1997) produced a substantial catalogue of works dominated by the *mélodie*. Texts and translations with IPA of all published songs. Discussion of each song, with Leguerney's instructions for performance.

Robert Gartside, *Interpreting the Songs of Gabriel Fauré* (Geneseo, NY: Leyerle Publications, 1996). Gartside's thoughts on interpretation of all of Fauré's published songs, with texts, IPA, and word-for-word translations. Contains an introduction to the Phonetic Alphabet in French, and an introduction to Fauré's style and compositional techniques.

————, *Interpreting the Songs of Maurice Ravel* (Geneseo, NY: Leyerle Publications. 1992). Follows the same format as Gartside's book on Fauré, discussing all of Ravel's songs. Ravel set texts in seven languages and the IPA symbols for some of the trickier languages (for example, Greek, Aramaic and Sephardic Hebrew, and the French Limousin dialect) are provided.

Reynaldo Hahn, *On Singing (Du chant)*, trans. Léopold Simoneau, O.C., Reinhard G. Pauly general editor (Portland: Amadeus Press, 1990). A compilation of Hahn's essays about singing and singers. Fascinating narrative.

Graham Johnson and Richard Stokes, *A French Song Companion* (Oxford: Oxford University Press, 2000). An invaluable reference book with composers' biographies, texts and translations, and a history of the *mélodie*.

————, with translations of the song texts by Richard Stokes, *Gabriel Fauré: The Songs and Their Poets* (Burlington, VT: Ashgate Publishing Co., 2009). All of Fauré's songs, with texts and translations, are discussed. Each song is put in historical context, and in the chronology of Fauré's life. The poets are not neglected, nor is performance practice. An exceptional resource.

Timothy LeVan, *Masters of the French Art Song* (Metuchen, NJ: Scarecrow Press, 1991). Texts, translations, and IPA of the complete songs of Chausson, Debussy, Duparc, Fauré, and Ravel.

Barbara Meister, *Nineteenth Century French Song: Fauré, Duparc, and Debussy* (Bloomington: Indiana University Press, 1980). Discusses every published song by Fauré, Chausson, Debussy, and Duparc from the standpoint of text setting and noteworthy musical elements. All of Fauré's texts are given with Meister's translations.

Roger Nichols, *Ravel Remembered* (New York: W.W. Norton Co., 1987). An absorbing kaleidoscope of writings about Ravel by those who knew him best, including Jean Cocteau, Francis Poulenc,

Igor Stravinsky, and Manuel de Falla. First hand descriptions and anecdotes throw some light onto his musical compositions.

Jean-Michel Nectoux, *Gabriel Fauré: A Musical Life*, trans. Roger Nichols (Cambridge: Cambridge University Press, 1991). Distinguished Fauré scholar Nectoux's excellent study of Fauré's life and musical compositions.

Sydney Northcote, *The Songs of Henri Duparc* (London: Dennis Dobson, 1949). A small but mighty book. Succinct but excellent discussion of all of Duparc's *mélodies*. Includes a fine biographical essay of Duparc's life.

Frits Noske, *French Song from Berlioz to Duparc* (New York: Dover, 1970). A study of nineteenth-century French song. Analysis of the *mélodies* of Berlioz, Liszt, Gounod, Bizet, Délibes, Massenet, Saint-Saens, Lalo, Franck, Fauré, Duparc, and others.

Arbie Orenstein, *Ravel: Man and Musician* (New York: Columbia University Press, 1975). Excellent biography. Includes discussion of Ravel's song output, catalog of works, and historical recordings.

Charles Panzéra, *Mélodies Françaises: Fifty Lessons in Style and Interpretation* (Brussels: Schott, 1964). Brief lessons in style and interpretation by one of France's major singers. Fauré dedicated his last cycle *L'Horizon chimérique* to Panzera who knew and worked with many of France's 20th-century composers. A fascinating book. Musical examples, French and English.

Francis Poulenc, *Diary of My Songs (Journal de mes mélodies)*, trans. Winifred Radford (London: Victor Gollancz, 1989). The composer's thoughts on all his songs—origins, performance/interpretation—in diary form.

Emile Vuillermoz, *Gabriel Fauré* (Philadelphia: Chilton Book Co., 1960). Fine biography of the composer which contains interesting material on his songs.

Arthur Wenk, *Claude Debussy and the Poets* (Berkeley: University of California Press, 1976). Excellent discussion of Debussy's settings of Banville, Verlaine, Baudelaire, Mallarmé, and Loüys.

American Art Song

Judith E. Carman, William K. Gaeddert, Gordon Myers, and Rita M. Resch, Art *Song in the United States, 1759–1999,* 3rd ed. (Lanham, MD: Scarecrow Press, 2001). Extensive annotated listing of art songs for solo voice and piano. Contains 2,401 numbered title entries, a key to Song Anthologies and Collections (172 entries), a Discography (338 entries), a Composer Index (602 entries), a Poet Index (1,062 entries), a Special Characteristics Index (30 categories), and a Title Index (4,700+ entries). Helpful source reference tool for studio voice teachers and singers.

Keith E. Clifton, **Recent American Art Song: A Guide** (Lanham, MD: The Scarecrow Press, Inc., 2008). A study of approximately 1000 art songs by some 200 composers, written since 1980. Organized alphabetically by composer, entries give complete brief biographical information with major works and links to print resources; composer websites when available. Vocal range, musical style, and appropriate voice type for individual songs are provided. Discography, bibliography, and indexes listing works by poet, song cycle, title, voice type, and level of difficulty. An essential resource on American song. Foreword by Paul Sperry.

Ruth C. Friedberg, **American Art Song and American Poetry** (Metuchen, NJ; Scarecrow Press, Inc., 1981). Three volumes. Volume I: *America Comes of Age*: Edward MacDowell, Charles Loeffler, Charles Griffes, Charles Ives, Roy Harris, Aaron Copland, Douglas Moore, Ernst Bacon, and William Grant Still; Volume II: *Voices of Maturity*: Virgil Thomson, John Duke, Ross Lee Finney, Paul Nordoff, Sergius Kagen, Mary Howe, and Charles Naginski; Volume III: *The Century Advances*: Hugo Weisgall, David Diamond, Jack Beeson, Richard Owen, Jean Eichelberger Ivey, William Flanagan, Ruth Schoenthal, Richard Cumming, Vincent Persichetti, Ned Rorem, Richard Hundley, John Corigliano, and Robert Baksa. Selected examples of American songs by selected American composers, focusing on the interrelationships between composer and poet.

Barbara B. Heyman, **Samuel Barber: The Composer and His Music** (New York: Oxford University Press, 1992). Excellent biography of Barber and his musical style.

Carlton Lowenberg, *Musicians Wrestle Everywhere: Emily Dickinson and Music* (Berkeley, CA: Fallen Leaf Press, 1991). A catalog of 1,615 musical settings of Emily Dickinson's texts by 276 composers written between 1896 and 1991. Songs are listed alphabetically by composer with song title, publisher, publication date, instrumentation, and number of poems. Back matter provides an index of poems by first line and another index of poems by number (Johnson edition). A very useful reference.

Jane Manning, *New Vocal Repertory: An Introduction* (New York: Taplinger, 1987). A selection of suggestions for extending the English-language repertory with specific pieces grouped according to technical difficulty. Composers include Babbitt, Musgrave, Carter, Bernstein, Sessions, and Rands.

Victoria Etnier Villamil, *A Singer's Guide to the American Art Song: 1870–1980* (Lanham, MD: Scarecrow Press, 1993). Villamil's valuable book gives brief biographies and selected song listings (with annotations) for 146 American composers An excellent, user-friendly reference. Useful appendices, and a foreword by Thomas Hampson.

British Art Song

Anne Williams Allman, *The Songs of Frederick Delius: An Interpretive and Stylistic Analysis* (Unpublished doctoral dissertation, Columbia University Teachers College, 1983). Examines forty-four of Delius's sixty-five songs, including biographical background, analysis, bibliography, and available printed editions (at time of writing).

Stephen Banfield, *Sensibility and English Song: Critical Studies of the Early 20th Century* (New York: Cambridge University Press, 1985). Two volumes examining British song and its composers. Volume 2 contains extensive song lists by composer.

Liane Curtis, ed. *Rebecca Clarke Reader* (Bloomington: Indiana University Press, 2004; also a 2005 reprinting by the Rebecca Clarke Society, Inc.). Considers the life, works, and career of the English composer Rebecca Clarke (1886–1979). Leading scholars present original research on Clarke's songs, chamber music, and contemporary musical milieu supplemented with new editions of rare writings by Clarke herself. Transcriptions of four interviews with the composer in which Clarke speaks candidly about her fascinating life. Also see the Rebecca Clarke Society: www.rebeccaclarke.org

Trevor Hold, ***Parry to Finzi: Twenty English Song-Composers*** (Woodbridge: The Boydell Press, 2002).

Graham Johnson and George Odam. ***Britten, Voice and Piano: Lectures on the Vocal Music of Benjamin Britten*** (Guildhall Research Studies, 2003). A collection of eight "lectures" by pianist Graham Johnson, based on a series of concert talks given at the Guildhall School of Music and Drama as part of the Benjamin Britten festival in 2001. Drawn from letters and diaries, the book's focus is on Britten's songs, starting with his earliest compositions in the genre. Johnson suggests that the nature of Britten's creativity is especially apparent in his setting of poetry—that Britten becomes the poet's alter-ego. Informative and excellent resource.

Elise B. Jorgens, ***The Well-tun'd Word: Musical Interpretations of English Poetry 1597–1651*** (Minneapolis MN: University of Minnesota Press, 1982). The relation of text to music in songs by England's lutenists.

Michael Pilkington, ***Gurney, Ireland, Quilter, and Warlock*** (Bloomington: Indiana University Press, 1989). Covers all songs (in print or not) of these four composers, giving ranges, voice types, commentary, specific technical problems, publishers.

———, ***Campion, Dowland, and the Lutenist Songwriters*** (Bloomington: Indiana University Press, 1989).

Italian Art Song

Ruth C. Lakeway and Robert C. White, Jr., ***Italian Art Song*** (Bloomington: Indiana University Press, 1989). Brief history of solo Italian song. Deals specifically with representative songs of composers Alfano, Respighi, Pizzetti, Malipiero, Casella, Davico, Wolf-Ferrari, Cimara, Santoliquido, Castelnuovo-Tedesco, among others.

Spanish Art Song

Suzanne Rhodes Draayer, *A Singer's Guide to the Songs of Joaquín Rodrigo*. (Lanham, MD: Scarecrow Press, 1999). Word-for-word translations, idiomatic translations, and IPA transcriptions of all of Rodrigos's eighty-seven songs. Biographical information and interviews with Rodrigo's only child, Cecilia.

————, **Art Song Composers of Spain** (Lanham, MD: The Scarecrow Press, 2009). More than 90 composers are discussed in detail with complete biographies, descriptions and examples of their song literature, and comprehensive listings of stage works, books and recordings, compositions in non-vocal genres, and vocal repertoire.

Josep M. Sobrer and Edmon Colomer, *The Singer's Anthology of 20th Century Spanish Songs* (New York: Pelion Press, 1987). Concert songs of Enrique Granados, Manuel de Falla, and Frederic Mompou. Some discussion of composers and poets. Word-for-word and poetic translations, IPA transcriptions.

South American Art Song

Maya Hoover, ed., *A Guide to the Latin American Art Song Repertoire: An Annotated Catalog of Twentieth-Century Art Songs for Voice and Piano* (Bloomington, IN: Indiana University Press, 2010). Reference guide to the art song literature of composers from Latin America. Divided by country into twenty-two chapters, each containing an introductory essay on the music of the region, a catalog of art songs for that country, and a list of publishers. Helpful and informative resource lesser-known song repertoire.

Russian *Romans*

Natalia Challis, ed., *The Singer's Rachmaninoff* (New York: Pelion Press, 1989). Includes original Russian texts, with English translations and IPA.

Scandinavian *Romanser*

Beryl Foster, *The Songs of Edvard Grieg* (Brookfield, Vermont: Scolar Press, 1990). Select bibliography, discography, and chronological list of songs.

Kathleen Roland Silverstein, **Northern Lights: Swedish Songs for Studio and Concert Stage** (Stockholm, se: Gehrmans Musikförlag, 2013). Contains a guide to Swedish diction, IPA/phonetic translations, and a CD of spoken poetry. 25 songs, 12 composers, including Alfvén, Rangström, Frumerie, Peterson-Berger, Linde, Liljefors.

Websites

In addition to print books, readers should search the Internet for websites of specific composers, artists, song foundations, song repertoire, texts and translations. Listed below are some sites that are good places to begin. The Internet is always changing, so this list is by *no means* exhaustive. Most of these websites will provide links to others.

Consider this list as your "starter list" and bookmark the sites you find interesting and helpful. Continue to add links as you find more sites that suit your research purposes. For the sake of brevity, the list does not include performing artists, but there are numerous websites of both singers and pianists. Many have multiple links on the Internet. Keep researching!

Composers:
Lori Laitman (www.artsongs.com)
Daron Hagen (www.daronhagen.com)
Tom Cipullo (www.tomcipullo.com)
Ned Rorem (www.nedrorem.com)
Libby Larsen (www.libbylarsen.com)
Ricky Ian Gordon (www.rickyiangordon.com)
Judith Cloud (www.judithcloud.com)
Richard Pearson Thomas (www.richardpearsonthomas.com)
Jake Heggie (www.jakeheggie.com)

Publishers:

Hal Leonard Corporation (www.halleonard.com)
Classical Vocal Repertoire (www.classicalvocalrepertoire.com)
Leyerle Publications (www.leyerle.com)

Specific Song Literature:

Russian song (www.russianartsong),
The American Art Song (www.americanartsong.org)
Song of America (www.songofamerica.net)
Swedish song (www.SwedishSong.com)

Foundations and Societies:

Lotte Lehmann Foundation (www.lottelehmann.org)
Marilyn Horne Foundation (www.marilynhornegfn.org)
Hampsong Foundation [Thomas Hampson] (www.hampsong.org)
Art Song Preservation Society of New York (www.aspsny.org)

Texts, translations, diction:

The Diction Domain (www.dictiondomain.com)
The IPA Source (www.ipasource.com)
The Lied, Art Song, and Choral Texts Archive
(www.recmusic.org/lieder/)

About the Author

CAROL KIMBALL is the author of *Song: A Guide to Art Song Style and Literature* (Hal Leonard Corp.), a widely used text and reference that has become the principal one-volume American source on the topic. She is the editor of several music anthologies: *The French Song Anthology; Women Composers: A Heritage of Song;* and *Art Song in English: 50 Songs by 21 American and British Composers* (Hal Leonard Corp.); and co-author of *Interpreting the Songs of Jacques Leguerney* (Pendragon Press). Among her other publications are numerous articles and reviews on opera and song literature in many professional journals as well as liner notes for a number of CD recordings.

As a performer, Dr. Kimball earned a reputation as an expressive and versatile performer in concerts, recitals, and musical theater. Recognized as a gifted recitalist, her imaginative programming and the unusual scope of her repertoire garnered critical praise. A specialist in French repertoire, she has studied and coached with Pierre Bernac, Gérard Souzay, Martial Singher, Thomas Grubb, and Dalton Baldwin, and regularly presents master classes and lectures on French *mélodie*.

Dr. Kimball is an Emerita Professor of Voice and a Barrick Distinguished Scholar at the University of Nevada, Las Vegas. She is a member of the Board of Advisors of The Lotte Lehmann Foundation, the Advisory Board of The Art Song Preservation Society of New York, and a recipient of the Nevada Governor's Arts Award for Excellence in the Arts. Other honors include the Nevada Board of Regents' Creative Excellence Award for the Nevada System of Higher Education and the UNLV Alumni Association's Outstanding Faculty Award. Retired from full-time teaching in 2008, she remains active as a writer, lecturer, and clinician.